JOHN BASTIN, *specialist on British and Dutch colonial history in Southeast Asia, is Reader in the Modern History of Southeast Asia,* School of Oriental and African Studies, University of London. *He is the author of five other books including* Essays in Indonesian and Malayan History *and* The British in West Sumatra, 1685–1825.

HARRY J. BENDA *is Professor of History at Yale University. An authority on internal developments in the history of Southeast Asian countries, he has written four other volumes including* The Crescent and the Rising Sun: Indonesian Islam under the Japanese Occupations, 1942–1945.

A History

of

Modern Southeast Asia

Colonialism, Nationalism, and Decolonization

JOHN BASTIN

and

HARRY J. BENDA

PRENTICE-HALL, Inc. Englewood Cliffs, N. J.

A SPECTRUM BOOK

Library of Congress Catalog Card Number: 68–17832

PRINTED IN THE UNITED STATES OF AMERICA

Current Printing (last digit):
10 9 8 7 6 5 4 3 2

Prentice-Hall International, Inc. (*London*)

Preface

While the collective concept of "Southeast Asia" was long familiar in Chinese and Japanese usage as *Nanyang* and *Nampō* (the region of the Southern Seas), it is of very recent vintage as far as Westerners are concerned. In all likelihood, it only emerged during the closing stages of the Second World War with the creation of a Southeast Asia Command. Once born, however, the concept rapidly gained widespread currency until the many-faceted political crisis of the mid-twentieth century turned it into an all too familiar collectivity. That crisis, in turn, has brought in its wake a fast-growing scholarly awareness of the significance of an area that had received little academic attention in prewar years. This is not to deny that patient and in many ways still unrivalled scholarship had been devoted to some of the peoples and cultures of the Southeast Asian region before the middle of the twentieth century. But it tended to focus not on the area as a whole, but on its constituent parts, reflecting the parochial isolation in which most Southeast Asians lived during the colonial era, as they had for centuries before. At least equally important, the peculiar and restrictive climate of colonialism—most prewar scholars were officials of colonial governments—had led to an almost exclusive preoccupation with the local and the distant, rather than with the broader and more modern, aspects of Southeast Asian developments. This is particularly true with regard to modern historical studies which have barely started to come into their own in the past two decades or so. No serious student of Southeast Asian history will wish to ignore, let alone denigrate, the painstaking work bequeathed to our generation by the scholars of colonial Southeast Asia. Without their labors, we could not even begin to strike out in new directions. But the time has clearly come to move beyond their accomplishments to wider horizons.

This short book is by no means the first effort in such a direction. Valuable syntheses of the sweep of Southeast Asian history by such authors as D. G. E. Hall and John F. Cady must be placed side by side with briefer, but important, books by Brian Harrison and Nicholas Tarling.* Only the last of these is primarily concerned with the modern era, which is the main subject matter of our volume. Ours differs from Tarling's account, and implicitly also from the others, in two major respects. In the first place, it is the joint product of two authors living in different parts of the world, and, more important, specializing in different aspects of Southeast Asian history: one is primarily concerned with Western expansion in Southeast Asia and with the modes and instrumentalities of colonial governance; the other has been drawn to the study of internal developments within the area's indigenous societies, in particular of their variegated responses to the colonial "input" in modern times. Both approaches, we feel, are not only valid but essential and complementary to any proper understanding of the course of Southeast Asian history. In the second place, we have endeavored to view Southeast Asian history as more than a mere chronological account of disparate events occurring among a variety of colonizers and colonized. Without forcing these events into rigidly preconceived molds, we have tried to fit them into a broadly comparative frame of reference.

We are well aware that our approach, whatever its merits, entails certain risks. Quite apart from anything else, the brevity of this interpretive essay is bound to impose some burdens on the reader. Indeed, the more serious student is advised to seek fuller information in the above-mentioned syntheses as well as in the titles listed and described at the end of our volume. There is another problem: as a result of our method, the reader may feel that we have done violence to the clear forward march of chronology. We have in a sense carved up the modern history of Southeast Asia, first discussing the foreigners in the region and then

* D. G. E. Hall, A *History of South-East Asia* (London and New York, 1964); J. F. Cady, *Southeast Asia: Its Historical Development* (New York, 1964); B. Harrison, *South-East Asia: A Short History* (London and New York, 1966); N. Tarling, A *Concise History of Southeast Asia* (New York, Washington, and London, 1966).

analyzing the indigenous Southeast Asians' responses to their actions. Of course many if not most of these events happened simultaneously, and they are usually treated in such fashion. But we hope that such deviations from the norm may be amply compensated for by the comparative treatment we have accorded our twin themes. Finally, we must admit that we have not been able to do more than pinpoint some of the most significant events and themes in the distinct histories of the various peoples and civilizations of Southeast Asia. Like all historians, we have chosen our emphases (and our deletions) in accordance with what we have felt to be significant. We have similarly been rather arbitrary in assigning space to the various phases of the region's modern history. Thus, to some it may seem disproportionate to devote as much space as we have to the brief Japanese occupation era; but we believe that it played such a determining role in the decolonization process that a reasonably full treatment appeared desirable.

What is attempted here is a broad interpretive account of the process of Western colonialism in Southeast Asia, beginning with the arrival of the Portuguese in the early years of the sixteenth century and ending with the withdrawal of the Western powers and the establishment of independent Southeast Asian governments after the Second World War. The latter period—the period of decolonization—although relatively short in terms of the time taken to dismantle the apparatus of Western rule, is a period which is essentially open-ended since the immediate, if not permanent, effects of the centuries-old process of Western colonialism are not yet fully revealed. Certainly it would be a mistake to regard decolonization as a simple matter involving the withdrawal or expulsion of the Western colonial powers from Southeast Asia in the years immediately following the War. Postwar developments in Southeast Asia, after all, are only one facet of the new power relationships in Asia as a whole, just as the region's incorporation into the Western colonial system was part of a larger historical process.

The latter process spread over a long period of time and involved many peoples, including those of the Iberian peninsula, the Netherlands, Britain, France, the Scandinavian countries, and the United States. Some of those peoples played a much more significant role in Southeast Asia than others, and it is and will remain an absorbing subject of study to trace the rise and fall of the fortunes of the Westerners as they engaged one with another to gain their objectives in Asia. During the course of time those objectives changed in often subtle ways, and the historian must be wary of easy generalizations intended to embrace a complex of events ranging over centuries. In its latter phase Western colonialism in Southeast Asia was something very different from what it had been at the beginning. In fact, the word "colonialism," which is a relatively modern term, does less than justice to the variety of historical phenomena discussed in this book.

Just as the Western colonial experience differed in time and place in Asia, so too did the Asian reaction to it. In Southeast Asia this reaction, until the twentieth century at any rate, was more quiescent than it was in China and India; but, again, such a generalization cannot hope to embrace the variety of responses in the individual countries of the region. What at least is becoming increasingly obvious as the subject is studied in greater depth is that Western colonialism, though diverting much of Southeast Asian life from its peculiar, indigenous course, did not necessarily cancel out age-old traditions and institutions. Thus while the Western impact, particularly during the nineteenth and twentieth centuries, introduced great technological, political, and economic changes in the region, it did not necessarily affect the fundamental character of Southeast Asia itself. Indeed, the alien nature of the Western impact often precluded its accommodation to the fabric of indigenous life and in this sense represents something different from the age-old cultural influences which had emanated from China, India, and the Middle East.

We should like to thank the following colleagues who have read various parts of the manuscript and have made valuable suggestions, many of which we have gladly incorporated: Professor Paul Wheatley (University of London), Professor David K. Wyatt (University of Michigan), Professor Oliver W. Wolters (Cornell University), Professor W. F. Wertheim and Dr. O. D. van den Muijzenberg (University of Amsterdam). Parts of the Introduction are based on Harry J. Benda's article, "The Structure of Southeast Asian History," which originally appeared in *Journal of Southeast Asian History* (Vol. III, #1, March, 1962, pp. 106–38), while the last section of Part Two was first published, in slightly different form, as a contribution by Harry J. Benda to *Imperial Japan and Asia: A Reassessment*, a symposium edited by Grant K. Goodman (New York: The East Asian Institute, Columbia University, 1967, pp. 65–79). The Editor of the *Journal of Southeast Asian History* and the Director of The East Asian Institute have been kind enough to permit us to use these materials in the present book. And last, our thanks go to Mr. Christopher S. Gray for the preparation of the index.

John Bastin
Harry J. Benda

Contents

Introduction

The Southeast Asian World

I

Southeast Asia is a modern term used to describe those territories to the south and east of the land masses of India and China that go to make up North and South Vietnam, Cambodia, Laos, Thailand, Burma, Malaysia, Singapore, Brunei, Indonesia, Portuguese Timor, and the Philippines. Together these countries cover an area of nearly 1½ million square miles and contain more than 220 million people, almost half of whom live in the three thousand islands of Indonesia. Likened by a nineteenth-century Dutch writer to a girdle of emerald flung round the Equator, the Indonesian archipelago forms, along with the seven thousand islands of the Philippines, and the Malaysian states of Borneo, a vast island world which is separated from the mainland at its nearest point by the Straits of Malacca and Singapore, and at its furthest by the great expanse of the South China Sea.

Mainland Southeast Asia is to some extent geologically separated from the remainder of the Asian continent by the chain of mountains extending from the Himalayas eastward into southern China. South of this eastward axis the less rugged mountain ranges of mainland Southeast Asia fall generally in a north-south direction, while those in the islands run from west to east. The north-south direction is evident in the mainland ranges among which the longest rivers in Southeast Asia, the Salween, Chao Phraya (Menam), Mekong, and Irrawaddy, develop parallel courses. These rivers, carrying their heavy loads of water and

1

silt deposits, constitute one of the most important elements in the agricultural cycle of mainland Southeast Asia.

Lying for the most part between the Tropic of Cancer and twelve degrees south of the Equator, the Southeast Asian countries share a generally heavy rainfall; and the constant high temperatures, which never vary much more than ten degrees from eighty degrees Fahrenheit, produce a continuous and luxuriant plant-growth which covers a great deal of the region with rain forests. The density of these forests has been a significant factor, though by no means the only one, in determining the concentration of settlement along the rivers, which even today are still an important means of movement and communication.

In prehistoric and historic times the rivers were the highways along which the Southeast Asian peoples effected their southward migrations. Following the primitive Australoid and Negrito peoples, a small number of whom still survive in Australia and certain regions of the Philippines, Indonesia, and Malaysia, the more advanced Indonesian or Austronesian races began their slow southward movement from southwest China during the second and third millennia B.C. Constituting the main elements of the present-day population of Malaya and island Southeast Asia, the Indonesian type peoples form two broad, though by no means exact, categories, the Proto-Malay and the Deutero-Malay, the former of which, with its Mongoloid strains, are represented in the Jakun of Malaya, the Torajas of Sulawesi, the Dyaks of Borneo, and the Bataks of Sumatra; the less homogenous "Deutero-Malay" family finds its representatives in the Malays of Sumatra and Malaysia, the Javanese, Sudanese, Balinese, and Madurese of Indonesia, and the Bisayans, Tagalogs, Ilokanos, Bikols, and Pampangans of the Philippines.

During and after the period when the Indonesian type peoples were achieving their wide dispersal in the south, the Austro-Asiatic Mons migrated into the coastal regions of Lower Burma from the valley of the Chao Phraya, and the related Khmers moved into the Mekong valley. The ethnically related Vietnamese, who during the first Christian millennium were subject to direct Chinese political control and cultural influence, migrated into the Red River delta from southern China, and shared with the Chams, a Malayo-Polynesian type people, the upper parts of the coast of Annam. The early Pyu and Burmans settled in the central Irrawaddy valley during the early Christian centuries, and the Shan or Thai peoples, who occupied the upper reaches of the Mekong and Red rivers, slowly dispersed over a wide region extending from Assam in the west to Tonkin and the borders of Cambodia in the east.

Despite this ethnic variety, the early peoples of Southeast Asia shared a fairly common pattern of material culture. Thus the Mesolithic cultures, as represented in the Bacsonian semipolished chisel-edged stone tools of Tonkin and related artifacts found on sites in Thailand, Malaya, and Sumatra, were replaced by the quadrangular adzes of the Neolithic or New Stone Age after the Indonesian type peoples began their southward migration into Southeast Asia during the third and second millennia B.C. Widely distributed finds of Neolithic pottery with strong stylistic similarities also suggest a long period of cultural sharing which was followed in the centuries immediately preceding the Christian era by the Bronze-Iron Age culture commonly referred to as the Dong-s'on. The distinguishing feature of this culture, which drew its main inspiration from China, was the large bronze drum, examples of which have been found widely scattered throughout Southeast Asia. Designs of the older Megalithic culture were sometimes fused with the newer Dong-s'on forms to produce decorative motifs acceptable to the Southeast Asian peoples; in other regions, particularly those adjacent to China, purer Dong-s'on designs prevailed.

Metals were not used in the manufacture of improved instruments of husbandry in Southeast Asia until a later stage, but when they were it represented an important step in the economic development of the region. At first entirely self-sufficient and based largely on hunting and fishing, the early economy of Southeast Asia was extended slowly by the adoption of primitive agricultural methods involving shifting dry cultivation on successively cleared forest lands. This form of agriculture, still widely practised in Southeast Asia, later gave way in areas like central Java to wet rice cultivation in permanently irrigated fields. The plough and domesticated animals such as the buffalo and ox became essential tools of the rice cycle, and settled habitation and an increase in production led to the extension of the static economy through a simple division of labor utilized for local cloth and metal manufacture. In those areas where wet rice cultivation developed, control of the water supplies for irrigation led to a marked degree of social cohesion and political order. Of course, this total evolutionary change in society, representing a move from one level of socio-cultural development to another, cannot be explained satisfactorily in terms of single elements. Southeast Asian society changed, and in so doing changed the way it adapted to its environment.

Wet rice cultivation, domestication of the ox and buffalo, the use of metals, and skill in navigation are recognized as the distinguishing material characteristics of Southeast Asian civilization before it was affected by outside influences, especially those emanating from India. Its spiritual characteristics were ancestor worship, the placing of shrines in elevated places, and beliefs which involved animism, a cosmological dualism between mountain and sea, and a numerology associated with magic. Although subject to considerable local variation and to subsequent modification by Hinduism, Buddhism, Islam, and Christianity, these cultural elements survived, and today provide the essential justification for the study of Southeast Asia in its own right and not merely as an appanage of China or India. Certainly it is becoming increasingly recognized that the process of "Indianization" did not represent simply the transmission of Indian civilization with a consequent displacement of local cultures, but a complex process involving the merging of foreign and indigenous elements to produce something that is distinctively Southeast Asian.

For the peoples of the region contact with Indian civilization meant their introduction to cultural forms based on Sanscritic writing and literature, to Hindu mythology and artistic motifs, and to Indian economic and political theories and practices. How the process of "Indianization" occurred is still a matter of considerable controversy. Hitherto, the generally accepted view was that Indian traders, who began visiting the embryo Southeast Asian ports possibly as a result of the Roman embargo on the export of precious metals in the first Christian century, were transmitters of Indian culture through marriage and other social contacts with the local people—a process that was often facilitated by the Indians' wealth and by their claims to magical powers. Against this, the opinion has been advanced that such traders, drawn from the lower social orders and engaged in peddler activities, could hardly have been the means by which the higher Indian cultural elements were transmitted to Southeast Asia, and that the agency was more likely to have been the Brahmans, who were invited to the courts of the Southeast Asian rulers to bolster their political authority, and who are known to have been knowledgeable in Hindu scriptures and literature. Once there, the Brahmans either assumed power by marriage or else extended their influence more subtly under royal protection. Other scholars, who feel that the degree and extent of "Indianization" in Southeast Asia cannot be explained solely in terms of this limited human agency, posit an intermediate stage through which small Indian trading centers developed slowly into larger "Indianized" cities and city-states.

These early cities of Southeast Asia, which were generally built on a common pattern portraying in terrestrial terms the Hindu or Buddhist universe, were surrounded by wooden palisades or stone-piled walls which gave protection to the wooden houses and royal palace inside and to the temples of brick and stone erected to the gods. The stone sanctuary representing Mount Meru, the focal point of the spiritual and secular forces of the state, was in the center with the wooden palace of the god-king and the residencies of the Brahman ministers nearby. Separating the palace from the dwellings of the subject-population were the buildings occupied by the soldiers and court retainers, including the domestic servants, craftsmen, and artists, who produced ornate weapons, jewelry, and carvings for the ruler, and the poets and story-tellers who surrounded him with language taboos and literary magic to consolidate his absolute power. The cosmological morphology of the early Southeast Asian city was subject to infinite variety of this basic pattern. But the general principle is clearly observable in the Angkorian complexes of the Khmers; in the Pyu city of Sri Ksetra, which legend ascribed to the work of the gods who modeled it on Indra's city on Mount Meru; in Mandalay, where the palace, enclosed within square walls and facing the cardinal points, had as its center a seven-tiered tower raised over the throne in imitation of the sacred mountain; in the capital city of Majapahit which, though not a walled town, was divided into a series of walled-in courtyards laid out in conformity to the spiritual and secular needs of the state; and in many other urban centers of the "Indianized" area of Southeast Asia.

II

Within this "Indianized" area, which included most of Southeast Asia except the Philippines and Vietnam, two basic types of political organization appear to have evolved during the millennium between the fourth and fourteenth centuries A.D. The first was the inland-agrarian "hydraulic" prototype, of which Khmer Angkor is one example and the Indonesian state of Mataram is another. On the other hand there was the riparian or coastal prototype of which Srivijaya was possibly one of the most important and highly developed. The former, perhaps the most prevalent polity in mainland Southeast Asia, displayed the typical division into court and peasantry, with virtually complete royal control over the agrarian economy, the absence of a substantial landowning class, and political power channeled through an appointive, quasi-bu-reaucratic nobility. The other prototype deviated sharply from this oriental-type despotism since it contained a more cosmopolitan population composed of merchants of various, including indigenous, races, an urban trading bourgeoisie, with substantial financial resources and, consequently, very likely possessing at least some degree of countervailing political power.

In the Philippines, which was only peripherally touched by the culture of India, social and political life down to the arrival of the Muslims and Spaniards revolved round the *barangays*, or territorial groupings of families, in which there was a sharp social demarcation between the four main classes of chieftains, nobles, free men, and serfs. The pattern of political relations existing between the *barangays* is unknown, and although there is some evidence of cooperation between them, it is by no means certain that such evidence attests to the existence of political organization on a supra-*barangay* level. In Vietnam, which from the first century A.D. really fell within a "Sinicized" sphere of influence, a Chinese social pattern of landed gentry and a political system based on Confucian bureaucracy were superimposed on indigenous molds. In all three cultural spheres of Southeast Asia, political power was essentially personal in character and therefore subject to extreme vicissitudes of fortune, so that the tendency toward social and economic cohesion within the framework of broader political units was counterbalanced by strong disruptive forces. The basic political pattern of early Southeast Asia was one of alternating periods of order and instability.

III

Until the beginning of the Christian era, when Chinese sources provide evidence of two powerful states in the Indo-Chinese peninsula, little material is available on the subject of political groupings in Southeast Asia. The first of the states mentioned in the Chinese sources was the "Indianized" pre-Khmer realm of Funan, which had its capital city near the village of Banam in the present-day Cambodian province of Prei Veng; the second was Lin-yi, later known as Champa, which was founded toward the end of the second century A.D. and had its center of power south of Hué. In the northern region of the Malay peninsula, possibly near the modern town of Patani, another "Indianized" kingdom, Langkasuka, was in existence about this period. Chinese records of the sixth century A.D. state that it had been founded four hundred years previously and that it had walled towns and produced eagle-wood and camphor.

The economic existence of Funan depended to a large degree on its trade through the port of Oc Eo, until it succumbed to the new Khmer kingdom of Chen-la in the sixth century. The powerful state which succeeded it in importance in Southeast Asia, Srivijaya, with its capital near Palembang in south Sumatra, also owed much of its commercial preeminence to the control it was able to exercise over western Java and the Straits of Malacca, and to its excellent geographical position between India and China. In the seventh and eighth centuries Srivijaya extended its political sway over the former independent state of Melayu (Jambi) in Sumatra, and apparently even over parts of southern Thailand, north Malaya, and west Java. It was accorded official recognition by the Chinese Emperor in the early eighth century, by which time it had long been noted as an important center of Buddhism of the Mahayana school.

The influence exerted by Mahayana Buddhism at this period in other parts of Southeast Asia, notably Malaya and Cambodia, was probably connected with the rise of the Pala dynasty in north India; the religion was specifically associated with a powerful new dynasty in central Java known as the Sailendras, who were responsible for the erection of a series of magnificent stone monuments, including the world-famous Borobodur, a replica of the cosmic mountain with a golden image of what is apparently a Sailendra king as supreme god at its summit. Sailendra influence extended beyond Java, possibly as far as Cambodia. In central Java, Mahayana Buddhism gradually gave way to Brahmanism, or merged to produce the Siva-Buddha cult, on which spiritual base rose the east (and later central) Javanese kingdom of Mataram. This state extended its sway over Bali during the tenth and eleventh centuries and, after a period of conflict with Srivijaya, continued to flourish until divisive forces ultimately split the realm. Both the increasing incursion into Southeast Asia by the Cholas of southern India and the recurring challenges presented by the successor Javanese states eventually weakened Srivijayan power, and its earlier dominant role in island Southeast Asia came to be exercised by the last of the Hindu-Javanese kingdoms, Majapahit, in the fourteenth century.

In Cambodia, evidence of Sailendra influence during the late eighth century is partly confirmed by local tradition and by later Arabic sources, and may well account for the spread of Mahayana Buddhism in the region at that particular time. A strong new centralizing Khmer power arose in Cambodia during the ninth century, and its monuments of imposing grandeur and beauty, built at a later period, survive to this day. During the eleventh century the new state quickly overran the Mon

ople along the Menam River, and in the following century reduced
for a time Funan's eastern dependency, Champa. The latter quickly
recovered and in turn set about the invasion of Cambodia. The Khmer
capital was captured toward the end of the twelfth century, but the
Chams were forced to withdraw and the final sacking of Angkor in the
first half of the fifteenth century was left to the Thai peoples who,
having been forced gradually southward from Yunnan by Chinese pressure since the seventh century, made their escape routes along the river
valleys of the Salween, Irrawaddy, Menam, and Mekong, where they
came into conflict with the Khmers. Angkor was abandoned and Khmer
power afterward began to center around Phnom Penh, the present-day
capital of Cambodia.

The southward movement of the Thai peoples resulted in the establishment of small states in Assam, Upper Burma, and Siam in the
twelfth and thirteenth centuries, during which period the Thais came
into open conflict with the Mons and Khmers, from whom they derived
much of their artistic and cultural heritage. It was not until the founding of Ayuthia in the middle of the fourteenth century that Thai principalities were in control of the territory now known as Thailand. The
new state of Ayuthia quickly consolidated its power and extended its
sway over the northern regions of the Malay peninsula, Tenasserim and
Tavoy.

Continuing conflicts with the northern Laotian states occurred in
the succeeding century, and after the reestablishment of the Burmese
monarchy in Pegu in the early sixteenth century, Thai attacks were
directed against that state also. The opportunity presented by a counter-
invasion of Thailand by the Burmese in the middle of the sixteenth
century was seized upon by the Cambodian ruler to annex several of
the border provinces, but the retaliatory sacking of the Cambodian
capital by the Thais toward the end of the sixteenth century marked the
beginning of a long period of decline for Cambodia. In the following
century a succession of Vietnamese and Chinese invasions against the
Thai-controlled provinces of Cambodia met only with mixed success,
and it was not until the Thais were engaged in a life and death struggle
with the Burmese in the mid-eighteenth century that the Vietnamese
were able to attempt a process of annexation that proved so successful
that the Cambodian ruler was obliged to offer tribute to both Thailand
and Annam. Cambodia continued to play the pawn between the Thais
and the Vietnamese until the middle of the nineteenth century, when

the Thai-supported ruler was elevated to the throne after a long period
of bitter warfare.

IV

The involved interprincipality relations and rivalries in Southeast
Asia have generally been explained in terms of the personal ambitions of
individual rulers, but it may well be that the inner dynamics of the
dynastic struggles are to be found in the existence, side by side, of different social and political structures. In Java, for example, it would appear that it was the struggle between inland and coastal polities that
accounts for part of the history of both Majapahit and Mataram; and
the constant clash between Vietnamese, Chams, and Khmers may also
be explained in terms of a basic polarization between different, if not
hostile, social and political systems.

Religion provides another important criterion for establishing basic
structural differences in the Southeast Asian realms, especially in the
context of the relationship between ecclesiastical and secular authority.
Religion in the Philippines up to the end of the fifteenth century—that
is, before contact with either Islam or Hispanic Catholicism—appears to
have been structurally rather simple, with neither an elaborate clerical
establishment nor a sophisticated creed exceeding animism or nature
and ancestor worship. By contrast, both the "Indianized" and "Sinicized" areas of Southeast Asia experienced profound contact with highly
sophisticated religious systems. In the "Sinicized" realms Taoism, Mahayana Buddhism, and Confucianism had been introduced from China.
More important, the shifting balance of power between the Buddhist
clergy and the Confucian mandarinate (the latter representatives of a
civic, religious-political cult), that occupies such a fascinating and complex place in the history of China, had apparently likewise been transmitted to the recipient Southeast Asian regions. Buddhism in Vietnam
should therefore be seen in a Chinese, and only secondarily in a comparative Southeast Asian, context. "Indianized" Southeast Asia was
Buddhist, too, but its Buddhism, of either Vehicle, was a direct importation from India which had not passed through the sieve of Chinese
Mahayanism. Buddhism in the "Indianized" regions is, in fact, often
hyphenated with Hinduism or Brahmanism, and is sometimes, as in the
Javanese context, referred to as Siva-Buddhism.

The crucial structural difference between the Buddhist establishments in the two areas may well have been that in "Sinicized" Annam and Tonkin the Buddhist monkhood, after several vicissitudes in its position, ceased to form an integral part of the politico-religious elite. From the mid-thirteenth century onward, it thus came to play a more or less peripheral role in the scholar-gentry dominated center, though not necessarily at the village level. In the "Indianized" principalities, on the other hand, Buddhism had seemingly adapted itself to, if it had not actually merged with, the Brahmanic court order to such an extent that Brahman and Buddhist monks reinforced each other, or in other words, came to form one elite group at courts revolving round deified kings who presented themselves now as Hindu gods, then as reincarnations of the Buddha, if not as both simultaneously.

Another comparison of religion in the "Indianized" and "Sinicized" areas deserves attention. Both Brahmanism and Buddhism in the "Indianized" realms were court religions, or more properly, ecclesiastic establishments undergirding and intermeshing with political authority. While Tantric Buddhism may have spread downward here and there to the peasantry, the "official" religion seems to have been a court affair pure and simple. The peasantry was probably forced to participate in the religious rites centering on the god-kings, but such participation was likely to have been passive, and the state religion as such did not cater to the villagers through its teachings or, more important from a structural point of view, provide a rural clergy for them. The peasantry, therefore, presumably continued to live in a spiritual, largely animistic world of its own. This, however, may have been the prevalent picture in the "hydraulic" inland principalities only. Whether or not Buddhism, in a thriving trading and maritime community and major center of Mahayana Buddhist learning like Srivijaya, did not play a somewhat different role for greater numbers of the population outside the court circle remains to be determined.

In the "Sinicized" area of Southeast Asia the separation of "state and church" (that is, the ultimate supremacy of the Confucian mandarinate over the Buddhist monks) at times seems to have brought the monks closer to the peasantry, without, however, endowing Vietnamese peasant religion with a lasting or profound Buddhist element. Apparently Buddhist monks occasionally placed themselves at the head of peasant unrest, but seemingly they did not occupy a central place in the structure of the Vietnamese village. Buddhism in Vietnam was allowed to continue as a private faith but it was not nourished from peasant roots. At the same time, Chinese and later indigenous Confucian control

insulated Vietnam from the intrusion of other world faiths whose penetration and ultimate consolidation marked the beginning of the modern
period in other parts of Southeast Asia. Rural Vietnam thus came to
exhibit a religious vacuum, which in succeeding centuries allowed the
mushrooming of a plethora of religious beliefs and practices and, with
them, of a wide range of ecclesiastic personnel.

V

With the exception of Vietnam, Southeast Asia experienced significant changes in the period between the fourteenth and sixteenth centuries. In the Philippines, two world religions appeared, and with them
new social and political patterns were established. Muslims and Spaniards introduced both highly sophisticated faiths and a system of integrated principalities. Although Islam was pushed back from Luzon, it
maintained itself in the southeastern islands, and these came to constitute a religious frontier dividing the Christianized sphere in the north
from the Islamic world of Indonesia and Malaysia in the south. Equally
significant were the changes wrought in the "Indianized" areas of mainland Southeast Asia after the thirteenth century, when the Brahmanic
Mahayana Buddhist court civilizations gave way to Theravada-dominated
principalities. Neither in these realms nor in the Islamized sultanates
of island Southeast Asia did the new religions remove all traces of
Mahayana Buddhism and Brahmanism; indeed, in Indonesia and Malaysia Islam is often represented as a thin veneer on the courts still dominated by the spirit and practices of the earlier period. But wherever
Theravada Buddhism or Islam struck proper roots they proved immune
to displacement by other faiths.

Externally, the advance of these religions in Southeast Asia can be
explained by the missionary zeal of Singhalese Buddhism on the one
hand, and the worldwide resurgence of Islamic Sufism on the other; but
their advance was also facilitated by political and religious disintegration
within the Southeast Asian realms themselves. In Angkor, for example,
where the old order had seemingly fallen into disrepute and become the
object of fear and hatred on account of hardships imposed on the population by the building mania and other excesses of the god-kings,
circumstances were favorable to the reception, via Thailand, of Singhalese Buddhism of the Lesser Vehicle, which opposed individual person-
ality and therefore the attribution of deity to the rulers. Though by no
means the only factor, there is little doubt that the new religion con-

tributed in great measure to the rapid decline of the Khmer empire during the fourteenth century.

The innovations introduced by Theravada Buddhism were three-fold. In the first place, it created a quasi-egalitarian religious community of which even the monarchs themselves became, albeit for short times and mainly symbolically, members. Second, it is not unlikely that by virtue of their example and teachings the monks exerted a measure of restraint on the exercise of monarchial power. And finally, sociologically the most important innovation of the new faith lay in the new monk-hood which practiced the principles of otherworldly simplicity and frugality, in sharp contrast to the Mahayana monks of the classical era. In spite of the close liaison between the upper ranks of the Buddhist monastic order and the courts, the mass of the new monks became village "priests," permeating all aspects of peasant life and forming the undisputed centers of rural education and social activities. This amounted to a revolutionary change in the religious landscape of main-land Southeast Asia or, more precisely, in the traditional balance be-tween secular and ecclesiastic authority. The two were still intimately connected, but they no longer represented the twin aspects of court culture only; indeed, the new religious order had an obvious bearing on rural unrest in Theravada lands, which, as often as not, over the cen-turies came to be led by monks, the only spiritual and organizational leaders of the peasantry. In other words, the "beggars'" democracy was no longer leaderless or ideologically confined to its world of local spirits and traditions. Theravada Buddhism had forged a link—an ambiguous link, to be sure—between the Great Tradition and the Little Tradition, and therein lies its major significance in terms of structural change in Southeast Asia.

Close parallels, as well as interesting contrasts, exist in the Islamized parts of the former "Indianized" realms. The extent and depth of the consolidation of the two religions obviously differed to a marked degree, depending among other things on internal social factors. Thus in the agrarian principalities of the mainland, where the new faith was not associated with any particular social and economic class, "conversions" apparently proceeded smoothly and without encountering concerted opposition from defenders of the old order. As for Islam, while there is no direct evidence that this intrinsically egalitarian creed owed its spread to innate peasant opposition to the established regimes, its expansion was by no means unopposed by some of the powers-that-were. Islamiza-tion proceeded from the coastal mercantile principalities or dependencies—such as Malacca, Achin, and Bantam—to such inland agrarian polities as Mataram. The dynamics of Islamization would thus appear to be certainly bound up with the age-old rivalry between two kinds of societies, now sharpened by an increasingly wealthy and independent trading and commercial class and, in some instances, by its administrative allies. It is in this context that the history of Islam is best understood, as Mataram in Java clearly attests.

The sultans of Mataram won a temporary victory over Islam through the stratagem of *pro forma* adopting the new faith themselves. Having taken the wind out of the enemy's sails, so to speak, they proceeded to attack on the two fronts that most seriously threatened the *status quo*. The prime religious-political targets were the rebellious commercial port districts of the northeast coast whose systematic destruction by Mataram may have been greatly facilitated by the ceaseless and ultimately successful molestation of Indonesian traders by the newly arrived representatives of the Dutch East India Company. Mataram's second target were those overzealous propounders of the new faith, the *ulama*, who became formidable obstacles to the royal absolutism of the newly converted Mataramese sultans. In a crushing blow, Amangkurat I (1645–1677) reportedly had several thousand recalcitrant *ulama* slaughtered. With its dynamic coastal bases destroyed, its lines of communication with overseas Muslim centers cut by joint action of Mataram and the Dutch East India Company, and its most voluble propagators annihilated, Javanese Islam was forced into domestication and its long, syncretic slumber.

VI

While Vietnam survived virtually unchanged down to this period, the Philippines, Indonesia, and "Indianized" Southeast Asia experienced varying degrees of religious, social, and political innovation. The fifteenth, sixteenth, and seventeenth centuries constitute a watershed in the historical development of many parts of the region, although the elements of continuity during that period are much more evident than the elements of change. In the Philippines, Malaysia, and Indonesia, where Spanish, Portuguese, and, above all, Dutch influences directly and more or less importantly impinged on society, the traditional order changed more rapidly. Elsewhere, the Southeast Asian world moved, both internally and externally, within the broad confines established at earlier times. It is not until the mid-nineteenth century that ever wider parts of the area come to share intrinsically similar and profound social and political upheavals caused by modern Western imperialism and colonialism. It is only then that the various parts of Southeast Asia, without necessarily shedding their individuality and historical legacies, are welded more closely together.

Until that time one is faced with the problem of assessing the effect of early Western contacts on Southeast Asia, a subject that has aroused considerable controversy. In recent years there has been a tendency, more perhaps in theory than in practice, to pay greater respect to the majesty of the Southeast Asian infrastructure, and to view the Dutch, let alone their Portuguese predecessors and competitors, as mere tangential influences on the course of Southeast Asian history. Arresting and welcome as this corrective is, it is easily possible to overstate and exaggerate it. At the outset the Westerners may well have constituted no more than an additional factor in the age-old pattern of Southeast Asian trade, forced to carry out their commercial dealings in an essentially Asian matrix; but quite soon the Western economic agencies, especially the Dutch East India Company, became *primus inter pares*, to say the least. While its monopolistic control over Indonesian and Asian trade may have been more limited than previously thought, the Dutch Company nevertheless profoundly affected the economy and the social structure of those parts of Indonesia where it exercised quasi-sovereign political control. However salutary the warning against the application of European historical categories to the historiography of Asia, this must not bar us from examining the early centuries of Western intrusion into Asia as a possibly distinct, if only transitional, period in the history of Southeast Asia.

PART ONE

The West
in Southeast Asia

The Western Entry
into Southeast Asia

I

Heralds of the new age were the Portuguese, whose discovery of a sea-route to Asia round the Cape of Good Hope at the end of the fifteenth century was inspired by a mixture of religious, political, and economic motives. Important among these was a desire to participate in the spice trade of western Asia which was shared by the Muslim merchants of Gujerat, who collected the spices from the Malay *entrepôt* of Malacca, and by Indians, and Arabs who shipped them to the Levant by way of the Persian Gulf and the Red Sea. Although unable to close the latter route to Muslim trade, the Portuguese in Hormuz and Goa exerted a considerable influence on commerce and shipping in the Persian Gulf and Indian Ocean during the early sixteenth century, as well as on the maritime arteries of the Southeast Asian spice trade once they had captured Malacca and established bases in eastern Indonesia. The competition of Javanese and Malay merchants prevented them from monopolizing this branch of commerce as the Dutch were to do later, but they managed to secure large quantities of spices from the Moluccas, Ambon, and Banda, and a major share of the sandalwood trade of Solor and Timor. By the mid-sixteenth century they were regulating the export of cinnamon from the maritime provinces of Ceylon, and functioning in Macao as important intermediaries in the trade of eastern Asia. Later, after the control of Nagasaki was handed to the Jesuits (1571), they acted for a time as bullion brokers between Japan and China, exchanging large amounts of Japanese silver for Chinese gold.

Despite these impressive achievements, the impact of the Portuguese on the economy and organization of trade in Asia is frequently represented as negative. Compared with the Dutch, who are said to be the true progenitors of Western colonialism in Asia as they were the first to apply the principle of capital investment to overseas ventures, the Portuguese are characterized as medieval, concerned only with conquest, religious conversion, loot, and tribute. Yet the large amounts of private capital subscribed by Italians and Germans to finance early Portuguese expansion, and the active part played by European merchants in *Asia Portuguesa*, make it dangerous to exaggerate the novel financial features of the Dutch and English East India Companies or their unique contribution to the development of Western commerce in Asia. Apart from the authority exercised by the Crown, and the conquistadorial and missionary spirit which influenced its growth, the Portuguese seaborne empire in Asia was based on economic and political principles which, far from being markedly different from the secular trading organizations of northern Europe, were often emulated by them. The establishment of forts and trading factories, the conclusion of treaties with Asian rulers regulating the delivery and price of produce, and the system of issuing official passes to direct the flow of Asian shipping, were only some of the more important Portuguese practices which were taken over and extended by the British and Dutch. The latter certainly controlled more avenues of trade and affected Asian production in a more fundamental manner than their predecessors, but the influence of the Portuguese on various sectors of the commercial economy of Asia during the sixteenth and early seventeenth centuries should not for that reason be minimized.

Although the Portuguese colonial empire in Asia was basically maritime in character, it was sustained by a chain of fortified posts and trading settlements stretching from east Africa to the Timor Sea. With the possible exception of Ceylon, these possessions did not embrace much territory, and as a result the Portuguese were never confronted by local administrative problems of the magnitude which faced the British, Dutch, and Spaniards as they extended their territorial holdings in South and Southeast Asia during the seventeenth and eighteenth centuries. All the same, the Portuguese were not averse to interfering in the affairs of their Asian neighbors and on occasion influenced the course of political events out of all proportion to their resources and numbers. In

Malacca they never exceeded six hundred, yet their presence undoubtedly stimulated the rise of the powerful north Sumatran sultanate of
Achin by initially diverting Muslim trade to Pasai and later Kutaraja,
and this in turn led to a bitter and protracted struggle with the Achinese
for political and commercial hegemony in the Straits of Malacca. The
Portuguese were also obliged to take an active interest in the politics of
the Johore empire, partly to counter Achinese influence in the Malay
peninsula, and partly to restrain Johore's own economic ambitions in
the south. The curious power struggle between Malays, Portuguese, and
Achinese, which is so marked a feature of the political and economic
history of the West Malaysian region during the sixteenth and early
seventeenth centuries, ended as abruptly as it began when the Portuguese
were driven out of Malacca by the Dutch, and the Achinese sultanate
passed into the hands of the first of four weak female rulers. The equally
interesting role which the Portuguese played in the sixteenth century
political and religious conflicts in the Moluccas is better known, and
affords further evidence of the significant consequences which flowed
from Portuguese intervention in Southeast Asian affairs.

Whatever the overall economic and political impact of the Portuguese in Asia, their success in shipping to Lisbon vast quantities of
spices and pepper soon engaged the attention of their fellow Iberians
who, because of a series of papal bulls, briefs, and donations, were
debarred from direct access to Asia by way of the Cape of Good Hope.
The westward path across the Atlantic and Pacific oceans to the Philippines and the Moluccas blazed for Spain by Magellan in 1519–21 was
immediately disputed by Portugal, but it was nearly a decade before
the latter's claim to the Moluccas and to all territories lying within a
line drawn seventeen degrees to the eastward were formally recognized.
If faithfully observed, the Treaty of Zaragoza would have excluded Spain
from Southeast Asia altogether. As it was, the weakening of Portuguese
power in eastern Indonesia, especially in the face of Dutch opposition at
the beginning of the seventeenth century, enabled Spain to maintain her
possessions in the Moluccas until as late as the 1660s, and to extend by
conquest and treaty, after Miguel López de Legazpi arrived with ships
and supplies from Mexico, that seemingly unpropitious beginning which
had been made in the Philippines by Magellan forty years earlier. Luzon
was pacified, and the Spanish flag was carried to the Visayas, Mindoro,
and Catanduanes by the *conquistadores*, whose martial discipline, superior arms, and unquestioning faith more than compensated for their
lack of numbers. The work of conquest was consolidated and extended

by the evangelizing activities of the Catholic priests and friars, who were encouraged and sustained in their endeavors by the Castilian monarchy. Yet, as with the Portuguese, the Cross did not entirely dominate Spanish activities in Asia. By utilizing part of her supplies of New World silver, carried in galleons across the Pacific Ocean, Spain was able to effect such a profitable trade in the silks and porcelains of China that by the end of the sixteenth century Manila had developed into one of the most thriving commercial centers of Southeast Asia.

II

The activities of the Spaniards and Portuguese in Asia did not pass unobserved by the trading peoples of northern Europe. But there was at first no possible appeal against the papal bulls and briefs which conferred on the Iberian apostles of Christ a fairly equal share of the Atlantic and Pacific worlds, and even later, when Protestant feeling in England and the Netherlands came to challenge openly this territorial allocation, no amount of anti-Catholic rhetoric could supply the deficiencies in the nautical knowledge required to make the hazardous voyages to Asia. Only by the end of the sixteenth century, when the Netherlands had won from Spain her effective independence, when Spanish sea-power had been successfully challenged in the Atlantic Ocean, when Portugal had fallen under the constitutional control of Spain, when capital-saving from the north European trading ventures was available for new commercial outlets, and when the nautical secrets contained in the Portuguese rutters were becoming known, were the northern Protestant nations in any position to challenge seriously the trading preserves of the Iberians. The disclosure during the last decade of the sixteenth century of the detailed sailing directions and lists of harbors and islands frequented by the Portuguese was important in stimulating Anglo-Dutch interest in Asian commerce, but more important in giving it initial impetus was the disruption to the trade of Antwerp caused by Spanish activities in the Lowlands, and the embargo placed by the Spanish Crown on Dutch exports of spices from Lisbon.

Early British and Dutch voyages to Asia were financed by independent groups of merchants in London and the ports of Holland, but high investment costs and the hazardous nature of the trade soon led to the formation of two organizations which, despite subsequent radical modification, directed the course of British and Dutch activities in Asia for the next two centuries. As originally incorporated in 1600, the English

East India Company consisted of a General Court of stockholders, and a Court of Committees, or Directors, under a Governor and Deputy-Governor. The Court of Committees, numbering twenty-four members, comprised the executive branch of the Company, with power to initiate trading policy ratified by a majority of stockholders. As the Court of Committees had general administrative functions to perform, such as the provisioning of ships, it came to divide up into specialist subcommittees, each with its own task of collecting stores, armaments, trading goods, and silver for shipment to Asia. The General Court of stockholders took no part in these functions, but all important matters of trading policy had to go before it for decision. In the English East India Company the stockholders exercised considerably greater power than their counterparts in the United Dutch East India Company, which incorporated in 1602 the existing overseas trading organizations in the major Dutch ports. By the new arrangements these organizations, or chambers, were assigned a quota of the commercial operations of the United Company depending upon the amount of capital invested, but in certain matters they were subject to the Company's general policy as formulated by the Seventeen Gentlemen, elected by the chambers in proportion to their capital investment. The chambers retained their own distinct administrations, but as the Company grew more structurally uniform during the seventeenth century it was these Seventeen who became responsible for the determination of policy, their increasing power in this respect arising from the fact that they had in their hands control of the declaration and distribution of dividends.

The capital invested in the Dutch East India Company amounted to 6½ million guilders, of which Amsterdam subscribed more than half. The magnitude of this investment can be comprehended when it is realized that the first voyage of the English Company was financed with capital of only one-tenth of that amount. This marked difference in the amount of capital investment explains the strength and early successes of the Dutch Company in Asia compared with the less spectacular results achieved by its English rival, even when the latter abandoned the system of separate voyages in 1613 to form the first Joint Stock; but the relative initial strength of the two Companies is to be distinguished not so much in terms of actual capital investment, as in the fact that the Dutch operated on a continuing investment, and not on capital that was subject to withdrawal for division among the stockholders after the completion of specific voyages. To be sure, it was provided in the charter of the Dutch Company that investors had the right to withdraw their capital at the end of ten years' operations, but the Directors refused to recognize this provision, arguing that if investors wanted their money they could sell their stock to other speculators. This was the feature that marked the essential difference in the financial strength of the two Companies during the early decades of the seventeenth century and, when reinforced by greater state support, enabled the Dutch Company to gain such enormous initial advantages over both the Portuguese and British. Operating on a fixed capital, it was able to provide a bigger investment in Asia itself—in goods, ships, and men—and this ultimately proved to be the decisive factor.

Indonesia was the main center of operations for both the Dutch and English East India Companies during the early years of the seventeenth century, although attempts were made by the latter to develop avenues of trade in the Red Sea area and, after 1613, when a factory was established at Surat, in South Asia as well. In 1619 the Dutch moved their headquarters from Bantam to Jakarta, where their rights to construct a fort and lay out a town (Batavia) were enforced by conquest. Because of their superior maritime and economic resources they were able to make notable advances against the Portuguese and Indonesian powers, and, as they wished to establish monopoly conditions of trade, were not particularly tolerant of the English benefiting from their hard-earned spoils. Anglo-Dutch conflict in Southeast Asia was recognized by both Companies as inimical to their interests, and in 1619 it was agreed that there should be equal contributions to the cost of defense against the Spaniards and Portuguese in Asia, and a proportionate sharing of the trade in pepper and spices. Despite this "Accord," which in theory constituted a united Protestant front against the Iberian powers in Asia, friction between the Dutch and British officials in Indonesia continued. Matters came to a head in 1623 with the so-called "Massacre" of Amboina, in which a handful of British merchants and Japanese soldiers in the employ of the English East India Company were put to death on charges of plotting the capture of the Dutch fort. This event, so important in hardening Anglo-Dutch feeling, is generally represented as marking the end of British commercial connections with eastern Indonesia; but though the English Company's trade with the region was subject to interference, especially during such crises as the first Anglo-Dutch War (1652–54), it continued to flourish until as late as the 1680s, when a local dynastic dispute in the sultanate of Bantam provided the Dutch with the opportunity of expelling the British from Java altogether. The latter were able to maintain a footing in the pepper ports of western Sumatra, but in any case British interest was already centering more on the Indian subcontinent and on the trade with Persia, which was developed by way of Surat. Indian goods were also shipped directly to home markets, thus providing a new range of imports for sale in Europe. So quickly did this branch of commerce expand that by the end of the seventeenth century pepper and spices had given way to Indian textiles as the most important element in the European imports of both the English and Dutch Companies.

The British were able to maintain their position in western India despite Portuguese opposition directed from Goa, but it was left to the Hollanders to make the most notable advances against the Iberian powers in Asia. Periodic blockades of Manila by Dutch ships during the early decades of the seventeenth century disrupted the galleon trade from Mexico, and the pirating of Fukien junks bound for the city imposed severe strains on the Spanish sector of the Philippine economy. The recognition accorded by the Treaty of Münster (1648) of Netherland's independence and rights of free trade in Asia relieved the situation for Spain, but left the Portuguese exposed to mounting Dutch pressure elsewhere. The Hollanders failed to capture Macao in 1622, but they were soon able to establish themselves on the Pescadores and on Formosa, where they built a heavily fortified *entrepôt* rivaling Macao and Manila. Until they were driven out from there in 1662 by Chêng Chêng Kung (Koxinga), Castle Zeelandia was of immense importance to the Dutch East India Company for it served as the main distribution center of Japanese silver after the expulsion of the Portuguese from Japan in 1639. In one particular year silver worth 3 million florins was shipped into Formosa on Dutch ships, so it is hardly surprising that the Directors in Amsterdam at that period regarded the trade in specie as the most important branch of the Company's activities in Asia.

Further to the south the Dutch gained access to the tin supplies of the Malay peninsula by wresting Malacca from the Portuguese (1641), and at the same time they united with the Kandyian ruler in an effort to expel their enemies from Ceylon. After a bitter twenty-year struggle this was achieved in 1658, and the Dutch Company fell heir to the Portuguese domains in the maritime provinces and to a large part of the island's cinnamon trade. On the west coast of India, where important supplies of pepper could be obtained, the Dutch captured Cochin from the Portuguese in the middle of the century and immediately directed their attention to undermining the position of the English Company in the region. Their determined efforts were unsuccessful, and once the

Travancore rulers began interfering in the production and distribution of pepper, the Dutch had to abandon entirely all hope of establishing over Malabar pepper that effective monopoly they succeeded in imposing on the spice trade of the Moluccas after the last remaining loophole in the Celebes was closed in 1666–69. With the capture of Macassar, and the expulsion of the British from west Java thirteen years later, the main outline of their commercial empire in Asia was drawn. They continued the conflict with their British rivals in India, but a century later were reduced to playing second fiddle to tunes alternately improvised by Dupleix and Clive. With Goa, Macao, and Timor in Portuguese hands, and the Spaniards securely entrenched in Luzon and the Visayas, the Dutch had to remain content with their exclusive dealings with Japan, with the major part of the cinnamon trade of Ceylon, and, under growing British political hegemony, with limited commercial ventures in India. By the beginning of the eighteenth century their main endeavors were directed toward establishing the spice trade of the Moluccas on an efficient monopoly basis, and to extending the cultivation of coffee and sugar in Java, the most densely populated and highly developed of all the Indonesian islands.

III

During the early phase of Western contact with Southeast Asia, relations between Asians and Europeans were confined in the main to trading transactions conducted on a simple basis of exchanging silver and manufactured goods for pepper, spices, and other tropical produce required in Europe. As the real price of silver was higher in Asia than it was in Europe, this trade could be maintained advantageously by shipping silver, generally in the form of Spanish reals, direct to Asia. Mercantilist opposition to this system of trade was formidable, and inevitably led to an examination of other means of providing goods to exchange for spices and pepper. As the Asian market for European manufactured goods was limited, a partial solution, but one which became increasingly important, was found in the intra-Asian trade itself. By engaging in the carrying trade between Asian ports Western traders were able to reduce their dependence on specie, and so reduce the proportions of silver that would otherwise have been necessary if direct purchases for Europe had been made.

The local trade between Asian ports was particularly significant in the development of the Dutch and English East India Companies in Asia, and helps explain why these essentially mercantile organizations became territorial in character. In order to provide for the collection of trading goods it was necessary to establish permanent commercial centers, and to station at them European agents, or factors, who collected throughout the year goods necessary for shipment to Asian or European markets in the ensuing trading season. These "factories" represented the beginnings of Western territorial holdings in Asia, and led to the adoption of local administrative arrangements which subsequently blossomed into full governmental instrumentalities. The later English system of Governor-in-Council had its genesis in the President and Council arrangements in Bantam and Surat during the early seventeenth century, and these in turn had their origin in the appointment of a Factor-General and Supervisor of Factories in 1614, and the joining with him three years later of two persons to give him advice. In the case of the Dutch officials in Asia, there was after 1609 a Governor-General who was intended originally to have only presidential powers over a Council of the Indies which was to be the real governing authority; but under the forceful direction of some of the early appointees, power came to be concentrated in the hands of the Governor-General, and the exercise of this power was circumscribed only by the fear of dismissal at the hands of the Directors at home and, later, by the appointment of a Governor of the northeast coast of Java following its cession to the Company by the central Javanese principality of Mataram in the mid-eighteenth century.

With the extension of Dutch territorial control in Java, large quantities of products which had hitherto been paid for at market prices began to be received on more advantageous terms under contracts and treaties concluded with the Indonesian rulers. In addition to demanding specific amounts of rice, sugar, pepper, and coffee from the people of Java, the Dutch also required personal services in the manufacture of salt, cutting of timber in the forests, dredging of canals, construction of roads and bridges, and all kinds of public works. Moreover, the officials of the Company exploited this source of labor for their own private purposes. It is not possible on the basis of existing economic data to estimate precisely what proportion of goods and services were rendered by the people of Java to their Dutch masters, but it has been calculated that in the Preanger districts of west Java, where the people were engaged in the forced cultivation of the coffee shrub, individual cultivators received less than one-fifth of the total market value of the coffee which they handed to their own rulers for the Dutch. The Indonesian rulers retained for themselves about one-half of this produce and delivered the remainder to the Company.

The traditional economy of Java was regulated by an indigenous social structure which the Dutch freely adapted to their own purposes. The demands made by the Company were not laid directly upon the Indonesians themselves but upon their rulers, over whom the Company came to exercise a large measure of control. Called "Regents" by the Dutch, after their own officials in the Netherlands, these rulers of the northeastern coastal districts of Java were obliged to enter into treaties of alliance with the Company which bound them to obey the Dutch officials and to deliver to them the requisite amounts of produce. They promised to conform to the commercial regulations of the Company, to live at peace with their neighboring Regents, to submit all dissensions arising between them to the Company for decision, and not to form separate alliances with other Indonesian rulers or with any European power. In the Preanger districts of west Java, over which the Company claimed a greater degree of sovereignty, the Regents were issued with certificates of appointment which made them theoretically more dependent upon the Dutch. Yet despite the legal difference between the Indonesian rulers in the two parts of Java, the Company in practice dealt with them in much the same way, never hesitating to interfere directly in the administration of the country if Dutch economic and political interests seemed threatened. Nonetheless, official Dutch policy was strongly opposed to interference as the aim was to supervise rather than to exercise direct control over the people. Whatever its later theoretical justification, this system of administration in Java had the obvious advantage of being cheap, and, when linked with the commercial monopoly regulating the production and sale of spices in the Moluccas, was effective in yielding enormous quantities of produce to the Dutch Company for sale in Asia and Europe.

The Netherlands were not exceptional among the Western colonial powers in exploiting the labor and agricultural resources of their Southeast Asian possessions. During the late seventeenth and eighteenth centuries the British developed a system of forced pepper cultivation in western Sumatra that was basically the same as the Dutch coffee system in Java, and in the Philippines the Spaniards earlier introduced from their colonies in the New World the *encomienda* system which provided cheap Filipino labor and tribute. But whereas in western Sumatra every Indonesian family was obliged to cultivate two thousand (later one thousand) pepper vines annually, and deliver the produce to the British at stipulated prices, in the Philippines all adult males embraced in the *encomiendas* were subject to the payment of annual tribute, which the grantees (*encomenderos*) and their agents were often able to demand in the form of goods and services in excess of the official amount. Protests by the clergy about these abuses at the end of the sixteenth century led to the attempted regularization of tribute payments, and further revisions were made by the Spanish authorities at the beginning of the seventeenth century when it was provided that only a proportion of the tribute could be collected in kind, the remainder having to be received in specie. The system gradually degenerated into a family tax, a process that was facilitated by the liquidation of the private *encomiendas* by the Crown. In the original apportionment only one-third of the Filipino population was reserved for the benefit of the Crown, but during the seventeenth and eighteenth centuries an increasingly large number of private *encomiendas* were assumed by the Crown, and in 1721 it was expressly provided that all such *encomiendas* would automatically be taken over as they fell vacant. The annual tribute, which was increased during the nineteenth century, continued to be paid until the end of Spanish rule in the Philippines.

In addition to the exactions of tribute the Filipinos were also subject to levies of forced labor under the *polo* system (*polos y servicios*), which developed in the late sixteenth and early seventeenth centuries as a result of the burdens placed on the economy by the Dutch war. By this system all adult males, except members of the chieftain class, were obliged to give their services periodically to the state labor pool. Although they were supposed to be paid wages for this work, in practice they received only doles of rice sufficient for subsistence. *Polo* labor was supposed to be used for work of a military or naval character, but it was frequently utilized for public works, and therefore compares with the labor levies exacted by the Dutch in Indonesia. The Spanish authorities in the Philippines also demanded from their subjects the delivery of certain amounts of produce against fixed rates of payment; but as the colonial treasury was unable to meet its obligations in this respect the *vandala* system became in reality another form of direct taxation.

These revenue and labor systems, and the intricate commercial ties linking Mexico with China, were the supports of the colonial economy in the Philippines during the first two centuries of Spanish rule.

Following the British occupation of Manila between 1762 and 1764, attempts were made to diversify the economy by encouraging the cultivation of cotton, sugar, mulberry plants, tea, indigo, and spices, and also by expanding the manufacture of silk, hemp, and porcelains. The Economic Society of Friends of the Country was established in 1781 to encourage these objectives and to raise the necessary capital for the local enterprises. In an endeavor to free the Philippines from economic dependence on Mexico a tobacco monopoly was created by the government in 1782 in the Ilocos, Nueva Ecija, and Marinduque, with each Filipino family there being obliged to cultivate a specified number of plants annually, and to deliver the produce at fixed prices. At the same time (1785) the Royal Company of the Philippines was formed with the object of establishing direct commercial connections between metropolitan Spain and the Philippines instead of by way of Acapulco.

The radical reorientation of Spanish commerce with the Philippines proposed by the new arrangements was reflected in the abrogation of the decrees prohibiting the importation of Asian commodities into Spain, as well as in the Company's own privileges, which included not only a monopoly of the Philippine commerce with Spain but also the right to engage in direct trade with Asian ports. The Company was permitted to fly the flag of the Spanish navy and to purchase stores from royal naval arsenals at official prices; and, as a further mark of royal favor, the Crown supplied one-eighth of the Company's capital, the remainder being subscribed by banks and mercantile concerns in Spain and Mexico. Despite a brief period of prosperity the Royal Company of the Philippines experienced heavy losses, and, as it was unable to raise sufficient additional capital to cover them, was obliged to dispose of shares to foreigners. Moreover, because of the Company's failure to participate effectively in the intra-Asian trade—a failure which it shared with the Dutch East India Company—the Spanish authorities had to allow foreign merchants to import Asian commodities into Manila. The share capital of the Company was increased in the early years of the nineteenth century but it did nothing to remedy the poor administration and heavy overheads which had dogged the Company from the beginning. Its privileges were finally revoked in 1834 when Manila was thrown open to world trade. During the fifty years of its existence the Royal Company of the Philippines, in accordance with obligations under its charter, invested large sums in agricultural and industrial enterprises in the Philippines, and this capital did much to bolster the indigo, sugar, and textile sectors of the Philippine economy.

IV

It is perhaps not without significance that the Royal Company of the Philippines was incorporated by the Spanish Crown when the era of European mercantile companies in Asia was rapidly drawing to a close. A number of these companies had been formed in the seventeenth and early eighteenth centuries, including the Danish and Swedish East India Companies, the Imperial East India Company of Ostend, as well as a spate of French companies. Many of them had limited and far from profitable existences, but some, particularly the Ostend Company, caused the Dutch and English East India Companies considerable concern during their brief periods of operation. The English Company also had to contend with competition from rival organizations in Britain, and at the beginning of the eighteenth century it amalgamated with one of them under the name of the United English East India Company, which then enjoyed a continuous existence down to the Indian Mutiny of 1857. Though many of its commercial and political powers were severely curtailed during the late eighteenth and early nineteenth centuries, and by the end had ceased altogether to be a trading organization, the English Company nevertheless managed to survive fifty-odd years longer than its great rival in the Netherlands.

The economic fortunes of the Dutch East India Company experienced a marked decline during the second half of the eighteenth century, at which time its debts increased tenfold to the staggering total of 100 million guilders. These vast liabilities resulted from a number of factors, including the failure of the Seventeen to relate dividends to trading profits, the rising costs of territorial administration in Indonesia, losses caused by mounting competition from other Western nations in Asia, the Company's inability to adapt itself to the vicissitudes of the intra-Asian trade, and its rigid adherence to a system of commercial monopoly without the maritime resources to enforce it. During the American and French Revolutionary Wars Britain was able to isolate Java from its European markets by naval blockade, and the Company, lacking the financial resilience to survive, was forced to apply to the States-General for assistance. After the French invasion of the Netherlands the government dismissed the Directors and appointed a committee, later a Council of Asiatic Possessions, to administer colonial affairs. Shortly afterward, on January 1, 1800, the mighty Dutch United East India Company was officially dissolved and its properties and titles assumed by the Netherlands state.

Although the fall of the Dutch East India Company may be attributed to specific causes, its general decline can only be explained satisfactorily in terms of the growing commercial and maritime impotence of the Netherlands during the eighteenth century. With this went a proportionate increase in British economic and political power in Asia, especially after Clive's victory at Plassey and the acquisition of the *diwani* placed the revenues of the Bengal provinces of the Mughal empire in the hands of the English East India Company. This enormous expansion of territory and revenue resources, reinforced by a growing volume of trade with China and an industrial revolution at home, enabled Britain to establish herself as paramount power in India and from there to interfere more effectively in the affairs of Southeast Asia. By the time the Dutch East India Company was dissolved, Britain had become the most formidable Western nation in Asia, a fact which the Dutch were not slow to recognize; nor, for that matter, did it escape the notice of the French, who had struggled during the eighteenth century to attain the hegemony in the Indian subcontinent which Britain now enjoyed.

In the previous century France's main struggle had been to create a mercantile organization sufficiently powerful to compete with the English and Dutch East India Companies, but despite infusions of private Dutch capital, a general shortage of finance led to the demise of the early French trading ventures. A new organization was formed in 1642 (Compagnie d'Orient) but it never extended its field of operations beyond Madagascar, and it was not until a charter was granted to the Compagnie des Indes Orientales twenty-two years later that France was given a potentially formidable instrument for developing trade with Asia. Unlike the Dutch East India Company, which owed a considerable measure of its early success to the assistance it received from the States-General, the Compagnie des Indes Orientales was actually sponsored by the state, with only minimal support from French mercantile capital. So limited were its financial resources that by the end of the century the Company was obliged to forego its fifty-years' trading monopoly and throw open Asian trade to private French merchants on a commission basis. After a brief revival under the aegis of the merchants of St. Malo, the Company amalgamated in 1719 with other bodies to become the Compagnie des Indes, which controlled French trade with Asia until it was abolished fifty years later. Overall responsibility for the French Company's affairs was in the hands of a Conseil des Indes, appointed by the Crown. The King also selected the Company's twelve Directors, but neither they nor the eight Syndics who were supposed to look after the interests of the shareholders took much part in the determination of trading policy. The lack of commercial orientation in its management and the government's protectionist measures were severe handicaps to the Compagnie des Indes, but during the early decades of its operations good profits were made, and shareholders were paid a guaranteed dividend. However despite wild speculation in its original share issue, the Company's trading capital was never large, and after French reverses in Asia during the Seven Years War it was found impossible to raise loans to cover bad debts. In 1769 the Compagnie des Indes was liquidated and its assets in Asia were purchased by the Crown.

The royal direction of French economic affairs in Asia during the seventeenth and eighteenth centuries compares more with the Spanish than with the British and Dutch systems; and a further important comparable feature is the manner in which religion served to advance the political influence of the two nations in Southeast Asia. For, like Spain, France owed her position there more to the activities of her Christian missionaries than to her merchants, as is evidenced in the impressive gains made at the Thai court in Ayuthia during the second half of the seventeenth century by the Jesuits and representatives of the Société des Missions Etrangères. French political and economic power increased rapidly through the exchange of diplomatic missions and the grant of exclusive trading privileges, and was important enough in the 1680s to cause the severance of the long-standing Dutch commercial connection with Thailand. With the indefatigable votaries of the French Church active at court, and French troops garrisoning Bangkok and Mergui, plans were well advanced for the capture of the whole apparatus of the state; they were shattered with awful suddenness in 1688 with the execution of the Francophile Minister of Trade and the death of King Narai. The strong antiforeign reaction in Ayuthia swept the French out of Thailand.

The debacle of 1688 seriously affected French fortunes in Southeast Asia although they revived during the eighteenth century when commercial interest shifted to India and, for a time, to Vietnam, where French missionaries were active. Vietnam at this period offered great opportunities for French intrusion in the uneasy peace prevailing between the Trinh in Tonkin and the Nguyen in Annam. During the mid-eighteenth century the French made great efforts to extend their commercial interests in Cochinchina, but the opposition of local officials and the difficulties of providing satisfactory articles for trade hampered progress, especially after the eclipse of French economic and political power in India following the Seven Years War. The Tayson rebellion in 1773 afforded fresh opportunities for French intervention in Cochinchina during the closing years of the eighteenth century when a limited amount of military support was given to the hard-pressed Nguyen dynasty; but events in Europe again affected France's position in the region, and the final unification of Vietnam achieved by Nguyen Anh really owed little to direct French help. Although the French largely withdrew from Cochinchina during the Revolutionary and Napoleonic Wars, many of the missionaries remained, and it was they who were to provide the bridgehead by which France was to regain entry into the Indochinese peninsula in the mid-nineteenth century.

The Western Forward Movement
in Southeast Asia

I

By the beginning of the nineteenth century, Southeast Asia had experienced direct contact with the West. The nature and extent of Western power necessarily varied from one region to another, and was obviously much weaker in mainland Southeast Asia than it was in the islands where their greater maritime resources gave the Europeans a decided advantage. Because of this naval supremacy, the Westerners were able to capture or share an important part of the commerce of Indonesia, the Philippines, and the coastal regions of mainland Southeast Asia and, where necessary, divert it into new channels. They were also able to exercise in island Southeast Asia some measure of territorial control, and a degree of regulation over the means of production. How far the economic structure of the region was affected by this political control and commercial dominance is a matter for debate; but, except in parts of island Southeast Asia, the Western impact down to about 1800 was essentially limited. This all changed in the nineteenth century. However much historians may dispute the precise effects of Western influence during the earlier period, all are at least agreed that the character of the change wrought on the social, economic and political fabric of Southeast Asia during the nineteenth century was marked and readily apparent. Some historians are inclined to view this change as sudden and dramatic while others claim to discern its origins at an earlier period; but none dispute the fact that the rapid series of events,

33

characterized by the term "Industrial Revolution," which transformed the face of Europe within a few decades, also had profound and lasting effects on the world of Southeast Asia as it became increasingly subject to the political authority of the Western powers.

It was only in the Philippines and Indonesia that any effective measure of Western political control was exercised at the beginning of the nineteenth century, and even that was generally restricted to parts of the Visayas, Luzon, Java, Sumatra, Banda, and the Moluccas. Yet as limited as de facto sovereignty undoubtedly was, there had come into existence by then three colonial spheres of influence whose reality had been fashioned by a long series of wars and by political decisions in Europe which were often as decisive in determining the fate of the region as events of a more local character. Spain, after all, had established herself in Southeast Asia by hard-fought diplomatic contests in Lisbon, Madrid, and the Vatican, as well as by the sanguinary conflicts she had waged against the Filipinos in the Visayas. Holland also owed her position in Indonesia after the Napoleonic Wars to the fact that Great Britain, the third of the major colonial powers in Southeast Asia, was more interested in maintaining the balance of power in Europe than in retaining the Indonesian colonies captured from the Dutch during the period of European hostilities. Subsequently, Britain gained the more important objective of undisputed control of the Malacca Straits by securing Dutch recognition to the occupation of Singapore, and by exchanging her west Sumatran possessions for the Dutch colony of Malacca. The division between British and Dutch spheres of influence north and south of the Straits of Singapore effected by the 1824 Treaty of London ultimately proved decisive in demarcating the national frontiers of Malaya, Singapore, and Indonesia.

II

British power in Southeast Asia had expanded substantially in the period immediately preceding and during the Revolutionary and Napoleonic Wars. The capture and occupation of Manila in 1762–64 brought few positive advantages but was indirectly connected with the attempts made during the following decade to establish a commercial *entrepôt* on the island of Balambangan, south of Palawan, for the purpose of collecting Southeast Asian products suitable for sale in Canton. The failure of this venture was followed in 1786 by the founding of a British settlement on the island of Penang in the Straits of Malacca to facilitate the trade with China and provide a naval station for ships based on the Bay of Bengal during the northeast monsoon. To safeguard Penang's food supplies a strip of territory in the Malay peninsula, named Province Wellesley, was subsequently acquired from the ruler of Kedah. British acquisitions in Southeast Asia increased in the 1790s when Malacca, Padang, and the Moluccas were all captured from Holland. The Dutch possessions in eastern Indonesia were returned at the Peace of Amiens in 1802, but not before sufficient clove and nutmeg seedlings were transplanted to Penang, western Sumatra, and Ceylon to ensure that the Netherlands would never again be in a position to establish a trade monopoly of fine spices. Nine years later, in order to prevent the French from using the Dutch colonies as a center for hostilities, Java was captured. It was not intended that the colony should be permanently occupied, but the five years of British rule (1811–16) were to prove a significant phase in the history of Java's contact with the West.

Initially, the British attempted to continue the Dutch commercial system based on forced deliveries and contingents, but as hostilities in Europe closed the continental markets to produce collected by these means, a land rent system was introduced in the expectation that it would yield large territorial revenues to the state. Under the new system the Javanese cultivator, instead of delivering fixed quantities of produce every year, was to be left free to grow whatever crops he chose so long as he paid an annual cash rental for his lands. It was anticipated that, in addition to providing the British colonial government with much needed revenue, the new system, regulated on principles of free labor and cultivation, would stimulate the Javanese to industry and encourage the production of surplus crops for export, thereby affording Great Britain a new outlet for her manufactures. In theory there was nothing erroneous about these ideas, but the proposals for establishing freedom of labor and cultivation and for releasing the Javanese from traditional social and economic ties proved in practice too revolutionary, especially as the British did not have the administrative personnel to enforce them. The age-old economic structure of Java based upon the supply of goods and services to the indigenous rulers, and through them to their colonial masters, was not so easily overthrown by a system geared to the free circulation of money at the village level. The British land rent system functioned only in a defective manner, but it pointed the way in which a Western government, motivated by liberal economic principles, could exercise closer political control over the people of Java, and, as such, was retained by the Dutch when they returned to the island in 1816.

If the restitution of Java and its dependencies lost Britain one group of colonies in Southeast Asia, she quickly gained another by the occupation of Singapore in 1819 and the acquisition of Malacca five years later. Singapore was not long in proving its economic worth. During the first two and a half years of its existence 2,500 Asian craft carrying £1¼ millions' worth of cargoes called there, as well as 383 European ships with cargoes valued at nearly £1 million. In the succeeding two years the total value of Singapore's trade exceeded £4½ million. Better located to meet the needs of the China and archipelago trade, Singapore soon replaced Penang as a port-of-call and as the center of government of the British Straits Settlements (Malacca, Singapore, Penang and Province Wellesley).

When they first came under British rule, the islands of Penang and Singapore were relatively uninhabited so that their early administration presented few of the difficulties encountered in the more densely populated islands of Java and Sumatra. In the mid-1820s there was a population of only 60,000 in Penang and Malacca, and about one-tenth that number in Singapore; but during the middle years of the century the position changed radically with the influx of large numbers of immigrants from southeastern China, attracted by the growing commercial opportunities in the Straits and by the expansion of tin mining in the western states of the Malay peninsula. By 1840 there were already some 17,000 Chinese settled in Singapore, and twenty-five years later their number had more than trebled. By the end of the century more than 70 per cent of Singapore's quarter-million population was Chinese. The "Lion City" of the Malays had become the focal point of Chinese commercial enterprise in Southeast Asia.

The existence of the Straits Settlements depended primarily on trade, but limited revenues came by way of harbor dues and from opium, betelnut, and other "farms," and these went a long way toward meeting the expenses of administration. The commercial life of the colony was shared by Chinese, Indians, and other Asians, but the elite were the British merchants and businessmen who operated the powerful agency-houses, and who formed something of a pressure group in the colony itself. As the *raison d'être* of the Straits Settlements was trade, administrative and political problems revolved around matters of commercial organization. During the mid-nineteenth century the political question which engaged most attention was that of securing independence of the

Straits Settlements from control of the government of India which was deemed by some to be insufficiently attentive to local interests, especially insofar as they related to the protection and encouragement of regional trade, including that with the Malay peninsula.

Pressure to change the official policy of nonintervention in the Malay states began to mount after the Colonial Office in London assumed responsibility for the Straits Settlements in 1867. A temporary trade recession in the colony during the late 'sixties and early 'seventies, caused by the development of the steamship as an economic freight-carrier, the opening of the Suez Canal, the extension of the telegraph from India to Singapore, and new political and economic realignments in Europe and America, led to demands by British merchants for government assistance to develop new trading outlets in the peninsula. These became linked with the petitions of Straits Chinese for protection of their investment in the tin-mining industry of the western Malay states, where conflict between Chinese secret societies and Malays and Chinese for control of the profits of the mines had thrown the country into turmoil. In 1871 the Straits Settlements government was obliged to take limited action in Selangor because of these conflicts, but while this action received qualified approval in London no further interference was deemed necessary, despite the disruption to trade caused by continuing civil strife both there and in Perak, where Chinese secret society rivalry became enmeshed in a Malay succession dispute. Events took a somewhat dramatic turn in 1874 when the unrest in Perak led to the appointment of a British Resident to advise the Malay ruler on all matters of administration except those affecting Malay custom and religion, and similar arrangements were made shortly afterward with the rulers of Selangor, Sungei Ujong, and, later, with those of the Negri Sembilan and Pahang. British rule was initially resisted in Perak, where the first British Resident was murdered, and disorders also occurred after the establishment of Residential rule in Pahang; but the British officials soon contrived to introduce stability in the country and established conditions conducive to the rapid development of tin mining and, later, rubber planting.

While the instability of the western Malay states was an important factor influencing the British forward movement in the peninsula in 1874, the immediate reason for intervention was the somewhat unreal fear entertained by the Home government that another European power might utilize the prevailing unrest to gain a foothold in the Malay states and so threaten British strategic interests in the Straits. The government's decision does not appear to have been much influenced by the need to protect British investment in the peninsula or by any of the other classical determinants of economic imperialism. The capital invested in the western Malay states was probably much less than £1 million which was an infinitesimal amount compared with the total British overseas investment of £785 million. In any case, the bulk of it belonged not to local British firms but to Straits Chinese, representing surplus trading funds and not British export capital. Any notion that there was effective pressure from British capital to make the Malay peninsula a secure field for investment is belied by the events of the decade after intervention, when it proved exceedingly difficult to raise money in London to work Malayan tin deposits. In fact, the first tin-mining company floated in London to exploit a Selangor concession in mid-1874 was forced into voluntary liquidation in the following year largely because of its failure to interest British capitalists in Malayan tin mining, and also because the Straits government, supported by the Colonial Office, refused to recommend the company's concession for the approval of the Sultan of Selangor because of its monopolistic character.

If the British forward movement in Malaya in the 1870s was motivated by political rather than primarily economic considerations, it resulted in the long term from the existence of the Straits Settlements along the western Malayan seaboard. These Settlements were regarded as colonies of trade and not as instruments for exercising direct political influence over neighboring regions, but their intimate historic and economic ties with the peninsula made it virtually impossible for the British to escape involvement in Malay affairs. The acquisition of Malacca, for example, resulted in a futile and costly war with the Malay state of Naning in 1831–32 in assertion of controversial revenue rights, just as the proximity of Singapore to Johore led to participation in the succession problems of that state in the 1850s. Later, in 1862, complications arising from the civil war in Pahang caused the Straits government to adopt the spectacular if extreme expedient of bombarding Trengganu in an attempt to thwart Thai interference and so preserve the integrity of the eastern Malay states. These and other incidents, often involving the suppression of piracy, certainly constituted direct interference in the Malay states long before 1874. It was not only the proximity of the Straits Settlements to the peninsula that determined these events, but also the fact that the colony was a Western area of law and order fronting weak and, in certain respects, unstable Malay polities, unable to restrain turbulence from spilling over into the British Settlements.

The existence of elements of instability on a Western frontier of government was an important dynamic of nineteenth century European territorial expansion in Southeast Asia. In Burma, for example, the British, after contending for many years with border problems arising from the Burmese annexation of Arakan and interference in Manipur and Assam, declared war in 1824, to secure their frontiers in India. By the Treaty of Yandabo in 1826 the Burmese were obliged to renounce all claims to Assam and its dependencies, to cede Arakan and Tenasserim, and to pay an indemnity amounting to £1 million. The treaty gave the British security on their northeastern frontier and control over the northern maritime approaches to Singapore; it left the Burmese in possession of Upper Burma and the Irrawaddy delta. Eventually, however, the creation of a well-ordered British administration in Lower Burma itself created problems to which only further territorial acquisitions appeared to offer any solution, until finally, in 1886, the whole of Upper Burma was annexed by Great Britain.

The dynamic for expansion produced by the contiguity of areas of stable and unstable government is also evidenced in the extension of the territories in Sarawak ruled by the Brookes, which initially approximated to the present First Division, but which finally embraced the Rejang, Baram, Trusan, Limbang, and Lawas Rivers. These acquisitions by the White Rajas of Sarawak represented an important phase of the British forward movement in Southeast Asia even if the British government was reluctant to recognize the fact. It was not until 1863 that Sarawak was accorded official recognition as an independent state and not until twenty-five years later that it was granted formal protection by the British government. James Brooke, however, was given some mark of official approval by his appointment in 1847 as British Commissioner and Consul-General to the Sultan of Brunei and the independent chiefs of Borneo, and in the following year as Governor and Commander-in-Chief of Labuan, an island in Brunei Bay which Britain acquired in 1846, three years after Hong Kong, as a coaling station for British ships.

Brooke owed his position as Raja of Sarawak to the authority conferred on him in 1842 by the Sultan of Brunei, and it was at the expense of this sultanate that Sarawak's territorial acquisitions were made during the nineteenth century. In the north, Brunei was also subject to pressure from Western agencies formed to exploit the natural resources of the country. The most important of these was the British North Borneo Company, founded in 1881 on the basis of a revised cession obtained four years earlier from the Sultan and Temenggong of Brunei of some twenty-eight thousand square miles of territory. Part of the cession fell within the domains of the Sultan of Sulu, but in 1878, shortly before the Sulu archipelago was formally incorporated in the Spanish Philippines, he "ceded" (or "leased") his Sabah possessions to the British promoters on payment of a small annual subsidy. Three years later a royal charter was granted to the North Borneo Company, which ensured that it would remain British in character and domicile, and in 1888 the Company's possessions were accorded protectorate status. Subsequent acquisitions of territory by both the British North Borneo Company and the Sarawak regime left little of the sultanate of Brunei, which was also granted British protection in 1888 and a British Resident in 1906.

The cession of North Borneo by the Sultan of Sulu in 1878 was regarded as illegal by the Spanish, who claimed sovereignty over the Sulu archipelago. Spanish claims to Sulu and other islands in the Philippines were more generally assumed than made explicit by formal acts of incorporation, but when in 1844 there occurred the unexpected and, as it turned out, unsuccessful French intrusion into the Sulu archipelago for the purpose of developing Basilan as an *entrepôt*, the authorities in Manila reacted sharply by attempting to formalize their rights over the islands south of Mindanao. This was to take them a considerable time to achieve. The Sulu fortress of Jolo was captured in 1851, but local resistance continued and Sulu maritime power remained formidable. Even after 1878, when the Sultan of Sulu finally acknowledged Spanish suzerainty, it required constant policing by gunboats to hold the islands loyal to Spain. Great Britain recognized Spanish rights to the Sulu archipelago in 1885, when Spain abandoned her claims, derived from her Sulu dependencies, to the British territories in North Borneo "ceded" in 1878.

III

The expansion of British influence in Malaysia during the nineteenth century was matched by an equally impressive growth in Britain's political and economic power in Burma. The maritime provinces acquired by the Treaty of Yandabo in 1826 were first administered under the authority of the Governor-General in India, but Arakan was later placed under the government of Bengal and in 1828 its Superintendent was made subordinate to the Commissioner of Chittagong. Tenasserim, on the other hand, remained under the Governor-General for a further six years, at which time the judicial and revenue branches of the administration were placed in the hands of the Bengal government. In order to meet the costs of administration, the British resorted to a land tax levy similar to that adopted in Java and, as there, introduced the principles of free cultivation and labor in place of the traditional system regulated by the Burmese rulers. Unlike the Javanese cultivators, the Burmese were accustomed to payment of taxes on the produce of their lands, but whereas it had amounted only to about 6 per cent under indigenous rule, it was now increased by the British to 10 per cent. Even this failed to cover the costs of administration, so that in succeeding years the levy continued to rise. Moreover, despite the liberal economic ideas motivating the colonial administration, *corvée* labor was utilized, fees charged for the hire of convicts, and taxes imposed on bazaars and on the Karens and Solons. In addition, export duties, which largely affected the European merchants, were laid on the shipment of teak.

The Treaty of Yandabo provided for the appointment of an accredited British minister to the Court of Ava so as to protect Western interests, but relations between the two powers deteriorated and finally resulted in the withdrawal of the Residency. The despatch to Rangoon of a strong naval force by the government of British India in 1852, following complaints about discriminatory practices against British traders, led to hostilities and the annexation of the remainder of Lower Burma, including the whole of the delta area and territories extending beyond Prome and Toungoo. Martaban was administered by the Commissioner of Tenasserim while Pegu was placed under a separate Commissioner. But in 1862, following the abolition of the East India Company and the assumption of its responsibilities by the British Crown, Pegu was amalgamated with Arakan and Tenasserim and, as the Province of British Burma, placed under a Chief Commissioner residing in Rangoon. Unlike Arakan and Tenasserim, which were something of an economic encumbrance to the British, Pegu gave considerable scope for the extension of rice cultivation in the delta region and for the exploitation of rich teak resources. British trade with Burma flourished, especially after the opening of the Suez Canal in 1869 when many agency-houses, similar to those already established in Singapore, were opened in Rangoon. Roads were built and communications developed. Lower Burma was slowly drawn into the world economy.

Upper Burma also prospered under the efficient administration of King Mindon, who maintained fairly harmonious relations with his British neighbors. But, after the accession of Thibaw in 1878, British commercial groups in Rangoon, who found their trading connections with independent Burma becoming increasingly affected by the royal monopolies, began to agitate for British annexation. The Home government resisted this pressure, as it had resisted the clamors for political intervention in the Malay states in the 1860s and 1870s. But when the Franco-Burmese Treaty of 1885 gave apparent substance to fears that French expansion in Indo-China would spill over into Upper Burma, the government took the rejection of its demand for international arbitration of the Bombay Burmah Trading Corporation dispute as a convenient pretext for annexing Upper Burma and incorporating it within the British Indian Empire. Possibly more by accident than design, the annexation of Upper Burma occurred at a time when French attention was diverted by a series of reverses in the Red River delta of Indo-China.

IV

France had long shown an interest in the Indochinese peninsula but had only acquired territorial power in the region after her intervention in Vietnam during 1858–59, ostensibly in the interest of persecuted Christian missionaries but also in the hope of gaining economic advantage and national prestige. The persecution of the French fathers and Spanish Dominicans in Tonkin, which provided the occasion for intervention, was largely the outcome of their own enormous success in winning converts. Already by 1839, when primacy in the Oriental mission field was withdrawn from the Portuguese and accorded the French Church, the Christians in Vietnam were said to have numbered nearly half-a-million. This high conversion rate aroused fears in the Court of Hué and led to the adoption of repressive measures against the missionaries, a number of whom were killed during the 1830s. Subsequent martyrdoms led to increasing pressure for government intervention and this became reinforced by a desire to develop French commercial enterprise in the region, especially after the failure of the Basilan venture in the Sulu archipelago. Rejection of French demands for religious toleration and for permission to establish a consulate and trading agency at Hué finally led to the despatch of a joint Franco-Spanish expedition against Tourane (Danang) following the conclusion of the Tientsin treaties with China. The spirited resistance of the Vietnamese, aided by bad military planning on the French side as well as by the continuance of the China war, resulted in protracted hostilities, and it was not until 1862 that the Vietnamese ruler finally agreed to the cession of three of the southern provinces of Cochinchina, including Saigon, the opening of three of the northern ports to trade, freedom of worship, and the payment of a large cash indemnity. Five years later the French formally annexed the western provinces of the delta.

Expansion did not stop there. Asserting rights which they claimed fell to them as masters of Cochinchina, the French actively intervened in Cambodian affairs in order to counter Thai vassalage claims. A treaty placing Cambodia under French protection was signed by the Cambodian ruler in 1863, and four years later the Thais formally renounced all claim to the country, except the provinces of Battambang, Sisophon, and Siemreap. French power in Cambodia was substantially consolidated when full control over the territorial revenues passed into the hands of the French Chief Resident in 1884.

Once it became clear that direct commercial relations with China could not be established along the Mekong valley, the French began to focus attention on the Red River route through Tonkin. By the 1870s strong French interests were demanding the establishment of a protectorate over the delta region and the free exercise of French suzerainty over the whole of Vietnam as provided in the 1874 treaty with Hué. The attempts made to reduce Annam to protectorate status led to direct conflict with China's claim of sovereignty over Vietnam; but in 1885 French protectorate rights to the country were finally conceded, and Chinese forces withdrew from Tonkin. Four years later, despite Thai protests, the province of Sipsong Chi Thai was annexed.

As the French pushed their boundaries further westward into the border provinces of Indochina, Thailand was being subjected to increasing pressure on her southern frontiers from the British. During the early 1870s, when King Chulalongkorn was attempting to follow further along the path of modernization already blazed by his father, preservation of the territorial integrity of Thailand between the Franco-British blocs in Southeast Asia seemed remote. The extension of Residential rule in western Malaya inevitably drew Great Britain into direct contact with the Thai vassal states of northern Malaya, and in 1882, after the ruler of Trengganu died, Straits officials protested at Thai interference in the succession and called for pressure to be exerted in Bangkok in order to restrain Thai influence in the region. At the same time another dispute with Thailand about the Reman boundary with Perak brought the whole weight of official opinion in Singapore on the side of resolving the problem in Perak's favor. However, while the Colonial Office gave general support to its own officials in the Straits, who contended that British influence in the Malay states should be clearly demarcated, the

Foreign Office, under pressure from its consular officials in Bangkok, urged restraint for fear that any attempt to limit Thai territorial control in the south would be counterbalanced by French encroachments on Siam's eastern frontiers.

Annexation of Burma in 1886 turned British attention to the question of establishing an eastern border with Thailand along the Salween or further south, and at the same time of avoiding a direct frontier with French Indochina. Certain sections of British opinion were in favor of the Burma frontier being advanced so as to provide contiguity with the northern Malay states; but the 1889 Anglo-Siamese frontier commission adopted a more equitable arrangement by which the trans-Salween states were incorporated into British Burma, but the territories south of Mergui in the Kra isthmus were left under Thai jurisdiction.

Difficulties with France had still to be resolved. Both European nations were generally in favor of preserving Thailand as a buffer state between their respective colonial spheres, but there was disagreement about what, on its eastern marches, constituted Thailand. Thai claims to the Laotian provinces were long established but France refused to recognize them, and in 1893, in a swiftly executed military and diplomatic coup at the expense of Great Britain, exacted from the Thais recognition of French territorial rights east of the Mekong. Subsequent disputes between Britain and France about the exact division of their imperial domains nearly precipitated war, but in 1896 Britain withdrew all claims to territory east of the Mekong in exchange for a joint Anglo-French guarantee on the independence of the remainder of Thailand stretching along the valley of the Menam. After a somewhat critical period during the last years of the century, this guarantee was observed by the two powers, and at the conclusion of the Entente Cordiale in 1904, they entered into separate negotiations with Thailand about residual matters in dispute. In the same year, under the terms of a new Franco-Thai Treaty, Siam renounced her suzerainty over Luang Prabang and agreed to establish a joint commission to settle the problem of the Cambodian frontier. Three years later, in return for the surrender of extraterritorial rights claimed over French subjects in Thailand, France was able to secure the abandonment of Thai claims to the Cambodian provinces of Battambang and Siemreap. By a sacrifice of similar rights with respect to its own subjects, and the provision of a loan for railway construction, Great Britain obtained in 1909 a treaty with Thailand by which she secured sovereign claims to the Malay states of Kelantan, Trengganu, Kedah, and Perlis.

By recognizing the expansive forces of Western imperialism and making timely territorial sacrifices, as well as by pursuing a deliberate policy of selective modernization both for its own sake and in an endeavor to remove any cause for direct Western intervention, Thailand was able to preserve her independence. And if she did not entirely escape the impact of the Western forward movement during the nineteenth century, she alone of the Southeast Asian states escaped formal Western political control.

V

The Western forward movement in Southeast Asia was not a unique phenomenon, but was related to the European acquisition of territories in other regions of the world. No single explanation satisfactorily accounts for this complex of events because the motive power of nineteenth-century imperialism varied in time and place, not least within Southeast Asia itself. But the actual extension of European territorial boundaries in Southeast Asia, with its concomitant administrative responsibilities, was due as much, if not more, to political than to economic factors. At the same time, the imperialist process was not merely characterized by an increase in territories and a more precise demarcation of political frontiers: equally important was the growing efficiency of the Western powers in exploiting the economic resources of their colonial acquisitions. In this respect the Dutch in Java stood preeminent.

After their return to the island at the end of the Napoleonic Wars the Dutch decided to retain the British land rent system, despite substantial arrears in payment, but to modify it so that assessments were made on a village basis and the rents calculated by a process of bargaining. In the Preanger districts of west Java forced cultivation of coffee continued, but the people were freed from levies of head-money and other family taxes. Except for the element of compulsion in the coffee culture and in the cutting of timber in the teak forests, the Dutch aimed at establishing a liberal colonial system based upon free labor and cultivation. The old economic order regulated by the social obligations of the people to render goods and services to their indigenous rulers was to be progressively revolutionized, and the island opened up to competitive Western enterprise.

The role of Western entrepreneurs in the new system was regarded as a matter of some importance by the colonial theorists in the Netherlands, but by the authorities in Batavia as incompatible with the welfare of the Javanese. European capitalists were therefore prevented from hiring out villages and utilizing occupied lands; and, in order to prevent speculation in the produce of the state plantation system, access to the Preanger districts was denied them. Increasing restrictions on their operations along the northeast coast led to their leasing lands in the independent principalities of central Java, but official action in 1823 also curtailed their activities there. Governmental interference of this kind was scarcely calculated to win the support of the doctrinaire liberals; it found even less sympathy among members of the Indonesian nobility who were obliged not only to repay the monetary advances made by the lessees but also to make financial restitution for all improvements effected on the lands. The sense of grievance arising from this action was one of the major causes of the war which racked central Java between 1825 and 1830.

Even before it had incurred the heavy debts connected with this and other wars in Celebes and western Sumatra, the Dutch colonial government was faced by an embarrassing lack of funds. The land revenue system returned 3¼ million guilders in 1818 and was approaching double that amount seven years later. But disbursements remained high, and hopes that Java would eventually yield large surplus revenues for the homeland soon faded. Even the Netherlands Trading Society, which had been established in 1825 for the purpose of confining colonial trade in Dutch hands, did not live up to the immediate expectations of its founders. The heavy burden of colonial debt was more than enough to harass the home authorities who were faced with the secessionist revolt of the Belgians and a national debt that had increased by one-third during the previous fifteen years. The time was ripe to lay aside liberal economic dogmas and experiment with a new colonial system designed to yield immediate financial returns to the Dutch nation.

The Culture System, which was introduced into Java after 1830, was, in certain respects, modeled on the arrangements already in existence in the Priangan where the cultivators were exempted from land rent levies but obliged to deliver fixed amounts of coffee to the state. It was now proposed that, instead of the village paying land rent in cash or unsaleable produce, approximately one-fifth of its lands would be set aside for the cultivation of export crops, the value of which would be deducted from the land rent assessments. If the value of the produce exceeded the assessments, the government would pay the cultivators the difference; if not, the village was obliged to make good the deficit. It was estimated that in normal circumstances one-fifth of the rice lands of a village would yield sufficient produce to meet the equivalent of the land rent; but it was not intended that the mere setting aside of this proportion of land would automatically provide exemption from the payment of land rent. The latter remained the criterion against which the produce delivered under the new arrangements was to be measured, so that liberals who later criticized the Culture System for imposing on the Javanese a system of double taxation—part levied in export produce and part in land rent—were in fact describing only its intended method of operation.

It was first proposed to establish the Culture System on a voluntary basis but the element of compulsion was soon introduced, and during the 1830s and 1840s large areas of arable land in Java were appropriated for the production of coffee, sugar, indigo, silk, tea, tobacco, and other articles suitable for the world market. Between 1830 and 1835 exports from Java increased by more than 100 per cent, and they more than doubled again during the following five years. By 1840 approximately 133 million pounds of coffee, an equal amount of sugar, and something in excess of 2 million pounds of indigo were being shipped out of Java, most of it by the now prosperous Netherlands Trading Society. The profits accruing to the Dutch state from the sales of this produce were immense. During the 1830s an average of 9 million guilders was paid annually as colonial contributions to the home treasury, and this figure rose to 14 and 15 million guilders during the ensuing two decades. By the time contributions ceased in 1877 something like 832 million guilders had been remitted from Indonesia to the Netherlands, where the money was used to redeem public debts, reduce taxation, and finance public works.

While the Netherlands derived great benefits from the Culture System, its effects on the people of Java are in dispute. The system has been painted in the most somber colors by the Dutch liberals and Indonesian nationalists, but at least one Dutch conservative historian has gone so far as to describe it as the greatest boon which the Netherlands conferred on Indonesia. There is probably much to be said for this latter view. At a time of rapid population growth in Java the Culture System undoubtedly placed large amounts of money in the hands of the people, thereby enabling them to enjoy a higher standard of living than would otherwise have been possible. Imports of cotton goods, for example, increased more than threefold between 1830 and 1840, and they remained at a generally high level during the following decade. But if such economic criteria point to one conclusion about the effects of the Culture System, there is considerable evidence which suggests another. Examples of bad planning on the part of the colonial government in the allocation of crops, of famines occurring because of too much land being devoted to the production of export crops, and of labor being unequally apportioned in their cultivation, are not difficult to discover. It is, of course, not really possible to arrive at a simple conclusion about a system so complex in its working. What at least can be said is that the Culture System affords an example *par excellence* of increasing Western exploitation of Southeast Asian economic resources during the nineteenth century.

The exploitation of Indonesia was carried on by the Dutch along a very narrow front. Only part of Java was directly affected by the Culture System, the outer islands scarcely at all. The economic and political inroads made by the Dutch in the archipelago were, in fact, very limited compared with those made in Java. During the 1830s and 1840s, in the light of the success of the Culture System, it was becoming increasingly obvious that, with the exception of the Moluccas, Sumatra, and the tin-producing islands of Bangka, the outer islands of the archipelago constituted something of a drain on Dutch resources. Compulsory cultivation of coffee was introduced into western Sumatra during the middle years of the nineteenth century, at which time more effective rule was also extended over the Lampong districts of south Sumatra. But even as late as the 1860s, when the cultivation of tobacco was making impressive headway in eastern Sumatra, the administration of the country was only indirectly exercised by the colonial authorities in Batavia. The same was true in the other islands. In Borneo, Dutch Residents at Sambas, Pontianak, and Banjermassin represented almost the sum total of Dutch power in the island, and their task was simply to show the flag with the object of both preserving peace in their territories and preventing incursions by other Western nations.

The activities of private British adventurers like James Brooke in Sarawak came as something of a shock to the Dutch, who placed a more exclusionist interpretation on clause twelve of the Treaty of London than the British, and probably operated as a spur to them to round off territorial frontiers in the archipelago. Certainly the interest shown by British merchants in the rice trade east of Java during the 1840s led to the despatch of an expeditionary force to Bali to secure an acknowledgment of Dutch supremacy. For the most part, however, the Dutch forward movement in Indonesia proceeded on a piecemeal basis and generally in response to purely local circumstances as, for example, in western Sumatra where the colonial authorities at Padang were drawn into a long and bitter conflict with the Muslim *padris* of the Minang-kabau highlands. It was really not until the closing decades of the nineteenth century, when the French and British were also engaged in extending their commitments in Indochina, Burma, and Malaysia, that active measures were adopted by the Netherlands to consolidate territorial holdings in the islands. In 1873, only two years after Great Britain had formally renounced all earlier claims, the Dutch resolved to bring northern Sumatra more directly within the sphere of *Pax Neerlandica*; but it was to take another thirty years before Achin was pacified and other pockets of Indonesian resistance overcome in central Sumatra, Borneo, Celebes, and Bali. In 1898 the Short Declaration, which replaced many of the earlier imprecise treaties, bound the Indonesian rulers to a recognition of Dutch authority over their territories.

VI

Whereas at the beginning of the nineteenth century only the periphery of Southeast Asia had come into direct contact with the West, by the end of the century virtually the whole of the region, except Thailand, had been brought under Western political control. However, a number of territorial problems still remained. It was not until 1909 that the northern Malay states were removed from Thai vassalage and placed under British protection, and not until some years later that certain anomalies were clarified in the treaties, agreements, and contracts entered into by the Netherlands with the rulers of the outer islands, and Indonesia became, in terms of strict international law, a Dutch colony. In the Philippines, moreover, the territorial and legal rights acquired by Spain during three centuries of occupation became vested in the government of the United States under the provision of the Treaty of Paris of 1898, which ended the Spanish-American War, and these rights were further strengthened by the defeat of the forces of the short-lived Philippine Republic which proclaimed independence after the Spanish withdrawal. In these two countries, as also in Burma, Indochina, and Malaysia, Western administration was conducted on different principles and exercised through a variety of political instrumentalities, and it is to a consideration of these that we must now turn our attention.

Consolidation
of the Western Colonial Regimes
in Southeast Asia

I

The different colonial policies and practices of the Western powers reflected distinctive European attitudes to colonial rule, the diverse social and economic conditions in the Southeast Asian countries themselves, and the multifarious economic relationships existing between the colonies and the metropolitan centers. The actual length of time during which rule had been exercised was also important in accounting for the markedly conservative nature of Dutch and Spanish policies in Indonesia and the Philippines compared with those of the other Western colonial powers in Southeast Asia. It is true that the peculiar nineteenth-century blend of *laissez-faire* economics and humanitarian ideals, which demanded the full extension into the colonial territories of Western economic and political influence, found formidable advocacy in Indonesia, but it is also true that the older policies, which had their origin in little more than expediency, showed an amazing capacity to survive. Buttressed by equally strong humanitarian considerations, the cardinal principle of Dutch colonial practice, the conservation of Indonesian societies from total integration into the Western world-order, resisted the growing tendency to conduct administration on thoroughgoing European principles of government.

The ideal of utilizing indigenous institutions and adapting them to the process of government also received due recognition from the British in Malaysia and Burma, but they were led rather faster than the Dutch in the direction of bureaucratic centralization and direct rule. In the Malay states of Perak, Selangor, Negri Sembilan, and Pahang, which came under British protection between 1874 and 1889, government was supposed to be in the hands of the Malay rulers who were to accept the advice of the British Residents on all matters except those relating to Malay custom and religion. In theory this exception was important, for there were few aspects of local administration which did not fall within the area of religion and, especially, custom. In practice, however, the limitation proved unreal, for power to control revenues and offer "mandatory" advice to the sultans gave the Residents full executive authority in the states. The association of the Malay elite with government was attempted by the incorporation of the sultans and Malay officials in State Councils to assist the Residents on all important questions of government, and these Councils evolved as the sole legislative and supreme judicial organs in the states, with jurisdiction over Malay headmen, the appointment of *Kathis,* and the administration of Muslim law. But while the outward appearance of the Residential system suggested that British rule was exercised indirectly through the indigenous hierarchy, in reality administration was in the hands of the Residents. The sultans reigned while the Residents ruled, subject only to the general supervision of the Governor of the Straits Settlements and to the instructions of the Colonial Office transmitted through him.

Increasing British political involvement in the protected Malay states resulted in their federation in 1896, when a Resident-General was appointed for the purpose of promoting financial cooperation between the states and achieving some degree of administrative uniformity. The new official, with his federal secretariat in Kuala Lumpur, gained a large measure of executive authority over the states, which were drawn into a pattern of strong centralized government. A common system of law was developed through the practice of the federal legal adviser drafting laws for transmission to the State Councils, and the rule of law was extended and strengthened by the appointment of federal judicial commissioners and by the reorganization of the police. Other federal departments dealing with public works, forests, and agriculture were established, and the financial structures of the various states were unified. In the process the functions of the State Councils suffered, and the Councils themselves were reduced to little more than registering bodies. The Residents also suffered a real loss of power, and the Malay rulers, though brought together occasionally for discussion at ceremonial durbars, had very little executive say in the actual administration of their states.

To restrict the influence of the Resident-General and to allow the Malay rulers to participate more directly in government, a Federal Council was established in 1909, which consisted of the Governor of the Straits Settlements in his capacity as High Commissioner for the Malay States, the Resident-General (renamed Chief Secretary), the four sultans and their Residents, and four unofficials nominated by the High Commissioner. The Federal Council was given legislative functions, and state enactments remained valid only to the extent that they were not repugnant to the laws of the Federal Council. The latter also controlled the expenditure of the State Councils by approving draft estimates of revenue and expenditure. Insofar as its purpose was to achieve some devolution of power to the states, the Federal Council failed entirely, and administration remained centralized in the office of the Chief Secretary. The power and influence of the State Councils and the Residents continued to decline, and the Malay rulers gained little direct benefit from membership of the Federal Council, the proceedings of which were conducted in English which few of them understood.

In a further attempt to reverse the process of centralization in the Federated Malay States, proposals were made during the 1920s and 1930s to abolish the post of Chief Secretary and distribute his powers and those of the federal departments among the states. But the idea of reconstituting the state governments with effective power of administration and financial control was opposed by the British and Chinese businessmen in the Straits who feared that the loss of the intermediary influence of the Chief Secretary would subordinate the interests of the Straits Settlements to those of the Malay states. It was also feared that decentralization would reduce security for investment in the Federation. Nevertheless, in 1927 the sultans were removed from the Federal Council and their places taken by four Malay unofficials. Eight years later the post of Chief Secretary was replaced by that of Federal Secretary, junior in rank to all the Residents. Complete financial autonomy was not given to the states, however, but the Federal Council no longer controlled their detailed expenditure but simply allocated a block grant, leaving it to the states to decide how it was spent—subject to the proviso that the Residents' original estimates had first to be submitted to the High Commissioner. The State Councils were also revitalized by the appointment of British, Chinese, and Indian unofficial members, and by the practice that the unofficials in the Federal Council were selected from members of the State Councils. Financial and legal uniformity between the states was achieved by making the federal financial and legal advisers members of the Perak, Selangor, Negri Sembilan, and Pahang State Councils.

In the other five states of the Malay peninsula which came under British protection as a result of the Anglo-Thai Treaty of 1909, a large measure of local autonomy was retained by the sultans' refusal to enter the Federation and by their ability to keep in Malay hands effective executive authority. The State Councils in the Unfederated Malay States exercised real powers of government, including the allocation of finance, and the British Advisers (as distinct from the Residents in the Federated Malay States) rarely attempted to do more than advise. If this advice was not to their liking, the sultans of the Unfederated Malay States possessed the right of appealing beyond the High Commissioner to the Crown.

Despite very real and important differences between the Federated and Unfederated Malay States, it is possible to regard their administration as conforming to one general pattern of British colonial rule, which differed markedly from the systems which evolved in the other Malaysian territories. In the Straits Settlements, which comprised a Crown Colony, the administration was in the charge of a Governor assisted by an Executive Council, and a Legislative Council in which officials and unofficials after 1924 were equal in number but with the Governor possessing a casting vote. In Sabah, which did not possess a formal constitution until it became a Crown colony after the Second World War, local administration was conducted by a Governor, subject to general control exercised by the directors of the British North Borneo Company in London. In the 1880s he was assisted by a small and irregularly convened Advisory Council, which gave way in 1912 to a Legislative Council consisting of official and unofficial members. In Sarawak, which also became a Crown colony after the Second World War, power was in the hands of the Rajas Brooke, who brought the principal Malay officers in Kuching and a small number of British officials together in a Supreme Council, which represented the legislative and judicial authority of the raj. Later a State Council was established, consisting of the principal native officers of Sarawak and the British Residents, but this met only triennially and possessed no political power.

Although the above summary does scant justice to the complexity of the instrumentalities employed in the government of the Malaysian territories, enough has been said to show the variety of patterns of British colonial rule. This variety resulted partly from the manner in which British influence developed in Malaysia and partly from the different agencies employed in the extension of that influence. In Burma the British colonial system also reflected the piecemeal manner in which the country was brought under British rule during the nineteenth century, as well as the fact that that rule stemmed directly from India.

In the decade after the annexation of Upper Burma in 1886 administration was in the hands of a Chief Commissioner, subject to the authority of the government of India. The fact that Burma was tied politically to India was reflected in the area of local administration, where the Indian pattern of village government was advanced at the expense of the traditional Burmese circle system under headmen, *thugyis*, who led the resistance to the extension of British rule in Upper Burma. By regulation and enactment, statutory duties were imposed upon the villages for the maintenance of order and the collection of revenues, and during the decade 1909–19 many villages were amalgamated with a consequent reduction in the number of headmen. The village, which in traditional Burmese political structure had no legal function, became an artificial administrative entity under the British; and the development of the village system at the expense of the circle led to an undermining of common social bonds and the whole corpus of Burmese customary law to which it was tied. Burmese social and political organization was disrupted, and the autonomous government of former times gave way to an alien system which imposed new obligations without any compensatory conferment of former rights and privileges. The old system of indirect rule through local circle headmen was replaced by local control through government officials.

Burma's political connection with India was reflected in the rate of constitutional change. The Chief Commissioner was replaced by a Lieutenant-Governor in 1897 and a Legislative Council was established consisting of nine nominated members. The Council was given an unofficial majority in 1909 when its membership was increased to thirty. Fourteen years later the Legislative Council was increased to 103 members, four-fifths of whom were elected on a democratic franchise. Under what was referred to as the "dyarchical" system, the Indian government continued to control such matters as defense, communications, external affairs, finance, and revenue, while the remaining responsibilities were shared by the Governor, with an Executive Council comprising two nominated members in charge of the "reserved" subjects, and two ministers answerable to the Legislative Council in the "transferred" subjects. This system in turn gave way in 1935, when Burma was separated from India, to a bicameral form of government with an elected House of Representatives of 132 members and a semi-elective Senate of thirty-six members.

II

In the Philippines proposals to establish a bicameral legislature were already made by the first Philippine commission in 1900, two years after the United States assumed sovereignty in the islands from Spain. Fresh to the task of exercising colonial dominion, the Americans entered the Philippines in a mood of high idealism to sweep clean the alleged Augean stables of the Spanish regime and to train the indigenous peoples in the art of self-government. The Filipinos' attempt to seize power and proclaim a republic independent of American control tended to blunt this initial mood and led to the creation of a military government which did not give way to a civil administration until 1901. In the belief that the Filipinos were not yet prepared or equipped to shoulder the responsibilities of independence, the first American commission recommended the establishment of a territorial government with a partly elective bicameral legislature, and a largely autonomous system of municipal and provincial administration. In 1900 a second commission was appointed with full legislative and executive powers (except those retained by the military governor). It enacted a large body of legislation creating a civil code, a civil service, a police system, departments of education, agriculture, and forestry, as well as a system of municipal and provincial government.

This latter system represented an adjustment to the new conditions of the old Spanish municipal organization. More than six hundred municipalities were constituted with powers to raise and disburse local revenues for schools and police. Above the municipalities were the provincial governments, forty in number, whose governors were elected for two-year terms by a joint convention of the municipal councillors in the province, and whose supervisors and treasurers were first appointed by the American commission. The provincial government had the right, subject to certain limitations, to levy taxes in the provinces, direct public works, and supervise municipal administration.

While the provincial government afforded no real representation of the people (two of the three members of the provincial board were appointed by the American commission), the municipal councillors were theoretically elective. But as it was provided that electors had to have held certain offices under the former regime, or possess real estate, pay taxes, or read or speak English or Spanish, the municipal government was by no means so democratic as at first sight it might appear. And, despite the infusion into its working of American political ideals, it continued to operate with much of the inflexibility of the old order, providing little practical experience in local democracy. One contemporary critic of the American system of government in the Philippines likened its working to that of a British Crown colony without its important advantage of administrative efficiency through the concentration of power in the hands of a single Governor.

At the higher level of government the United States' authorities pressed forward with political reform. A Philippine Assembly of eighty members, elected on a limited franchise, came into being in 1907, and this acted, in the general constitutional framework, as the lower house with limited powers to legislate for the Christian majority, while the American commission continued its functions as an upper house with authority over the non-Christian minority population. In budgetary matters both bodies had equal powers. Six years later a Filipino majority was introduced into the Commission, and in 1916, when all literate males in the Philippines were given the vote, this body was replaced by an elected Senate. Veto powers on all legislation was retained in the hands of the American President and the Governor-General, and legislation affecting tariffs, mining, and lands, was reserved for the assent of the United States President. Finally, in 1935 the Philippines were given a large measure of self-government (except foreign affairs, defense, and tariffs) in a Commonwealth with the promise of independence after ten years. In the same year were elected the first Filipino President and Vice-President, whose political party constituted the majority of the elected members of the National Assembly.

III

As the long-term aim of American policy in the Philippines was to confer on the Filipinos democratic institutions similar to those possessed by citizens of the United States, there was an obvious preoccupation with reform at the purely political level which was made all the easier by virtue of the fact that there was already in existence in the Philippines a Westernized elite. Yet so strong were the cultural forces emanating from American rule that in certain respects the results were not very different from France's policy of cultural assimilation in Indochina. Indeed, of all the countries of Southeast Asia subject to colonial rule, none afford more obvious evidence of the imprint of metropolitan cultural and social influence than do the Philippines and Indochina.

Unlike the Americans, who fell heir to the apparatus of a functioning colonial system, the French in Indochina had initially to adapt their rule to indigenous forms of government, especially in the protectorates of Cambodia, Annam, Tonkin, and Laos. It was, in fact, not until the end of the nineteenth century that any real attempt was made to fashion a fully integrated system of colonial administration. In the early 1890s civil government had been functioning in Tonkin for only a few years and the country was still in a state of disorder; French protectorate status in Annam and Cambodia was only nominal as no colonial administration existed; Laos had only recently been acquired, and Cochinchina, where effective civil government existed, was displaying separatist tendencies. Yet within a decade a unified civil service was created, the administration of Tonkin was reconstituted, and the government of the Laotian territories fully organized.

The traditional vice-royalty offices in Tonkin were abolished, with a consequent diminution in local autonomy, and administrative powers placed in the hands of the French Chief Resident; the protectorate, in fact, became something like a directly controlled colony. Laos and Cambodia were also placed under Chief Residents, responsible to the Governor-General who exercised overall power. The Superior Council of Indochina, which had hitherto enjoyed few functions, was reconstituted with a large official French majority, including the Lieutenant-Governor and President of the Council of Cochinchina, the Chief Residents of Tonkin, Annam, Cambodia, and Laos, the heads of the Governor-General's departments, and members of the French Chambers of Commerce. Indigenous membership of the Council was limited to four. The Superior Council not only formulated general budgetary policy but exercised control over local revenues and, indeed, over all local legislation. Four committees of the Council with specialist functions controlled naval and military affairs, public works, railways, commerce, and agriculture, and, in substance, constituted departments or bureaus under the Governor-General who was, in turn, responsible to the French Ministry of Colonies.

In certain respects this system of administration, which reduced the autonomy of the local governments in the five territories, was similar to that which the British evolved in the Federated Malay States. As in the latter, where the sultans continued under the restraining influence of the British Residents, so in the protectorates of Annam, Cambodia, and

Laos the kings and their administration continued to function along-side the French Chief Residents. In each of the protectorates, provincial government was controlled by the French Residents, but the form of rule, even allowing for the spurious façade of indigenous administration, was much less direct than in the colony of Cochinchina.

Local participation in the higher levels of government was granted only slowly and reluctantly by the French authorities. Consultative assemblies were established in Annam and Tonkin after the First World War, but the electorate was limited and the assemblies themselvs had little real power. Even when the Council of Cochinchina was reformed in 1929 to allow the election of twenty of the twenty-four members, half of those actually elected were French citizens of the colony, some of whom were admittedly Vietnamese. Increasing pressure for political reform during the 1930s was met by firm French resistance.

IV

In Indonesia political control continued to reside in the hands of the Governor-General and members of the Council of the Indies, although this power since the mid-nineteenth century was directed by a Colonial Minister responsible to the Dutch parliament. The territories ruled by the Governor-General and his Council were divided into Government Lands, where the people owed allegiance directly to the central government, and the Native States, where the people's loyalty was to the indigenous rulers who in turn recognized Dutch suzerainty. In theory, the former territories were governed directly by Dutch political instrumentalities while in the latter territories indigenous forms prevailed. In practice, however, there was a considerable difference between the application and techniques of direct and indirect rule, as in some of the Government Lands the people were left under the control of native heads and in a number of the Native States the indigenous rulers were placed under the direct supervision of Dutch officials. Generally speaking, though the exceptions were important, the geographical proximity of the territories to Batavia determined the degree of direct political power exercised by the Dutch government and its officials. Generally, also, the Dutch preferred to adapt their administration, particularly in Java, to smaller territorial units than the larger districts which formed the basis of the British colonial system in India and Burma. This factor alone tended to produce a tight form of Western control which was reinforced by a tendency, always strongly marked in Dutch colonial practice in Indonesia, toward paternalism.

Agitation for a larger measure of Indonesian participation in government coincided with the proclamation in 1901 of a new colonial policy. The spirit of free Western economic development that had increasingly influenced Dutch policy since the 1870s lost much of its appeal when severe depressions in the 1880s and 1890s caused an apparent diminution in the wage and consumption levels of the people of Java. The promise by the Queen of the Netherlands to inquire into the diminishing welfare of her subjects in the Indies marked the transition from the liberal experiments of the past to the introduction of the so-called "Ethical" policy, aimed at promoting Indonesian welfare through the provision of funds from expanding Western economic enterprise, and the utilization of the village as an instrument for raising local production and for promoting a degree of local self-government. These aims proved difficult to harmonize, for the attainment of a higher level of welfare implied a considerable extension and intensification of the activities of the central government which in turn conflicted with pressure to decentralize administration so as to encourage local initiative and political endeavor.

The view that greater efficiency in administration was more likely to result from an increase in local autonomy than from control by a centralized Dutch bureaucracy found considerable support, but various decentralization measures introduced at the turn of the century, with the object of creating a popular element in local government, achieved few positive results. The attempt made in 1906 to change the village into a form of minor municipality with power to regulate matters like property and land was directed partly toward training the people in the elements of self-rule but primarily toward allowing them some voice in the determination of measures affecting their immediate welfare. Although this device did not produce much in the way of democratic local government, since resolutions generally originated in suggestions made by Dutch officials, it at least provided a basis for a growing political structure aimed at incorporating an indigenous element in discussions on governmental policy. Councils were formed for larger rural areas and urban centers, and in 1918 there came into existence a central representative body, the Volksraad or People's Council, which embraced all territories, and which exercised a greater degree of control over matters of a purely local nature than was initially intended.

Between 1926 and 1930 the regencies of Java were formed into three provinces under separate governors, on much the same model as the provincial governments in the Netherlands. These and other changes in the political structure affected the traditional pattern of quasi-indirect rule in Java, inasmuch as the Regents, who represented a strong conservative element in the administration, tended to be ignored by the Dutch officials who worked increasingly through the subordinate ranks of the indigenous civil service. This change in the basic pattern of rule was further accelerated by the growth of specialist governmental agencies, concerned with such matters as education and agriculture, which relied on subordinate Indonesian officialdom. A still further result of the application of the new policy was the attempt made to move away from the dual system of administration, by which the Indonesians and Dutch were left under their own laws and customs, and toward a common system of law administered by both European and Indonesian officials. One facet of this particular policy was the so-called "liberation" of the Regents from the direct control of the higher Dutch officials; but the divorce of the constituent agencies of Regency government produced no obvious beneficial effects and was so disliked by both the Dutch officials and the Regents that it was abandoned in 1931.

With the establishment of the *Volksraad*, all legislation relating to internal affairs was effected by agreement between the majority voice and the Governor-General, subject to the overriding jurisdiction of the legislature in the Netherlands. The *Volksraad* met annually for four months in two general sessions. The limited annual tenure of the colegislative body was intended to keep its officials in touch with their own localities, but it necessitated the institution of an executive body, the Committee of Delegates, comprising one-quarter of the larger body, with authority to exercise the full powers of the *Volksraad* except in budgetary matters. The sixty-one members of the *Volksraad* reflected the diverse ethnic groups of the Indonesian archipelago, but as nearly half of the seats were allocated to Dutchmen and only half the total membership was elected (the remainder being directly nominated by the Governor-General), the institution was an obvious target for the criticism of the extreme Indonesian nationalists.

V

The constitutional changes outlined above marked important, albeit hesitant stages in the development of representative and, in certain cases, democratic government in Southeast Asia during the 1920s and 1930s.

The changes reflected an increasing tendency on the part of the colonial regimes to dispense political power through Western instrumentalities at the center so that despite earnest attempts to revitalize and reshape traditional institutions to allow indigenous participation in regional and local government, the latter were inevitably denied real and effective power. The authority of the traditional leaders declined and the contention for preferment at the center brought to the fore in Burma, Indonesia, and also Vietnam during the years before the Second World War a new political elite which for the most part dominated the events leading to independence. Whatever its shortcomings, the centralization of government and bureaucracy did at least manage to achieve some measure of political unity in countries where centrifugal forces in the past had produced disunity—forces, indeed, which had often been exploited by early Europeans for their own advantage. But if latter-day Western colonialism in Southeast Asia brought political cohesion to such diverse territorial conglomerations as Indonesia and the Philippines, it was also responsible for the introduction of powerful disruptive elements in the social and economic fabric of the region.

In this respect perhaps the most important element, and certainly the one most productive of continuing social disharmony, was the immigration of large numbers of Chinese and Indians which, if not always directly encouraged by the colonial regimes, was at least stimulated by the new economic opportunities arising from the introduction of Western capital and from the political stability effected by Western rule. The problem of social pluralism caused by outside immigration varied from country to country, and had its origin at different points of time. In Indonesia and the Philippines, for example, there were already large numbers of Chinese engaged as middlemen in the trade of Batavia and Manila during the seventeenth and eighteenth centuries, and later as entrepreneurs in rice mills and sugar manufactories. There were also significant groups of Chinese traders in the British Straits Settlements from the early nineteenth century. For the most part, however, the mass immigration of Chinese (and Indians) into Southeast Asia was the product of the late nineteenth and early twentieth centuries and was the outcome partly of individual initiative to participate directly in retail trade, tin mining, and agriculture, and partly in response to the needs of the Western plantation industries for labor, which, in the case of Malaya, was largely supplied under indenture from India.

In Malaya, where social pluralism is still present in its acutest form, there were already close to ¾ million Chinese in a population (including the Straits Settlements) of 2 million at the beginning of the twentieth century, at which time Indians in the four Federated Malay States, where Western economic development was principally confined, numbered about seventy-five thousand. By 1931, when the population of Malaya had increased to 3¾ million, the Chinese comprised 34 per cent of the total and the Indians 15 per cent. Burma, which escaped Chinese immigration on the scale experienced by Malaya, attracted large numbers of Indians who found employment in rice cultivation, on the railways and docks, while the Chettyars found ample opportunity to engage their money-lending propensities among the Burmese rice growers. At the beginning of the present century a quarter of a million Indians were arriving annually in Burma, a figure which nearly doubled in thirty years. Most of these immigrants did not remain long, returning to their homeland after two or three years. Even so, by 1941 of a total population of 17 million, nearly one million were Indians and three hundred thousand were Chinese. Despite, or perhaps rather because of their smaller number, the Chinese in Burma were more deeply integrated into the social and economic life of the country than anywhere else in Southeast Asia. There were certainly instances of anti-Chinese feeling, notably in the riots of 1931, but because a majority of Chinese spoke Burmese, and because they did not figure so prominently as the Indian element in the economy, they escaped much of the obloquy that attached itself to their compatriots elsewhere in Southeast Asia, particularly in Indochina where, despite the fact that they comprised less than 1½ per cent of the total population of 23 million, the Chinese managed to monopolize much of the rice, fish, and river-carrying trade.

While the French gave no special encouragement to Chinese participation in the economy of Indochina, in Indonesia the Dutch gave initial support to immigration from China in order to supply labor for the Western mining and plantation industries which developed in the outer islands during the late nineteenth and early twentieth centuries. The consequence was a marked employment differentiation between Chinese in Java, where most were engaged in commercial activities, and those in the outer islands where the majority before the Second World War were employed as plantation and mining coolies. The increase in Chinese immigration into Indonesia in the twentieth century contributed substantially, as it also did in Malaya, to the economic advance of the country. But whereas by 1941 the Chinese in Malaya* outnumbered the Malays, in Indonesia they constituted less than 2 million in a total

* Including the Straits Settlements.

population of 70 million. In the Philippines the number of Chinese was also proportionately small, totaling only slightly more than one hundred thousand before the War, due mainly to the strict control exercised over immigration by the United States, which applied to the islands its own immigration laws. Even so, their small number did not prevent the Chinese in the Philippines from controlling more than 70 per cent of the country's retail trade and from owning 75 per cent of its rice mills.

Although social pluralism in Southeast Asia was largely, though by no means exclusively, comprised of common Chinese and Indian elements, it presented widely differing features in the individual countries of the region. In the Philippines, for example, 45 per cent of the total Chinese population was actually resident in Manila or its environs prior to the Second World War, so that only tiny pockets of Chinese settlement existed in the outer provinces. The problems arising from this concentrated settlement were therefore different from those in Malaya where more than a million Chinese were domiciled in the west coast states and Johore. The degree of Chinese (and Indian) participation in the economies of the Southeast Asian countries also varied considerably, thus presenting a corresponding variation in the levels at which communal cleavage occurred. However, despite a heavy concentration of economic resources in Chinese, and in Burma Chettyar, hands, it was not so much their activities as those of the Europeans which produced the greatest imbalances in the economic structure of the region.

In the first place, the destruction of the traditional Southeast Asian handicraft industries caused by the importation of cheap Western manufactured goods produced injurious short-term effects by the removal of employment opportunities for seasonally disengaged agriculturists, and in the long term by preventing the growth of modern indigenous textile industries. More serious, however, were the consequences arising from the concentration of Western plantation and mining enterprises in regions with easy access to the seas, which resulted in a correspondingly heavy concentration of dock facilities, railways, and other communications. Western capital inflow into regions like east Sumatra, west Malaya, Java, and the Irrawaddy, Menam, and Mekong deltas led to their integration into the Western export economy, with its attendant advantages and disadvantages, while the larger but more inaccessible regions of Southeast Asia retained their relative isolation and remained tied to local subsistence agriculture and to traditional economic practices. The marked regional differentiation in economic development was also repeated in the actual areas of Western enterprise, being reflected in functional terms between estate wage labor and subsistence farming. In the countryside the distinction was often blurred, but the development of Western enterprises in towns led to the growth of an urban proletariat increasingly divorced from the agricultural hinterland and its economy. The existence side by side of two economic orders resulted in a basic cleavage between town and countryside, and the concentration of Western investment in relatively confined areas produced a disequilibrium which militated against overall social and economic evolution.

At the same time, the development of the economic resources of Southeast Asia, both in the short and long term, owed much to Western skill and investment, and to the stable conditions produced by Western rule. The latter factor for instance enabled the Chinese to bring the Malayan tin mines to a high level of productivity during the late nineteenth century, and increasing British investment in the industry from that period resulted in Malaya becoming the major supplier of the world's tin. The rubber industry, first developed by the British in Malaya, and subsequently extended by the Dutch to Indonesia and the French to Indochina, was essentially the outcome of Western initiative and investment, although in the last years of colonial rule the role of the Asian small holder, especially in Malaya and Indonesia, became increasingly important. Other agricultural enterprises which owed their origin and commercial development to the West included coffee, which was brought to Java by the Dutch at the end of the seventeenth century, and oil-palm, which was introduced into Malaya and northeastern Sumatra from West Africa by the British and Dutch in the nineteenth century. Because of the need for expensive machinery to extract its by-products, the cultivation of oil-palm remained largely the concern of the Western estates. The exploitation of mineral oil from Indonesia, Burma, and Brunei was also achieved by heavy Western capital investment in the late nineteenth and early twentieth centuries. The cultivation of rice, on the other hand, largely remained in indigenous hands during the colonial period, although in advancing techniques of irrigation and water control, and in facilitating export opportunities, the West also made important contributions. It has been estimated that in the final phase of colonialism—that is, in the decade before the Second World War— Southeast Asia produced no less than 90 per cent of the world's rubber, rice, and cinchona, 75 per cent of its copra, 55 per cent of its palm oil, and 60 per cent of the international supply of tin.

The economic advantages accruing to the colonial powers in Southeast Asia from this production were obviously great, although any overall estimate of profits against investment is virtually impossible to arrive at. It is equally if not more difficult to strike a balance between the benefits which Western economic activities brought to the countries of Southeast Asia, and the serious social and economic dislocations caused by those activities in the region as a whole. Criteria for assessing the economic impact of the West in Southeast Asia vary, but it is at least clear that, whatever its shortcomings, Western colonialism was able to sustain, admittedly with varying degrees of success, the six- or sevenfold increase in population which occurred in the region during the nineteenth and twentieth centuries. How far that population explosion was itself due to conditions produced by Western colonialism is a matter for debate, but there is no doubt that it could not have occurred without adequate resources being developed to support it and, especially, without the extension of peace and order achieved by Western rule.

PART TWO

The
Southeast Asian Response

Southeast Asian Societies
and Western Dominance

The imposition of Western economic and administrative instrumentalities did not necessarily cancel out age-old traditions, institutions, and, above all, Southeast Asian modes of thought. Both the severity and the alien nature of the Western impact, in fact, may well have precluded its gradual accommodation to and domestication in the fabric of native life. Unlike the long periods of confrontation with outside cultures—Indian, Chinese, Islamic—that in earlier centuries had impinged upon Southeast Asia and ultimately led to a measure of syncretic absorption by the host societies, the interlude of Western predominance and dominance was in most instances too short to yield similar results on a large scale. Yet if the transfer of cultural values, in particular, was relatively limited, the changes wrought by the West were in many other respects quite profound. However much of the old may have survived to reassert itself after the departure of the colonial powers, the West had, like a social engineer, diverted much of Southeast Asian life from its peculiar, indigenous course and forced it here and there into entirely new channels.

I

Nothing is more striking than the extent of the demographic revolution set in motion by foreign territorial control. Alone among Asian areas, Southeast Asia had for centuries exhibited a marked underpopulation. The traditional realms, even in the most fertile regions, had been small, largely because of the inherent administrative weaknesses, inadequate communications, and, above all, by the scarcity of population. This sparseness, in turn, had very likely been one of the most important motives of the incessant and often ruinous internecine wars so characteristic of premodern Southeast Asian politics.

The *Pax Europeana*, which for the first time established internal and external security and thus interdicted Southeast Asian warfare, laid the groundwork for population growth, further stimulated by health measures introduced on an ever larger scale during the twentieth century. The removal of these two prime "Malthusian checks" led to an unevenly spread population "explosion," from an estimated total of under 26 million in 1830 to perhaps 123-odd million in 1940. The introduction of such new crops as corn and cassava also played a significant role in rapid population growth. By mid-century, parts of Southeast Asia—Java most prominently—had been brought to the point of dangerous overcrowding; for other parts of the area, this dramatic change in the human landscape has only started to assume threatening proportions, in the mid-twentieth century.

Sheer numerical increment was, furthermore, accompanied by shifts in population, largely as a result of improved land and water communications and of Western entrepreneurship and technology. As Southeast Asia progressively came to supply agricultural and mineral staples for the world market, either new centers of economic gravity came into being or the ecological patterns of existing ones underwent significant changes. In both cases this affected the distribution, numerical and ethnic, as well as the density of the native populations, and for that matter the rate of immigration of nonindigenous groups. The almost tenfold increase in sugar production in Java between the 1860s and the 1910s constitutes a striking example. Originating in the days before the arrival of the Dutch East India Company, it was greatly stimulated by that Company in the eighteenth century, received additional impetus during the period of the Culture System in the 1830s, to be further expanded by private estate corporations after the 1870s. Sugar cultivation was perhaps the single most important factor—followed by crop diversification—accounting for the phenomenal population growth in the central and eastern parts of the island. Even before, but especially after the annexation of the Philippines by the United States, sugar cultivation produced similar demographic consequences in the province of Pampanga in Central Luzon, and in the Visayas on Negros.

In mainland Southeast Asia, demographic innovation was graphically expressed in an agricultural frontier rapidly moving southward into the delta regions of the Irrawaddy, Mekong, Chao Phraya, and Red Rivers. It was spurred by the conquest and subsequent pacification of these areas by the British in Lower Burma and by the French in Cochinchina, and followed by a similar trend in independent Thailand. Into these delta lands streamed peasants, clearing jungles—in Burma with initial financial and technological support from the colonial government—and establishing flourishing paddy fields that yielded vast rice crops from the late nineteenth century onward. The production of large-scale food surpluses made mainland Southeast Asia the continent's only staple food supplier and exporter; during the first four decades of the twentieth century, both rice acreage and rice exports more than doubled, yielding a total of almost 6½ million tons for export in the early 1940s. This was in and of itself one of the most notable innovations, accompanied, once again, by remarkable population growth.

The demographic changes so far discussed involved and occurred predominantly among ethnically homogeneous populations—Javanese, Filipinos, Burmese, Thai, and Vietnamese. Simultaneously, however, the opening up of territories for the cultivation of new exportable commodities, as well as the more thorough and methodical exploitation of existing resources, brought into being new settlement patterns in other parts of Southeast Asia. We have seen that the middle of the nineteenth century was especially remarkable for the rapid penetration of Western enterprises into parts of Sumatra (where it was sometimes preceded by European missionary activities) and Malaya. One concomitant of this penetration was the breaking down of the relative geographic and cultural isolation in which some of the Sumatran peoples—Batak and Minangkabau especially—had continued to live for so long.

But this internal migration was of less immediate consequence than the overall sparseness of population which, from the nineteenth century on, brought Chinese laborers in growing numbers to the burgeoning tin mines on the Sumatran offshore islands of Bangka and Billiton and, more strikingly still, in western Malaya. Labor also had to be obtained for the Sumatran tobacco estates and for the rapidly expanding rubber plantations in Sumatra and Malaya, as well as for those in Cochinchina. These demands were largely met by the recruitment of a nonlocal rural coolie proletariat from the crowded regions of Java, southern India, and Southwest China.

The primacy accorded Western economic needs by the colonial governments, combined with the difficulty of persuading local sedentary peoples to abandon their traditional livelihoods in favor of wage labor, thus led to a major trans-Asian migration pattern by no means limited to South and Southeast Asia; eastern Africa at one end, and such Pacific islands as New Caledonia and Fiji at the other, likewise received substantial numbers of Asian immigrants, as did, even farther away, the Dutch and British West Indies. Though in most Southeast Asian countries these foreign immigrant communities remained numerically limited, the human landscape of Malaya, West Borneo, and Bangka, Billiton, and Riau islands emerged radically altered, the number of Chinese almost equaling that of the indigenous populations in the twentieth century. On a lesser scale, Burma, part of Britain's Indian empire until the mid-1930s, found itself flooded by a sizeable foreign minority, amounting to some 8 per cent.

II

These quantitative changes in the population pattern, brought about by Western military, administrative, and economic control, led to equally significant if not more portentous qualitative changes in the social and political structures of most Southeast Asian societies. The most striking innovation was the introduction of a new, white ruling class into Southeast Asia. Until the middle of the nineteenth century, only the Dutch in Java and the Moluccas and the Spaniards in the greater part of the Philippines had foreshadowed the later colonial order, but even there the parallels are not always exact.

However dominant economically and politically, Iberians and Dutchmen had for centuries constituted small European enclaves living in essentially Asian environments which they sought to control rather than to transform. Until the early nineteenth century Spanish rule was concentrated in and around Manila, economically nourished by the galleon trade rather than by the exploitation of Philippine agricultural products. And while in Java the exploitation of local resources had been more or less systematically pursued from the eighteenth century onward, the Dutch had relied on the existing indigenous order to gain their economic ends. Socially, in both these early colonial areas, *mestizo* populations—Eurasian and Sino-Indonesian in the Indies, Eurasian but more importantly Chinese-Filipino in the Spanish realm—had come to play important intermediary functions between the small Western minorities and the bulk of the native peoples.

The newly emerging colonial pattern was not only staffed by far larger numbers of Westerners, but by Westerners of a rather different kind: trained, professional colonial civil servants, modern entrepreneurs, and the managerial personnel of the extractive and service industries. Whereas in earlier days the isolated European had settled into a patrician way of life largely modeled on the ostentatiousness of oriental nobles, surrounded by a numerous retinue as well as by native or *mestizo* womenfolk, the latter-day transient colonial establishments tended to become languid copies of Western middle-class family and social life. These purely Western enclaves, by and large self-sufficient and segregated from their Asian environment, underlined yet another major geographic shift in the map of Southeast Asia: while precolonial polities had as a rule centered on royal administrative capitals in the interior, the typically colonial capital city was located in a bustling port town. Batavia (Jakarta) had already displaced Jogjakarta and Surakarta before the onset of the modern era; Manila had become such a European center in the sixteenth, and Singapore in the early nineteenth century. Now Rangoon came to the fore, overshadowing Mandalay; Saigon and Haiphong bypassed imperial Hué; and Bangkok, chosen as their capital by the new Chakhri dynasty, developed into a seaward-looking emporium with a large Chinese population.

Riparian and coastal trading centers, it is true, had existed in premodern Southeast Asia. Most of them had declined, however, during the long centuries when westerners progressively wrested control of the sea lanes from their Southeast Asian and other competitors, diverting trade increasingly into new channels. Even in their heyday, moreover, many of the indigenous trading ports had existed more or less precariously in the shadow of the dominant agrarian states. The decline of these interior polities was accompanied by the rise of the new capitals and other commercial cities, with European officialdom and entrepreneurs constituting the top layers of the colonial social hierarchy.

The numerically, economically, and socially most prominent urban element below this Western elite stratum consisted of alien Asian immigrant populations, mostly Indian in Burma but otherwise predominantly Chinese; in some of the newly important centers—Saigon and Bangkok, for example—Chinese twin cities came into being. These foreigners, rather than indigenous Southeast Asians, provided European business firms, and here and there even colonial officialdom, with lower echelon skilled or semiskilled personnel. They also supplied the bulk of non-Western entrepreneurship and a whole host of ancillary service functions as well as artisans.

True enough, such foreign groups were by no means unknown in precolonial or early colonial Southeast Asia. Most ports, such as Malacca, had for centuries been visited by foreign traders and merchants—including the early Europeans—and in many of them the aliens had come to live in distinct ethnic quarters and virtually under the jurisdiction of their own compatriots. Chinese traders, in particular, had been appearing wherever Europeans built their "factories" and forts ever since the founding of Manila and Batavia; and in spite of occasional European massacres of Chinese, the two communities continued to coexist economically.

Yet once again these parallels are only partly relevant to the modern era. For one thing, the influx of Asian migrants was becoming far larger than ever before, and for another, Chinese and Indians—as well as other groups, including a small Japanese minority in the Philippines —spread out beyond the large urban centers as shopkeepers, artisans, and trader-financiers into many parts of rural Southeast Asia; we have already mentioned their large role in the labor market.

More important still than their geographical and occupational dispersal was the fact that, in the early decades of the twentieth century these communities grew into increasingly compact racial groups consciously separated from their Southeast Asian hosts. Just like the Europeans, Chinese and Indians now tended to intermarry less with the natives; cheap ocean passages greatly facilitated the importation of spouses from India and China. The emerging caste-like, ethnically and occupationally stratified pluralism that became the social hallmark of colonial Southeast Asia was further buttressed by the awakening of national consciousness in China, India, and Japan. The Westerners' racial exclusivism thus soon found its counterparts among the Asian minorities.

This, too, was a rather new phenomenon in Southeast Asia, where some degree of racial mixing, and indeed of cultural assimilation of foreign elements, had been the norm. Even the Chinese, often assumed to be unassimilable, had as a matter of fact for centuries literally entered the bloodstream of many Southeast Asian communities, most notably perhaps in Buddhist Thailand and in the Christian Philippines and, on a more modest scale, even in Muslim Java. These assimilationist instances apart, those Chinese who had been settled and intermarried for generations had in many parts of the area developed a peculiar culture of their own, which, though distinct, often contained more native than Chinese elements.

The mutual aloofness of the latter-day "plural society" was, however, caused not only by the size, composition, and separate orientations of the diverse racial groups; the colonial system itself was a major contributing factor. For with its consolidation, power—and, despite many outward trappings, glory—passed from the native court nobilities who in precolonial times had acted as strong magnets of assimilation. Like minorities everywhere, Southeast Asia's newly arrived Chinese and Indians tended to lean toward the centers of gravity in their host countries; but since Westerners eschewed assimilation and prized racial exclusivism in modern times, the minorities' choice was almost unavoidably along identical lines. (In noncolonial Thailand, where Chinese settlers had at one time been invited and granted privileged positions, twentieth-century Thai nationalists turned against them, thus interrupting a decades old process of assimilation.) Not only did it no longer pay, so to speak, to curry favor with Southeast Asians, but the immigrants' economic welfare and their place in colonial society depended almost entirely upon the white holders of power; and these, in turn, depended on the foreign communities for the proper functioning of the modern economy.

III

The colonial polities in a sense often appeared to turn the native populations themselves into aliens in their own lands. Whereas in precolonial times foreigners, whether Europeans or Asians, had been permitted to trade and gain wealth at the pleasure—and always to the partial profit—of Southeast Asian rulers, in the colonial "plural society" the roles were reversed. And where under the old order economic desiderata had been subordinated to political and social demands, modern colonialism generally ordained the primacy of economic demands over all others. The reordering of the social structure into an artificial racial mosaic was the clearest demonstration of this overriding fact; had it been otherwise, the large-scale immigration of foreign nationals, as for example in Burma and Malaya, could never have taken place. Not only did economic modernization primarily benefit aliens rather than natives, but, worse still, it occurred for the greater part outside native societies altogether. Most Southeast Asians became more or less passive onlookers while foreigners built a new world around, and largely without, them. Their ruling classes in particular became increasingly irrelevant to the modern colonial systems.

This was especially true of the nobilities and aristocracies in the most profoundly "Indianized" realms whose status, as we have observed, depended on royal favor rather than on independently owned wealth, whether landed or other. It was in these areas, too, that the entire culture and its value systems were probably least amenable to adapting to economic and technological innovation. By contrast, some members of the "Sinicized" gentry in Vietnam—the overt hostility and aloofness of the Confucian monarchy and its officialdom notwithstanding—had at least a secure base in landholding which made an adjustment to new economic opportunities possible.

In Cochinchina, where French hydraulic engineering and capitalization opened up vast new tracts of land for rice and rubber cultivation, a Vietnamese *bourgeoisie rurale* came into being which shared with the white colonial elite in the new agrarian prosperity. Likewise in the Philippines, where economic modernization had begun in Spanish times, and where for that matter cultural values did not overly stand in the way of change, the new wealth was shared between Western and native and *mestizo*—mostly Chinese-Filipino *mestizo*—landowners. Correspondingly, the alien Asians' role in the Vietnamese and Philippine economy, as for example in money-lending to the peasantry, was proportionately far smaller than it was in most other parts of Southeast Asia.

If the capitalist economy primarily benefited foreigners and by-passed many of the former ruling classes, large numbers of Southeast Asians were nevertheless drawn into its orbit. Within the new "plural societies" social change thus also occurred among the indigenous populations. We have already referred to the moving agricultural frontier in Lower Burma, Cochinchina, and central Thailand. Large-scale peasant migration—it was in fact not limited to the deltalands of continental Southeast Asia—proved that villagers could and did respond to economic stimuli. As often as not, it was the lure of new and fertile lands and of financial gain, combined with the prospect of law and order, that caused them to move into virgin territories.

But the demographic revolution was not followed by a true economic or technological one. Though the Burmese settlers turned from shifting to sedentary agriculture, the new frontier, far from giving rise to a Southeast Asian yeomanry, merely witnessed a spatial, though phenomenally sizeable, expansion of age-old agricultural techniques. In other words, what happened was a quantitative rather than a qualitative shift. While participating in the new export economy, Southeast Asian rice growers remained its passive beneficiaries in good times, its hapless victims in adversity.

Peasant indebtedness was apparent long before the worldwide depression took its toll in the late 1920s and early 1930s. Though rice exports continued to rise in quantity, prices fell quite steeply by more than half and did not recover their predepression levels throughout the remainder of the colonial era. Only in Thailand, where an independent Southeast Asian government followed a prudent fiscal policy, were the rice growers sheltered from impoverishment. In British Burma and also in French Vietnam, the small holders progressively lost title to their lands to the moneylenders—Indian *chettyars* in the former, Chinese and Vietnamese in the latter. At the mercy of foreign moneylenders and rice millers, peasants became tenants or landless agricultural laborers. This was particularly true of Lower Burma, where well over half of all delta farm land was in the hands of nonagriculturists after the early 1930s; and, deprived of the cohesive village institutions they had left behind, the migrants also suffered from psychological and social deprivations. Conditions were not quite so severe in Cochinchina and Thailand, whose rice growers had not immigrated *en masse*; but even there conditions were far from satisfactory, with widespread tenancy and rural indebtedness.

In island Southeast Asia social change was the result not so much of the spatial expansion of rice acreages as of the cultivation of other export crops, sometimes at the expense of rice, which in fact had to be imported from the peninsular countries, most notably in Malaysia and the Philippines but at times also in Java. In central and eastern Java, sugar cane had been introduced into the wet-rice village economy as long ago as the eighteenth century. Progressive intensification of sugar production went hand in hand with a steep increase in population to produce a peculiar ecological pattern which an American scholar has recently dubbed "agricultural involution." * Quite unlike the mainland migrants, Java's "involuted" peasantry remained settled, imprisoned, one might almost say, in its villages, dividing its time unevenly between subsistence and cash farming. While a few farmers did manage to

* Clifford Geertz, *Agricultural Involution: The Process of Ecological Change in Indonesia* (Berkeley and Los Angeles, 1963).

accumulate capital resources and larger landholdings, the bulk had to learn to subsist on less and less land and to share its poverty with increasing numbers of kinfolk. This overcrowding, in turn, placed severe strains on traditional institutions and loyalties.

Sugar was similarly the agent of change in parts of Luzon in the Philippines. Filipino tenants in Central Luzon and the Visayas progressively lost the security and protection of the old feudal order as landlords became capitalist entrepreneurs. The owners of the new sugar mills, or "centrals," in particular, sought to employ wage laborers, thus freeing themselves from time-honored, paternalistic obligations. Only Malay peasants and fishermen remained to a large extent cushioned from the tides of economic change by the large Chinese and Indian labor force in the rubber estates and tin mines; especially on the east coast of Malaya, economic modernization had minimal effects on the bulk of the indigenous peoples.

Wherever estates came into being in other parts of the region, they called forth a Southeast Asian agricultural proletariat, divorced from the villages from whence it had been recruited. In some instances, the members of this new working class had left their home districts, as we saw, and all too often they were eking out a marginal economic and social existence. An even more heterogeneous industrial, mostly urban, working class arose in the twentieth century. It clustered around the railroads and wharves, the Western business concerns, the oil wells in Burma and Indonesia, the tin mines of Indonesia, and the coal mines of Tonkin; here and there, native laborers competed against Indians and Chinese.

This is certainly not the whole story. That economic innovations had occasionally benefited segments of the native populations has already been pointed out in passing in connection with the South Vietnamese gentry-bourgeoisie and the Filipino landowning class, usually known as *caciques*. Not only had their enrichment been accompanied by the relative and absolute impoverishment of tenants and farm workers in their employ, it had also yielded little by way of developmental economic returns. Most of these new capitalists either continued to live in traditional manorial splendor or they indulged in conspicuous urban consumption either in the colonial capitals or abroad. What additional leverage their wealth provided was usually applied to political affairs rather than to experimental industrial investment.

These elite groups were, however, not the only indigenous beneficiaries of the new era in Southeast Asian economic and social history.

If the Burmese pioneers who cleared and settled the delta regions had reacted quite positively to the "profit motive," they were not altogether unique in their response to economic stimuli; similar initiative and adaptiveness had been displayed by peasants in many parts of Southeast Asia who had eagerly turned to small-holder rubber production. And there were others, especially outside the orbit of sedentary wet-rice cultivation, who had moved into commercial crop growing of such commodities as coffee and copra, into marketing, peddling, and even manufacturing. A minuscule Southeast Asian bourgeoisie, rural as well as (mainly small town) urban, was thus emerging during the first two decades of the twentieth century. Yet while enterprising peasant migrants and the new "middle class" shared a dependence on the trade cycles of the international economy, neither comprehended the distant mechanism which set that economy in motion.

So long as economic prosperity lasted, indigenous entrepreneurs managed to hold their own, and perhaps did even better than that; but the financial crisis of the early 1930s, an unprecedented disaster which virtually paralyzed the modern economic structure of the region, dealt them a virtual deathblow. It was then that they finally lost out to their ubiquitous foreign-born competitors in the "plural society." The depression wrought similar havoc in the agrarian sector of the export economy: the sudden decline of money income, as well as the "dumping" of unemployed estate workers on the subsistence village economy must have caused widespread hardship and declining rural living standards, even though they are harder to measure statistically than the effects of the crisis on rice exports. And, lest it appear that the entire burden fell on the indigenous population while the foreigners prospered at the natives' expense, it must be noted that drastic wage cuts if not outright loss of jobs also affected tens of thousands of Indian and Chinese laborers and coolies who could not even fall back on close-by home villages or kin; they could only reemigrate to their homelands.

What actually made matters far worse than they need have been was the fact that almost without exception the metropolitan governments shifted the major burden of the depression upon the colonies, thus virtually extinguishing the slow and halting advances in native economic modernization achieved before 1930. Such protective measures as were belatedly designed to salvage the colonial economies—sometimes in the form of international agreements restricting output and fixing minimum prices—almost invariably benefited the large European corporations rather than the small or medium-sized Asian cultivators. Only where native entrepreneurs were members of the Western economic power structure itself did they share in the benefits of financial crisis management: South Vietnamese landlords thus secured large-scale governmental credits alongside their French counterparts, while Philippine sugar exporters thrived on the price support extended by the United States. Thailand, with expert foreign advice, averted financial disaster by timely devaluation and appropriate fiscal policies that kept the Thai rice farmer from economic collapse.

In sum, it would seem that a half-century of economic and social change under Western aegis had benefited native Southeast Asians rather little. But this judgment must be tempered by some additional considerations. If colonial rule was primarily, and in several instances even exclusively, designed to provide economic benefits to vested interests in the "mother country" rather than to promote economic development for the benefit of Southeast Asians, there is little doubt that what modernization existed in the area was almost entirely accomplished by Westerners. The balance sheet admittedly looks forbiddingly adverse in terms of social dislocation and economic hardship. It must be borne in mind, however, that the former is a concomitant of change wherever (and under whatever aegis) it takes place, while the latter was largely caused by the phenomenal rise in population which tended to offset the benefits that economic innovation had started to yield. Even the most beneficent and altruistic government, foreign or indigenous, might have found it well-nigh impossible to cut through this vicious circle.

A wholesale indictment of the social and economic effects of Western colonialism becomes more tenuous still if it is simply predicated on the assumption that most Southeast Asian societies might have modernized more quickly, let alone more equitably, had they been left to their own devices. The transition from an agrarian to a more modern social order hardly ever proceeds smoothly, as Western European precedents amply demonstrate. *Anciens régimes* have in the course of history all too often resisted innovations stubbornly, and in some notable instances—as for example in the Iberian peninsula and in China—successfully. There is, indeed, little in the cultural and social traditions of most Southeast Asian societies—especially those most heavily "Indianized"—to indicate a propensity for self-generating economic innovation. Whether such aristocratic societies would or could have embarked on a social transformation along Western lines had they been offered adequate opportunities is impossible to know. In Thailand, where in the absence of Western political domination the choice was reasonably open, top priority was given to administrative and military, rather than to economic, modernization; the economy was in fact left to foreigners, mostly Chinese.

Again, it is one thing to observe the rise of a numerically and financially weak middle class in the shadow of twentieth century foreign capitalism; it is quite another to endow it, even had it not had to suffer from the depression, with the will and capacity to transform a native social system in which it was no more than a tiny "splinter." These middle-class elements were in any case overshadowed by other groups whose emergence owed less to the economic than to the administrative and educational innovations of the colonial era. It will be seen that these groups, though imbued with a measure of modernity, actually fitted into traditional patterns and categories far better than the emergent bourgeoisie, whose economic and social behavior often ran counter to established Southeast Asian mores and attitudes.

IV

The slow and cumulative effects produced by Western penetration on the demographic and other social facets of Southeast Asian life, stand in marked contrast to its dramatic and highly visible political consequences. Earlier chapters have chronicled the external history of the rise and consolidation of Western colonialism, and of the constitutional changes carried out by various colonial administrations. We shall now briefly assess their significance for Southeast Asian political structures.

Before turning to these internal factors, however, we must note that through the imposition of Western control Southeast Asia was incorporated into a new world system, that of the Atlantic powers. Divided as these powers were among themselves—their protracted quarrels over Southeast Asian territories showed this quite clearly—they nonetheless operated within an increasingly global system undergirded by a worldwide economy. This Atlantic order came to supplant an earlier, East Asian system centered in imperial China. For many centuries, China had at least de jure functioned as the—more or less distant—suzerain power in most of the Nanyang (the Southern Seas). It is no accident that the consummation of Western supremacy coincided with the decline of China, or for that matter that the abrupt end of that supremacy was caused by another East Asian claimant to power in the area, Japan.

At least equally important, the Middle Kingdom's relations with its Southeast Asian "vassals" (apart from contiguous, colonized, and "Sinicized" Vietnam) differed markedly from the military and administrative authority implanted by white overlords in their modern colonial realms. Unlike the Westerners, the Chinese had been satisfied to receive homage and needed commodities through embassies and trade missions; and with the exception of a few scattered and fruitless attempts at military intervention, the Chinese had over a long period of time been content to act as supreme political arbiter in the dynastic and interstate disputes of the Southeast Asian principalities. The change from Asian suzerainty to Western sovereignty was the more far-reaching since the Chinese power system had served as the model for relations between stronger and weaker principalities, as for example Siam's position vis-à-vis Cambodia and the northern Malay states.

The nineteenth-century acquisition of colonial domains, it may be recalled, had been a haphazard process, in several instances influenced by European diplomacy as much as by local conditions in the area itself. Indeed, involvements in Southeast Asia and the subsequent establishment of dependencies, especially on the mainland, were not necessarily ends in themselves for the Europeans; rather, they were but the prerequisites for closer contacts with China. Yet once acquired and consolidated, the colonial territories within the often arbitrarily if not accidentally drawn boundaries assumed the character of permanency. Neither traditional political divisions nor ethnic considerations necessarily played a decisive role in the demarcation of the new colonial realms. The incorporation of Burma into the British Indian Empire was as divorced from Southeast Asian reality as was, in another respect, the division of the Malaysian world among Dutch and British. Laos, to mention another example, was an artificial French creation without a proper past as a dynastic, united state.

One of the most important concomitants of this redrawing of the political map was the fact that the relations among Southeast Asian polities—peaceful as well as other—suffered an eclipse, to be superseded by links now forged between colonies and their distant "mother countries" in the Atlantic system. Each colonial territory came to focus and depend on its Western center of gravity—London, Paris, The Hague, and Washington. Thus, while many of the precolonial divisions in the area were, temporarily at least, submerged, a new factor of disunity was being introduced into Southeast Asia.

Within each colony, on the other hand, the emphasis was on the creation of territorial and administrative entities proper, in most cases accompanied by the integration of small units into a larger whole. The Philippines provides the earliest example of such Western-created integration, followed by the piecemeal formation of the Netherlands Indies and much later by the random and incomplete construction of a "British Malaya" (never as such a legal entity in colonial times) and of French Indochina.

Not only in sheer size, but in practically all other respects, too, the colonial "state" differed from the Southeast Asian polities of old. As was shown earlier on, these had been dynastic rather than territorial realms in which the luster of the court all too often stood in inverse relation to administrative efficiency. Usually limited in territory, they were subject to temporary expansion or contraction, if not to total dissolution. Though the traditional state was conceived in terms of cosmological sanction, it usually also served as the fulcrum of the keenest and bitterest internal political power struggle, as well as of dynastic and interprincipality conflicts. By contrast, the colonial state was equipped with unprecedented and unrivaled physical power. Its primary function was to exercise power as supreme policing agent, placed atop the colonial "plural" societies. As such, it drained its subjects of real political existence. (Foreign Asian communities, such as Chinese and Indians, usually remained more or less autonomous in their internal affairs, loosely supervised by the colonial authorities, but at no time properly integrated into colonial governance.)

Although by the late nineteenth century the modern colonial state had become a reality with many uniform characteristics in most of Southeast Asia, it impinged on native societies quite unevenly. These diversities were due to both internal factors and different colonial policies. As a result, the rupture between old and new, between traditional polity and modern bureaucracy, was certainly not a uniform phenomenon. It was most complete wherever colonial overlordship had extinguished or at least virtually replaced native rule, and it was least observable wherever Westerners had permitted the old forms to survive.

Even within this polarization—usually expressed in terms of "direct" and "indirect" colonial rule—the gradations were manifold and subtle, and for that matter far from static. True enough, in terms of political reality the distinctions between the various types of colonial administration were of little consequence: sovereign rights were securely vested in the Western power, whether it exercised them directly or through a "protectorate." But socially and even psychologically the two kinds of colonial rule gave rise to, or at least helped shape, differing historical factors and forces.

The distinctions between direct and indirect rule are of least relevance to the Philippines. Undeniably both Spanish and earlier American rule impinged directly on the islands, yet the gap between Western state structure and Asian population (or at least the elite among that population) was certainly far narrower in the Philippines than elsewhere in the area. Centuries of Spanish rule had not only absorbed and obliterated what little there had been of precolonial political life, but, alone among Southeast Asians, Filipinos (and *mestizos*) had become Westernized to a very high degree, especially those living in cities and towns. Cultural antagonisms between rulers and ruled were also muted by the fact that the natives, with the exception of the Muslim *Moros* in the South and some isolated tribal groups elsewhere, had been converted to Christianity. These factors markedly affected the Filipinos' response to both the Spanish and American colonial regimes.

In the other colonial domains, the differences between direct and indirect rule, combined with variegated internal factors, resulted in a wide spectrum of political patterns. Indirect rule, by preserving at least the outer scaffolding of the native status quo, provided a cushion against the corrosive effects of modernization. (This, incidentally, was also the rationale advanced by the European proponents of indirect rule, rather than the more obvious fact that it was more convenient and far less expensive than its opposite.) This was of course only the case where the inroads of economic change, in particular, were marginal or minimal. In its purest form, indirect rule was therefore limited to areas whose main significance to the European was strategic if not merely symbolic, serving to demarcate territorial control vis-à-vis other claimants or influences.

The French protectorates of Laos and Cambodia, the British-protected Unfederated Malay States, and a whole array of lesser Indonesian principalities contractually tied to the Dutch crown in the islands beyond Java were the clearest examples. In Tongkin and to a lesser extent also in Annam (Central Vietnam), as well as in some economically important areas of the Netherlands Indies, indirect rule progressively deteriorated into a legal fiction only thinly disguising increasing degrees of Western political control. This was, as we already saw, also largely true of the Federated Malay States, whose federal structure itself was of European design and at its higher administrative levels also predominantly British-staffed; yet within this foreign superstructure, these states remained far more viably intact than was true of other areas under nominal indirect rule, because economic modernization primarily involved Chinese and Indians, leaving the Malay communities as such almost untouched.

In several instances, indirect rule rather paradoxically went far beyond the mere conservation of the status quo. The guarantee of Western protection, though it betokened the native rulers' loss of independent political and, above all, military powers, carried with it a hitherto unknown degree of both internal and external security. Shorn of sovereign responsibilities, such "protected" potentates could and did devote their energies to what had, indeed, been their major preoccupation at all times—viz., dynastic matters, if not dynastic aggrandizement. In such Indianized" polities as Cambodia, for example, little more than French protection was needed to reinforce and refurbish the absolute, semidivine Khmer monarchy of old. But in many Malay states and also in some petty Indonesian realms European indirect rule actually helped create monarchical states proper during the nineteenth century; in many of them rajas and sultans had traditionally been nominal rather than actual rulers, sharing power to a considerable extent with local chiefs. Virtually all principalities under indirect rule thus experienced a strengthening of their courts, and they, in turn, grew into centers of substantial patronage.

Regardless of the actual political impotence imposed upon "protected" rulers, their survival as a highly visible traditional elite was of considerable importance in obviating or at least lessening the political alienation that occurred in other parts of Southeast Asia. Interposed between the mass of the population and the distant foreign overlord, in the eyes of their subjects still endowed with the charisma of legitimacy, and often enough provided with ampler financial resources than ever before, some dynasties under indirect rule also came to enjoy a virtual monopoly on the few avenues to modernization provided by the protecting power. Above all else, only younger men from these ruling families and their immediate entourages were privileged to attend Western schools and colleges.

Social evolution, slow and incidental as it was in most of indirectly ruled colonial Southeast Asia, thus gradually produced a younger generation aristocratic or gentry elite that combined traditional status with at least a modicum of modern education. Though the scales remained rather heavily weighted in favor of conservatism rather than modernization, this young "buffer-class" was in some countries to prove highly valuable in postcolonial times. (Even more striking developments along similar lines took place in independent Thailand, where the nobility remained the sole beneficiary of incipient modernization under direct royal auspices until 1932.)

Indirect rule also included many of the (mostly tribal) minority peoples who constituted ethnically and religiously separate nuclei in the midst of, or in close proximity to, major Southeast Asian communities. Such minorities were, for example, the various *montagnards* of Vietnam as well as the Shans and other groups in Burma. (Laos, in fact, comprised almost as many "minorities" as ethnic Lao, and noncolonial Thailand, too, contained several such minorities.) The inclusion of these minorities within the boundaries of the colonial state constituted a departure from premodern Southeast Asian practices. And since for the greater part the minorities continued to live in relative geographic and cultural isolation under a measure of colonial protection, they were destined to play a highly problematical role in the postcolonial era.

It was in the regions subjected to direct Western rule—most of them not only rich in natural resources but also the centers of major Southeast Asian civilizations—that modern colonialism wrought its most far-reaching changes. Its prime victims were, of course, the indigenous political systems with their courts and religious establishments. They either disappeared completely by European fiat, as was the case with the Burmese monarchy (destroyed in 1886), or else were doomed to gradual atrophy and impotence; this happened with the successor states in the Mataramese realm in Central Java whose progressively diminished authority was decisively broken after the Java War (1825–30). Long before their virtual demise, direct rule had come to extend all over the rest of Java, and in due course it was also introduced into several other parts of Indonesia. A similar fate befell the Vietnamese monarchy at Hué which, under the umbrella of a French protectorate, from the 1870s on rapidly declined to a shadowy existence bereft of all political influence; Tonkin in the north was detached to become a separate pseudo-protectorate in essence ruled directly, while the southern province of Cochinchina became an outright French colony under direct administration.

In the place of these eroded or decapitated indigenous state structures came the modern administrative state of Western design, in most respects their very antithesis. Above all else, direct rule destroyed the cohesiveness of the Southeast Asian political elites. This destruction was the unavoidable result of administrative modernization which, in turn, was the inescapable concomitant of intensive Western interference in the economies of the directly ruled regions. In spite of incidental efforts to maintain as much as possible of native social and administrative institutions, it proved almost impossible to square the circle by fitting a traditional system bereft of its peculiar *raison d'être* into a European bureaucratic apparatus. The demands of the modern colonial state, based on efficient territorial administration and on an increasing proliferation of technical and welfare services, simply could not be met by native institutions, whether at the level of the Southeast Asian monarchy or at that of local and village government.

Unavoidably, premodern institutions had to yield, as directly ruled colonies grew into Western-style administrative units. What native personnel was needed to staff the new colonial administrations—especially at the lower rungs—thus had to function within an intrinsically Western framework, regardless of its social origins and traditional functions. No longer status but qualification and efficiency became the chief criteria for employment in the colonial state. In most cases, as for instance in British Burma, the old hierarchies were simply ignored and bypassed, even if their individual members might find employment in the new order. At times, too, the old officialdom, particularly the Confucian mandarinate of Vietnam, retreated as a group before the colonial state into studied political isolation and cultural seclusion.

Even in Java, where the modern colonial state had taken long to mature and where regional administration had continued for centuries to be exercised by a traditional administrative corps, in the modern era it lost much of its usefulness, appearances notwithstanding: their earlier charisma considerably weakened, the Javanese regents had gradually deteriorated into a mere bureaucratic, hereditary adjunct to a Dutch administrative system for which most of them lacked adequate, modern training and expertise. If territorial administration as such was coming more and more to be cast in a purely Western mold throughout directly ruled Southeast Asia, this was truer still of the modern judicial organs and the manifold specialized services—forestry, irrigation, public health, communications, and many others—that the colonial state had increasingly called into being.

Recruitment into the various new agencies and instrumentalities thus called for Western-style training, and modern schools and colleges —whether operated by Christian missions or by colonial governments —soon attracted a fairly sizeable native clientele. While economic modernization had on the whole bypassed, and been spurned by, indigenous elite groups, educational modernization appealed to many of their members. Positions in the colonial government's services, but also in the liberal professions, promised status and prestige readily acceptable in terms of traditional aristocratic values. So great, indeed, was the social attraction of modern education that in the course of the twentieth century Western-style schools sprang up in most directly ruled colonies under private, native aegis.

Before long, the supply of educated or part-educated Southeast Asians exceeded the limited employment needs of the colonial state (and the even more limited requirements of Western enterprise) for clerical and administrative personnel. Both in numbers and in social significance, the products of the new education outdistanced by far the native bourgeoisie proper. They not only provided the lower echelons in the administrative and other services of the colonial states, but they also gave birth to an entirely new element in Southeast Asian social structure, the intelligentsia.

Since the institutions of higher learning were without exception located in the urban centers (especially the capitals) of the directly ruled territories, it was in them, too, that the new intelligentsia found its primary abode. Its members, it is true, shared a common exposure to modern education, but they were a heterogeneous group rather than a cohesive social class or segment of any one class. As we already noted, Western schooling in the indirectly ruled colonies benefited primarily the nobilities and aristocracies. The virtual destruction of the native political status quo precluded a similarly monopolistic mode of recruitment in the directly ruled regions.

Most intelligentsias did count young aristocrats and gentry among their membership, yet their numerical importance tended to decline as wider segments of the population—including those who had attained a modicum of wealth in the modern economy—were drawn into Western-type schools and colleges as the century proceeded. And even though in some countries, as in Java, the number of upper-class intellectuals continued to be disproportionately high, and aristocratic social values tended to influence intelligentsia mores and thought patterns, it was by no means the aristocracy as such that regained social and political ascendancy through modernization. Rather, it was the intelligentsia that emerged as the most versatile new group to fill, however slowly and hesitantly, the social and political vacuum created by direct colonial rule.

Intelligentsias were especially conspicuous in Burma, Tonkin, and Indonesia, where no other social classes had filled that vacuum; in Indonesia, the new intelligentsia was socially as well as ethnically "mixed," students from most of the directly ruled areas having gravitated toward the modern schools in Java. In French Indochina the beneficiaries of Western schooling included, in addition to Vietnamese from the three *pays* (with those from Annam in a minority), some few aristocrats from Cambodia and Laos; but the intelligentsia proper was far more in evidence in Tongkin than in Cochinchina, where French education had become the almost exclusive prerogative of the flourishing economic middle classes.

By the same token, it was the landed gentry, native and *mestizo*, that virtually monopolized the privileges of higher American education in the Philippines. Finally, the important Western-language educational centers of Singapore and Penang were of only marginal importance for the small Malay minority in the directly ruled Straits Settlements, most of their students being Chinese and Indians. For several decades, members of the ruling families in the indirectly ruled peninsular Malay States preempted British education; a nonaristocratic Malay intelligentsia proper only emerged later in the century.

Impressive as it was, the recruitment of Southeast Asians into Western governmental services and, indeed, into the Western intellectual orbit did not necessarily narrow the gap between ruler and ruled in the directly ruled territories. With the partial exception of the Gallicized Cochinchinese bourgeoisie and the Americanized Filipino gentry, the majority of Southeast Asians, including the newly educated ones, remained on the periphery of the essentially foreign colonial states. "Law and order" had become the far from hollow watchwords of these states; but it was essentially the foreigner's law and his apolitical order. Whatever the manifold shortcomings of the Southeast Asian polity might have been, at least it had enjoyed the legitimating sanction of tradition and religion. This the colonial state, for all its presumed or real advances, lacked. It could inspire obedience, awe and even respect, it could enforce its will—its taxing power especially—far more efficiently (though from the natives' point of view perhaps no less arbitrarily) than its predecessor, but it could not evoke true political loyalties among Southeast Asians, not even among its own public servants.

In the directly ruled colonies, especially, this basic alienation from the modern political order lay at the root of all opposition to colonial rule, tacit as well as overt, which will be our concern in the next chapter. It was highlighted rather than mitigated by the institution of various kinds of representative assemblies set up in most of these colonies in the course of the twentieth century. Once real political organs came into being, the colonial state could not (short of reducing them to mere caricatures) prevent them from becoming platforms from whence the abolition of the artificial and apolitical order itself would be demanded. This basic paradox continued as long as Western colonialism itself; if anything, it was heightened when native political consciousness and organizational life grew after the turn of the twentieth century.

The Southeast Asian Reaction
to the West

Southeast Asia's manifold ethnic, social, cultural, and political differences had been further complicated by the many-faceted and uneven Western inroads of modern times. These complexities and varieties were bound to yield widely divergent responses to the Western presence and dominance. By and large, those responses tended to be both most widespread and most vociferous wherever the perturbances in the native status quo had gone furthest, most strikingly in those parts of the region where economic penetration and direct Western rule had set in motion what might be best termed incipient social revolutions. In areas only peripherally affected by economic and administrative modernization, the responses were far less conspicuous and also far less shrill.

Our major concern in this chapter will be with the negative responses, particularly with various kinds of opposition to the Western impact, since these not only were its most dramatic and visible results but also were fraught with the greatest import for subsequent developments. By the same token, however, they should be placed in proper historical context lest they distort the sum total of reality. Even where social revolutions were gathering momentum in Southeast Asia, they often were doing so quite inconspicuously for several decades, only to erupt here and there in open, mostly short-lived revolts. Equally impor-

tant, areas already more or less profoundly troubled by internal upheavals were as a rule no more than isolated islands in seemingly (or
actually) still placid seas.

I

That latent opposition was widespread in colonial Southeast Asia
can easily be deduced from what we have discussed in the last chapter.
The increasing alienation of sizeable sectors of the native populations
from the modern economic and administrative order, especially in directly ruled areas, could not but engender discontent. But if the colonial
state lacked, as we have argued, the aura of proper legitimacy, it was at
the same time a harsh and inescapable reality, undergirded by administrative, police and military power. As such it had to be accepted and
obeyed. And while the foreign nature of that new reality made accommodation hard, the *Pax Europeana* was yet not devoid of tangible benefits.

More than anything else, internal security coupled with reasonable
economic stability must surely have made life tolerable to large numbers
of Southeast Asians. Colonialism, it is true, exacted a very high price
from its subjects: Westerners collected high taxes efficiently and even
ruthlessly, they alienated waste lands, and they created new and burdensome government monopolies, to mention but a few of the most deeply
resented innovations. But then, for all its legitimacy, the precolonial
dynastic polity had ofttimes been at least as arbitrary and oppressive as
its successor. Indeed, it was not so much opposition to authority as such
that was a new phenomenon in Southeast Asian history as its increasing
incidence and the changing forms in which it found expression. Admittedly the paucity of reliable data on precolonial social history makes
comparisons hazardous, but it may be as misleading to idealize the
precolonial era as it is to excoriate the colonial period.

The most common and general taproot of all native opposition to
Western dominance stemmed, of course, from the basic fact of the
aliens' intrusion into the social and political fabric of Southeast Asia.
It gave the impetus to the early, spontaneous responses to the Westerners' challenge as well as to modern developments. Yet the two kinds
of reaction must be clearly differentiated. In traditional Southeast Asia
neither society nor state were national entities in the proper sense of the
term, however deeply many of them were united by bonds of cultural

and political identity. "Indianized" as well as "Sinicized" states were dynastic rather than national polities, and it was this fact that had actually made it possible for Western power to penetrate with relative ease into the area's political arena: for Southeast Asian potentates thought and acted in primarily dynastic terms, as had been the case with premodern polities in Europe and elsewhere in the world. Westerners could thus exploit the region's dynastic instabilities, controversies, and jealousies, and, given their clearcut determination no less than their growing naval, military, and organizational supremacy, establish themselves as arbiters and, ultimately, as rulers in most of Southeast Asia.

The Europeans' path to hegemony had certainly been strewn with furious and at times bloody battles, many of them enshrined in the collective memory of Southeast Asians, and later extolled by modern leaders, writers, and historians. But Western advances had perhaps more often been smoothed by alliances with rulers and chiefs in many parts of the area; had it been otherwise, the European newcomers—small groups of social, racial, and religious outsiders—could have accomplished little.

It has often been argued that the religious factor played an outstandingly important role in fostering early anti-European sentiment, especially where it involved the encounter between Islam and Roman Catholicism, carried by Portuguese and Spaniards into the Indian Ocean. Some scholars have even speculated that the emergence of this militantly missionizing Catholicism rather paradoxically furthered and speeded the growth of Islam in island Southeast Asia. But if some Southeast Asian rulers—for example, the Muslim sultans of Acheh—raised high the religious banners, there were others who found it to their advantage to subordinate religious considerations to political, dynastic ambitions. (In this they were not unlike their European counterparts who, still in the era of the so-called religious wars of the sixteenth and seventeenth centuries, placed dynastic above religious interests.) Even the Iberian *conquistadores* were not always above sacrificing religious zeal to economic appetites. If this was true of two militant faiths locked in a worldwide, bitter confrontation, it was truer still where Europeans or Asians (or both) were less beholden to aggressive religious imperatives. Though both Islam and Buddhism provided common bonds—the only such bonds, in fact—transcending the individual native states, dynastic ambitions almost always stood in the way of a united religious front that could have obstructed the growth of Western power in Southeast Asia.

II

The Europeans' frontal attacks on native monarchies from the mid-nineteenth century onward inevitably brought the religious factor to the fore, since almost without exception native rulers combined secular with religious (or quasi-religious) functions. Armed opposition to the West was therefore from the very beginning heavily tinged with Buddhist appeals in Burma, whose monkhood, or *sangha*, was closely linked to the king. Similarly, the Vietnamese Confucian monarchy not only sought to rally support to the cause of dynasty and fatherland but also to the fight against the Christian faith that had—aided by French military might—steadily won adherents in the country. Among Muslims, generally prone to suspicions of "infidel" overlords, anti-Christian sentiment grew in response to Christian missionary zeal. This was particularly noticeable after the turn of the twentieth century in Indonesia, when missions obtained greater freedom of movement and official support from Dutch cabinets dominated by Protestant parties.

External and internal factors combined to enhance the importance of religion as a focal point for opposition to colonial rule. Buddhism and Islam, the latter in particular, experienced revitalization, largely kindled by developments abroad. New stirrings in the Muslim world, in reaction to the widening inroads of Western civilization—whether in its Christian or secular aspects—into Islamic lands in the Middle East (and also India), reached island Southeast Asia with increasing intensity, thanks to greatly improved sea communications.

Of special importance were the fundamentalist teachings of the Wahhabi sect of southern Arabia that had spread to some parts of the Indonesian archipelago. Its adherents preached an uncompromising return to the pristine purity of the faith, which in colonial Southeast Asia inevitably led to opposition, not only to the *kafir* overlords but also to the native traditional order of things, its syncretic religious laxity in general, and its visibly non-Islamic institutions in particular. The main propounders of this Wahhabi-inspired challenge to the status quo were *ulama*, especially those returned from or at least in touch with the Near East; their prime native targets were as often as not rulers and chiefs, in their critics' eyes representatives of a weak if not a declining and already compromised political system. Religious resistance found a very potent vehicle in mystical sects or brotherhoods (*tarekats*), which flourished in many parts of the archipelago from the closing decades of the nineteenth century.

In the face of such attacks, the old pattern of dynastic alliances with Western suzerains received fresh impetus, apprehensions of zealous religious innovators providing an ever stronger common motive on both sides. Wahhabi doctrine had in all likelihood provided the inspiration for the so-called *Padri* movement among the Minangkabaus of western Sumatra in the early decades of the nineteenth century; it was only with large-scale Dutch military support that the secular chiefs finally succeeded in destroying the Padris' militantly theocratic state, ultimately at the expense of their independence. Wahhabism may also have played a part in the far more complex Java War between 1825 and 1830, already briefly referred to in Part One. The chief protagonist of this anti-Dutch guerilla war was, however, Diponegoro, a royal prince of the house of Jogjakarta, and at the outset he enjoyed at least the tacit support of the nobility. Diponegoro's was, then, in the first place a case of dynastic opposition to foreign rule, and much of his vast appeal was due to the charisma of Javanese royalty and to traditional Javanese syncretic religious values. Yet a stern, more orthodox Islamic strain was quite clearly part of the rebellion, fostered by *ulama* in the princely entourage and discernible in organizational and other features of Diponegoro's short-lived "government." The Dutch encountered their most stubborn *ulama*-dominated opposition in the sultanate of Achin—for centuries a strongly Islamic realm—which it took from 1873 to 1903 to subdue. The victorious Dutch then proceeded to abolish the sultanate itself, just as they had undertaken the final dismantling of Javanese royal power after the capture and banishment of Prince Diponegoro in 1830.

It was in the areas under direct colonial rule that religion came to play the leading role in focusing and shaping anticolonial sentiment in the late nineteenth and early twentieth centuries. Religious leaders attained this prominence almost by default, since they were the only indigenous elites that had survived the virtual destruction of the old monarchical order at the hands of European colonialism. What is more, the religious groups represented something genuinely native, unfettered as they mostly were by compromises with the new foreign rulers. On that score, their prestige was far less tarnished than that of upper-class natives in Western administrative employ, whose collaboration and at least partial identification with the new, alien order—in later years also their Western education—seemingly estranged and almost divorced them from indigenous life and society.

Tensions between temporal and ecclesiastic power, known in at least muted fashion in premodern Southeast Asian polities, thus assumed a new character in the colonial setting. They were rendered potentially more dangerous still by the marked weakening of old organizational ties and disciplinary restraints. In dynastic states whose rulers combined secular and religious functions, acting as both supreme heads and chief benefactors of the religious establishment, the clergy was an integral part of the monarchy; in Theravada Buddhist lands, especially, clerical hierarchies were supervised and controlled by the state.

In sharp contrast to past Southeast Asian practice, many Western colonial administrators, whether imbued with the ideal of "separation of church and state" or guided by Christian prejudice, were in principle inclined to adopt a noninterventionist stance toward native religions. Left more or less to their own devices, religious leaders thus came to enjoy considerable latitude. This quite often brought in its wake doctrinal laxity, sectarianism, and here and there even near anarchy among the clergy. Such disintegration was most apparent in those rural areas where social dislocation and economic hardship provided excellent breeding grounds for agrarian unrest, as for example in Lower Burma.

Before we proceed to inquire into the nature of the religious factor in these rural upheavals, however, it may be worth dwelling briefly on at least two parts of Southeast Asia where divergent developments had resulted in different relations between religious and political elements. Not surprisingly, the divergence was greatest in noncolonial Thailand, where outside interference in the status quo was at a minimum. The two great Chakhri kings, Mongkut (1857–68) and Chulalongkorn (1868–1910), were as adroit in steering a diplomatic course aimed at safeguarding Thai independence amid the mutually jealous ambitions of two imperialist powers, Britain and France, as they were in strengthening their country's social structure the better to withstand external pressures. A veritable renaissance of Buddhism stimulated by royal patronage—not the first of its kind in Southeast Asian history—did much to purify *sangha* doctrine and teachings from the late eighteenth century on; under Mongkut, a devout Buddhist who had spent many years in the monkhood, it went hand in hand with organizational reforms that tied the monks ever more closely to the monarchy. In the latter part of the nineteenth century, the *sangha* played the leading role in the gradual modernization and expansion of vernacular civic education throughout the kingdom.

A similar strengthening of the ties between political and religious elites occurred in many of the Malay States. As we shall presently see, the currents of Islamic innovation were running strong in the Malayo-Indonesian world in general, and in the late nineteenth century strongest perhaps in the volatile Muslim communities of the Straits Settlements. But these were isolated enclaves, as it were, in the midst of non-Islamic cosmopolitan trading populations enjoying the benefits of unfettered free trade, worldwide communications, and direct British colonial rule. The situation was quite different in the peninsular states where Malay social and political conservatism flourished, protected, it may be recalled, by British rule. From the very beginnings of British involvement in the internal affairs of the Malay sultanates, the colonial power endeavored to exempt religious affairs from the purview of British officials; spelled out for the first time in the treaty with Perak, the so-called Pangkor Engagement of 1874, this stipulation was subsequently incorporated, in one form or another, in the compacts signed by the British with other Malay rulers.

Under its protective umbrella, these rulers proceeded in the course of time to establish official Muslim hierarchies that in size, organization, and administrative scope surpassed premodern Malay practice. The Malay states' waning political independence—especially in the Federation—was in a sense counterbalanced by enhanced internal prestige buttressed by religious sanction. This new-old conservatism, combined with the very slow rate of economic and social modernization among the Malays generally, sufficed to keep Muslim ferment, so important in the nearby Straits Settlements and in neighboring Indonesia, at bay. More Islamic than ever before, the Malay states found security and stability in a viable alliance between nobility and *ulama*.

These, however, were exceptional areas of tranquillity, especially on the rural scene, as were Cambodia and Laos and generally the more remote parts of colonial Southeast Asia, where modern influences had as yet barely reached. Elsewhere agrarian unrest became a more or less constant and conspicuous factor in the growth of opposition to colonial rule. As had been true for centuries before, the peasant upheavals derived their main spiritual and ideological inspiration from traditional folk religions. The penetration and "domestication" of Theravada Buddhism and Islam, already mentioned in the Introduction, had doubtless deeply affected the basic matrix of these peasant beliefs, as had also been true of Catholicism in the Philippines and, though perhaps less pervasively, of Mahayana Buddhism and Taoism in Vietnam. Yet within these separate worlds of major sophisticated world creeds, peasant religious sentiments and practices had retained much of the original and local

traditions, of which animism, the propitiation of spirits, and the veneration of ancestors were the major ingredients.

So strong were these local traditions that even the latter-day religious establishments, their official doctrinal orthodoxy notwithstanding,
had become permeated with heterodox beliefs and practices which, in
turn, lent a peculiar and differentiating flavor to, for example, Burmese
as against Thai Buddhism or to Javanese as against Sumatran or Malayan Islam. Still, the wide syncretic spectrum exhibited certain striking
similarities, uniformities it would almost seem, with regard to the peasants' primordial religious expectations.

Almost without exception, these were—as they still are—cast in a
utopian, messianic mold, with hopes for deliverance from the burdens
of earthly existence centering on the sudden appearance of a divine
harbinger of justice. It was these ever-latent longings, with their strong
overtones of religious-political opposition to the powers-that-were, that
found vehement expression—often in mystical societies—in the perturbed Southeast Asian countryside in modern times. What rendered
them politically more explosive than before was that they were now
directed against "unbelievers": not only rulers of a foreign religion, but
also prosperous alien Asian minorities in their midst. The age-old longings for the restoration of an imaginary blissful golden age now came to
draw a sharp religious line between past and present, and thereby became the most widespread popular base for anticolonial agitation.

Until the twentieth century, this rural agitation remained almost
wholly local and incidental, erupting when outside pressures, such as tax
levies, appeared particularly obnoxious and when local leadership was
readily available. There were literally hundreds of such localized, usually short-lived uprisings, some of them directed at Chinese no less than
at governmental authorities. Almost all of them were led by religious
leaders, including several of doubtful doctrinal purity; mystical and
other heterodox tendencies often played a very notable role. One Javanese case, the so-called Samin Movement of the late nineteenth and
early twentieth centuries, deserves special attention because, unlike most
rural uprisings there, it was inspired by pre-Islamic religious notions, and
also because of its unexpected longevity; Saminism, a simple, unorgan-
ized movement among the poorest peasant strata, actually survived the
banishment and death of its originator. A far more conspicuous Burmese
example is the Saya San rebellion of 1930, led by a former *pongyi* (Buddhist monk). Gathering his followers in the jungle, Saya San proclaimed

himself king with makeshift traditional paraphernalia and led the attack on the "unbelievers," only to be executed by the colonial authorities.

Its traditional contours notwithstanding, the Saya San rebellion (and others of its kind elsewhere) in a way marks a transitional stage in Southeast Asian agrarian unrest, as its leader had for some years been connected with an urban, more modern, and even (in spite of its name) more secular organization, the General Council of Buddhist Associations, founded by European-educated youths in Rangoon in the second decade of the century. Though Saya San himself forsook modernity in favor of the Buddhist-monarchical past, modern influences were sporadically reaching into the Southeast Asian countryside throughout the twentieth century. The traditional kinds of peasant commotion, it is true, perdured and very likely even increased in frequency throughout the colonial era; nor did they disappear when colonialism ended. More important, even when outsiders wittingly or unwittingly succeeded in rallying peasants to their cause, the rural response to such modern stimuli was as often as not traditional and utopian. Yet slowly, social change was mobilizing segments of the rural population into the wider stream of anticolonial agitation whose centers were urban rather than rural.

III

It was in cities and towns that new Southeast Asian elites were coming to the fore. In closer touch with the innovations of the colonial state, many of them educated in modern schools, they were also exposed to the political currents that were, often violently, abroad in other parts of Asia and farther afield. These young Southeast Asians were thus increasingly attuned to foreign intellectual and political influences, while at the same time confronting the Western material and spiritual—Christian or secular—inroads at home. Both impacts led them to seek new certainties to counter the challenge of Western dominance. Nor were they the only ones in quest of more modern values, for members of new or newly literate social and occupational groups, such as native government and private employees, merchants and traders, as well as wealthier landowners, were finding traditional mores, religious ones included, inadequate to modern times.

We shall presently see that these developments covered a wide, shifting and even contradictory variety of anticolonial orientations, differing from country to country over a span of several decades. Together, they helped to inaugurate a new chapter in Southeast Asian history. For where traditional reactions to colonialism had longingly looked backward to an allegedly perfect, golden past, almost all of the later movements expectantly looked to the future, however much inspiration some of them derived from older values. Their most significant accomplishment was the creation of a spirit of self-reliance and self-identification, achieved through journalistic and other writings, and above all through the mushrooming of all kinds of associations and organizations, many of them fashioned after Western models. Political maturation was an inevitable concomitant of all these activities. The literate political public as such admittedly remained rather small in proportion to the total populations. (Most colonial governments, moreover, barred civil servants, one of the largest native literate groups, from active participation in overtly political movements.) Incipient modernity was therefore for the greater part confined to urban areas, but vernacular education was also becoming modernized and attracted increasing numbers of pupils, so that new ideas were gradually spreading beyond their original confines, occasionally fanning, as we already saw, anticolonial sentiment even in the changing countryside.

It is not surprising that the first organized, clearly Western-inspired anticolonial movements should have occurred in the Philippines, where social evolution and Westernization had by the nineteenth century progressed far beyond the rest of Southeast Asia. Indeed, Philippine developments differed not only chronologically but in many other respects from those in other colonies, and hence remained more or less unique in spite of some parallels. Spanish higher education, for one thing, was available to selected natives and *mestizos* almost half a century before this became generally true elsewhere in colonial Southeast Asia; for another, almost all its beneficiaries were members of the Hispanized wealthier social classes whose emergence we have already referred to in the last chapter. Thus the Philippines in the late Spanish era resembled colonial—North as well as Latin—America rather than nineteenth-century colonial Southeast Asia, in that well-to-do, literate and socially prominent members of colonial society, often tied through bonds of intermarriage, found themselves denied political privileges by stubbornly unyielding colonial and metropolitan governments.

Of course, there were several quite peculiar Philippine factors, especially the prominent role played by the Catholic Church. Educated Filipinos—the *ilustrados,* as they were called—increasingly resented both

Spanish overlordship as such and Spanish clericalism, more particularly the great influence wielded by the Spanish regular orders that were far more powerful than the secular Church hierarchy. Friars had a virtual monopoly on parishes, which antagonized Filipino regular clerics; friars also owned some of the best agricultural lands and thus became the focus of bitter hostility on the part of their native tenants. It was, indeed, the peasantry which, subjected to ever greater economic and social pressures, was more recognizably Southeast Asian than any other segment of Philippine colonial society. All these variegated strands and tensions came to the fore in the momentous developments of the late nineteenth century.

Anticolonial agitation, at first cast in rather moderate, reformist language, originated not in the islands but rather among young students in Europe. These early reformers started to publish a newspaper, *La Solidaridad*, in 1889; the most brilliant and versatile among them was a young medical doctor, José Rizal, whose two novels, *Noli me tangere* (1887) and *El Filibusterismo* (1891) were smuggled into the colony, where their attacks on Spanish abuses, clerical ones in particular, no less than their appeals to Filipino nationhood, found a ready response among *ilustrados* and others.

The Spaniards, fearful of a repetition in Asia of their bitter experiences in the Americas, yet unable to learn from them, met the reformers' pleas and weak organizational efforts with the harshest repression, culminating in the execution of the repatriated Rizal in 1896. Almost at once the anticolonial movement passed from its reformist to its revolutionary phase. *Ilustrados*, who had played the leading part in the early years, receded into the background as new revolutionists—most notably Andres Bonifacio and later Emilio Aguinaldo—succeeded in mobilizing lower-class elements, peasants in particular, into the secret society called the *Katipunan*; significantly enough, Spanish temporarily yielded to Tagalog as the medium of revolutionary propaganda in the latter phase.

We can trace neither the complex course of Southeast Asia's first nationalist revolution, nor the contours of the area's first if short-lived independent republic, proclaimed in 1898. Both ultimately succumbed to the Americans, who not only defeated Spain but, after a harsh military campaign, established colonial rule over the islands. The only institution to survive—albeit considerably weakened as time went on—was one of the Revolution's important innovations, the Independent Philippine Church; not unlike the Anglican Church, it retained most of Catholic ritual but severed its ties with Rome, substituting the vernacular for liturgical Latin. Yet, extremely painful as the defeat of the Revolution was to Filipino patriots, its demise was, politically at least, temporary rather than permanent. A few years after the cessation of hostilities, Filipino-American collaboration took the place of the earlier, bitter confrontation. Though it was punctuated by acrimonious agitation every now and then, this collaboration carried Philippine political developments to the threshold of national independence on the eve of the Second World War, leaving other Southeast Asian colonies (with the only partial exception of Burma) far behind.

This harmony, unparalleled almost anywhere else in the area, derived from the peculiarities of the metropolitan power no less than from those of Philippine society. Compared to the French, British, or Dutch, the Americans had few economic stakes in their newly acquired colony; moreover, they came to imperialism late and with a distinct anticolonial legacy from their own revolutionary past. From the very beginning, indeed, there were American proponents—altruistic and egotistic—of Philippine independence. No less important, the main beneficiaries of the new colonial order were actually Filipinos rather than Westerners, as was mostly the case elsewhere. Protected access to the American market brought large new profits to wealthy native landowners and entrepreneurs, thus creating a propitious climate for a speedy *rapprochement* between *ilustrados* and Americans; and this climate improved further as American education and benevolent rule spread. After uncertain beginnings, the colonial authorities proved willing to transfer power to the proponents of a new, increasingly American-style nationalism, best exemplified in Manuel Luis Quezon, charismatic leader of the triumphant *Nacionalista* party and first president of the Philippine Commonwealth in 1935.

In sharp contrast to the spectacular near-consummation of the Filipino elite's political aspirations stood the virtually static if not worsening situation of the peasants. Their participation in the Revolution had brought no amelioration in rural conditions. The Americans, it is true, had removed one particularly hated social legacy of the past through the outright purchase of the extensive friar estates from the Vatican; but the bulk of these lands, offered for sale, went to the large native and *mestizo* landowners rather than to the creation of the sturdy yeomanry which some American administrators had hopefully anticipated. On the contrary, progressively rapid expansion of the Philippine export economy after 1910 brought in its wake a steady deterioration of rural conditions in several densely populated areas. Agrarian unrest, already chronic in late Spanish times, increased in incidence and temper. As in many other parts of Southeast Asia, it found expression in religiously inspired, utopian and messianic upheavals, but before long also in larger-scale movements under modern, urban leadership, as for example the *Sakda-lista* revolt in 1935.

Nowhere else in Southeast Asia had social evolution and partial Westernization reached a comparably high stage, and nowhere, for that matter, did the precolonial past loom less prominently than in the Philippines. As we turn to an examination of anticolonial movements in the rest of Southeast Asia, we must recall the comparatively recent impact of Western thought patterns on still strong indigenous cultural and religious traditions. Because of them, modern nationalist consciousness proper took time to mature in most colonial domains, especially where the colonial states were artificial creations; in the Philippines this artificiality—indicated by their very name—had perdured so long, and what had existed before had been by comparison so weak, that Filipino nationalism had, as it were, developed naturally over time, in spite of the survival of strong regionalisms. It was not so everywhere.

In most cases feelings of solidarity continued for a long time to center on smaller, primordial or at least parochial groupings rather than on the larger, national—and that often meant religiously and culturally heterogeneous if not also multi-ethnic—entities. And even in those areas where the colonial boundaries were more or less coterminous with those of the former dynastic state, political consciousness took decades to evolve toward modern nationalist loyalties. There is, then, in most of the twentieth-century anticolonial movements a gradual shift from prenationalist or protonationalist sentiments to the more fully developed and mature varieties of Southeast Asian nationalism. This shift is reflected in the changing patterns of leadership that emerged within the overall anticolonial movement in modern times.

The confrontation with the West forced many thoughtful Southeast Asians—with the exception of the dwindling proponents of a continued, stubborn retreat from modernity—to search for a new identity. To some of them—the Javanese aristocrat Noto Soeroto and the Vietnamese mandarin Pham Quynh for example—a synthesis of the best in native and European cultures appeared as the most desirable goal; such "associationist" views were also held by a few Dutch and French colonial administrators at the turn of the century. But far larger numbers preferred to delve more consciously and consistently into their own traditions in order to recast them as far as possible in more modern terms and organizational molds, without at the same time accepting foreign values as such. This search for a cultural renaissance clearly guided a good many youths in several parts of the region who had attended European missionary or secular schools.

The first modern, organized movement in Burma, the Young Men's Buddhist Association (clearly modeled on the Y.M.C.A.), founded in Rangoon in 1906 and subsequently developed into the more ambitious General Council of Buddhist Associations, exemplified one such case. While Buddhism prominently appeared in the names of both, its significance was symbolic rather than substantive: the partly Western-schooled leaders were not so much interested in religious matters or reform as in the search for Burmese identity, an identity in which "Burmese" and "Buddhist" were, as yet, interchangeable. *Budi Utomo*, the first modern association founded in Indonesia in 1908, served a rather similar purpose among young, Western-educated Javanese aristocrats. Of greater long-term significance was the rapidly growing *Taman Siswo* school system, whose originator, Ki Hadjar Dewantoro, was a member of the central Javanese court nobility; in his schools Western pedagogic methods and modern curricula were wedded to the inculcation of traditional moral values. Culturally and even socially parochial at the outset, both movements in later years joined the mainstream of Indonesian nationalism.

Indonesia's most spectacular anticolonial movement, *Sarekat Islam*, was a far more complex and many-faceted phenomenon, spanning old and new in a variety of ways. It originated in 1911 as an association of Javanese merchants whose main objective was organized protection against growing Chinese competition. While the nascent Indonesian urban bourgeoisie was, as we shall presently see, one of the main pillars of the modern religious movements in Java and other islands, once again it was not religious identification as such that underlay the original choice of the organization's name; "Islam" mainly served to stress the truly native vis-à-vis the foreign, non-Muslim, trading communities. In fact, the *Sarekat's* leadership very soon passed into the hands of far less parochially oriented men whose major preoccupations were with social and political amelioration, not with religious reform as such. As they steered the organization into ever more agitational channels, the bourgeoisie by and large withdrew its support and sought instead affiliation with distinctly religious movements.

For several years *Sarekat Islam* nonetheless grew rapidly into colonial Indonesia's only true mass movement with a membership of well over half a million in the late 1910s. It was recruited from a wide range of social groups, but above all from peasants, especially in perturbed rural areas. Though the organization's official program was only peripherally concerned with religious affairs, its name, and also its forensically brilliant leader, Umar Sayid Tjokroaminoto, must have exerted an almost magical, traditional spell in the Javanese countryside, not least among *ulama* who in many cases became its local standard bearers. Yet, uneasily poised between tradition and incipient modernity, *Sarekat Islam*, having temporarily and almost accidentally hyphenated urban leaders with agrarian unrest, declined as rapidly as it had risen, rather paradoxically in spite of conscientious efforts to infuse it with a truly Islamic, even pan-Islamic, content. Religious reform on one side, radical secular movements on the other, surpassed the *Sarekat* to become the dominant factors in Indonesian political life from the mid-1920s onward.

In the Burmese and Javanese movements we have so far reviewed, the leadership had been provided in the main by the early graduates of European schools, and their inspiration, direct or indirect, had been largely Western. In Vietnam (especially in Tonkin and Annam) this Western impact was for quite some time overshadowed by that of China, which had for centuries exercised a profound cultural and intellectual influence on upper-class Vietnamese. While French education was spreading and displacing the classical Confucian learning after the 1890s, Western ideas in fact had reached Vietnam by way of China (and in Chinese translations) before they became accessible to larger numbers of natives in French.

Not unexpectedly, the tremors that accompanied China's encounter with the West in the late nineteenth century found their echoes among educated Vietnamese, such as Pham Boi Chau. Even more important was the Chinese Revolution of 1911, which served as a model and inspiration to China-oriented youths, giving birth to a programmatic nationalism several years before it became the major ideological force elsewhere in Southeast Asia. Founded in the early 1920s, Vietnam's most prominent nationalist movement, the *Viet Nam Quoc Dan Dang* (Vietnamese Nationalist Party), was organizationally fashioned and ideologically guided by Dr. Sun Yat-sen's *Kuomintang* (Chinese Nationalist Party). Inspired by Chinese revolutionary fervor, the party launched an ill-prepared frontal attack on the French authorities in 1929, which caused its complete destruction.

Western influences were even more indirect and refracted among

Southeast Asia's Muslim religious communities, whose members consciously held aloof from European missionary and even secular schooling. It was, rather, continuing contact with the Islamic centers in the Middle East, brought so much closer to Asian believers after the opening of the Suez Canal in 1869, that generated a wave of new religious developments in the early decades of the century. Reformist and modernizing currents which resulted from the confrontation of Near Eastern Islamic civilizations with the Western world found their intellectual leader in Muhammad 'Abduh (1849–1905) at Cairo's renowned al-Azhar University, whence hundreds of Malay and Indonesian students carried them to island Southeast Asia. Where the earlier puritanical orthodoxy of the Wahhabis had spurned the modern world, 'Abduh's reformism sought to revitalize Muslim life by proving the compatibility of the Koran with intellectual and scientific innovation.

The combination of intellectualized piety and this-worldliness was bound to render the new teachings especially attractive to the flourishing Muslim trading communities in the Straits Settlements which had taken the lead in organizational and journalistic activities in the late nineteenth century. In turn, these activities radiated to Indonesia, notably to Sumatra and Java where they found ready imitators; we have already shown why Islamic reformist ideas were far slower to penetrate the peninsular Malay states. *Muhammadiyah*, founded in Central Java in 1912, soon became the leading reformist organization, with several hundred branches in most parts of Indonesia. In its far-flung modern-style school systems, but also through manifold other activities, it propagated the ideas of a viably modern, self-reliant Islam. Reasonable economic prosperity in the years after the First World War created an ever larger clientele for *Muhammadiyah* and other reformist or modernist groups. Growing Islamic sentiment also resulted from the rapidly increased volume of the Mecca pilgrimage, especially after the conquest and pacification of the Holy City by the Saudi dynasty in 1924; only two years later Indonesian registered *hajjis* reached a record total of over 52,000.

Reformism itself, however, was only one of the major causes of this impressive reinvigoration of Indonesian Islam. Another was the very reaction which the onslaught of its new ideas and practices elicited among the more tradition-minded *ulama*. Some of them felt the challenge of modernity strongly enough to adopt several of their opponents' organizational weapons, culminating in the creation of an association of their own, *Nahdatul Ulama* (Awakening of the Ulama), in 1926.

Its major strength lay in the heartlands of Java, where—especially in the rural areas—the traditional syncretic forms of Islam prevailed. The division between old and new thus mirrored to an important degree the growing rift between the more modern, urban segments in Indonesian society and the less rapidly developing, rural segments. But it also had its regional and ethnic ramifications, for reformism proved particularly acceptable in the less "Indianized" areas, such as West Java and several regions in the Outer Islands.

Moreover, while these religious developments, taken as a whole, undeniably strengthened and invigorated the consciously Islamic elements, they also brought about a sharpening of latent conflicts with those Indonesians who were averse to identifying themselves too strongly with Islam. Quite apart from the numerically small non-Muslim minorities, this applied above all to many nominal Muslims to whom the Islamic ideal of a more or less rigorously orthodox *ummat* (community of believers) appeared as an essentially foreign-inspired, Middle Eastern ideal alien to their own way of life.

This cultural cleavage had distinct social roots, for reformism in particular tended to find its most ardent adherents among the rising urban and rural bourgeoisie, while aristocratic families tended to look askance at it. And this, in turn, was reflected in growing ideological conflicts. Whereas Muslim leaders hoped for a truly Islamic community, members of the Dutch-educated intelligentsia—many of them of aristocratic backgrounds—found doctrinaire Islam parochially restricting; their goal was the development of an all-Indonesian nationalism. Muted as all these conflicts were by the common if tenuous bonds of anti-colonial unity, they nonetheless left deep marks on Indonesian history.

Religious modernization in the Islamic archipelago was without parallels in the mainland Buddhist countries which, in addition to other differences, lacked dynamic, religiously authoritative centers comparable to Mecca and Cairo. Thanks to fewer internal social and cultural divisions, Buddhists also escaped the kinds of conflict which Islamic reformism had brought in its wake. Too little is known about contacts among the Theravada *sanghas* in Burma, Laos, Cambodia (and Ceylon) in colonial times to assess the influence which may have been exerted upon them by the Siamese Buddhist "renaissance" promoted by the Chakhri kings, or for that matter by new trends in Japanese Buddhism.

As far as can be ascertained, Vietnamese Mahayanists did not experience a revitalization comparable to Theravada Buddhists, let alone to Muslims. In Cochinchina, however, where neither Confucianism nor

Buddhism had struck deep roots in precolonial times, new sects gained prominence from the 1920s on. The most remarkable and also most successful in terms of winning widespread support was Cao Daism, whose pantheon included a wide variety of Eastern and Western secular and religious "deities," blending in a remarkable synthesis elements of animism and Mahayana Buddhism with organizational borrowings from Roman Catholicism. Even then, the Cao Daists represented a regional phenomenon rather than a diffused, dominant strand in modern Vietnamese life as a whole. Its main protagonists were, in fact, urban elements with a modicum of Western orientation, dissatisfied with the colonial order. Another such sect, the Hoa Hao, recruited its adherents from among disaffected small peasants, tenants, and rural workers. It, too, enjoyed only a limited appeal.

IV

From the 1920s on, the ideological climate as well as the personnel in the anticolonial movements started to change perceptibly, as the influence of new foreign patterns of thought increased at the same time that the number of their Southeast Asian recipients rose as a result of spreading education. Furthermore, accelerated economic and social change in some parts of the region provided a steadily growing clientele for the multiplying political elites.

Overseas events had started to cast their shadows on Southeast Asia in the closing years of the nineteenth century. Quite apart from Islamic reformism with its important though geographically and socially limited appeal, the spectacular transformation of Japan into a modern nation state which by 1905 proved capable of inflicting a shattering defeat on Tsarist Russia stirred the imagination on a far broader and less parochial scale. We have already mentioned the repercussions of the Chinese Revolution of 1911 on neighboring Vietnam; but it, too, did not go unheeded elsewhere in the region (the more so since it impinged on Chinese minorities all over Southeast Asia).

But it was the First World War and, more poignantly still, the Russian Revolutions of 1917 that ushered in an era of markedly radical if not revolutionary expectations, in part also because of the influence of these events on the Congress movement's mounting anti-colonial agitation in nearby British India under the leadership of Mahatma Gandhi (which in turn affected Indian minorities in Burma and Malaya). Japan's growing stature, accompanied by the rise of totalitarian movements and the emergence of "strong men" not only in Russia but also in Turkey, Italy, and later in Germany—all these contributed to the growing restlessness.

By the 1920s, too, the number of natives exposed to these variegated foreign influences had assumed ever larger proportions, thanks largely to growing educational opportunities. Colonial institutions of higher learning—Rangoon and Hanoi universities and also the Batavia Law School, for example—had come into being during or immediately after the war, producing a steady if small trickle of graduates. To these must be added the growing number of students overseas—Europe in the first place but also Japan (especially chosen by Thai and Vietnamese) and British India (attracting Burmese students in particular). Foreign education, hitherto the privilege of the chosen few, gradually became a more and more collective experience. Such overseas student groups as the *Perhimpunan Indonesia* (Indonesian Union) in the Netherlands developed into politically active nuclei which, like the Madrid-centered Philippine *ilustrados* forty-odd years earlier, generated intellectual and ideological ferment.

In the colonies themselves, the expansion of Western but also of modern vernacular schools—the latter increasingly organized by private initiative—created ever wider circles in touch with modern developments. Nor was political consciousness limited to the direct beneficiaries of formal education. Employment in Western business and government offices offered thousands of natives a glimpse into new ways, while others came into contact with them through working, trading, and traveling within or outside the colonial boundaries.

Though the ferment was understandably greatest in the colonies, where it vitally affected the course and content of the anticolonial movements, foreign education at least indirectly caused a profound political upheaval in noncolonial Thailand. To an even greater extent than in indirectly ruled Southeast Asian colonies, modern education had for several decades been exclusively open to members of the Thai court nobility, in fact mostly to direct relatives of the monarchs. Yet the very modernization set in motion under royal aegis in the latter part of the nineteenth century had called forth the creation of a new army and navy, civil and diplomatic services. Recruitment into these modern instrumentalities called for promise of talent rather than proof of noble birth, and thus commoners were gradually drawn into modern schools and colleges—including Japanese ones—and into European military academies.

By the late 1920s, Thai junior officers and bureaucrats, having found intellectual inspiration abroad, started to express growing discontent with the absolute monarchy in which royal progeny continued to monopolize all decision-making functions, relegating the expertly educated to subordinate positions. In 1932 the reformers, practically all of them commoners, finally forced the king in a bloodless *coup d'état* to agree to the transformation of the state into a constitutional monarchy—in fact, a bureaucratic polity under military control. With the consolidation of the new authoritarian regime which outwardly upheld the traditional monarchy, Thai radicalism was expunged from the officially sanctioned political vocabulary, its erstwhile proponents having become the pillars of the modern state.

Where in Thailand the recruitment of students into overseas centers had been dictated by planned modernization, in colonial countries it proceeded in a far more piecemeal and accidental fashion. In indirectly ruled Malaya and Cambodia, for example, the carefully selected overseas students came from ruling (or at least reigning) families; invariably, their small numbers and noble births assured them of the few privileged positions available to the modern-educated in their homelands. Paradoxically, it was in directly ruled Burma, Vietnam, and Indonesia (where Java dominated all modern political life) that the intelligentsias were most numerous and at the same time in least demand. For the colonial state's needs for modern-trained Southeast Asians at higher levels were severely circumscribed by the presence of European (and Eurasian) administrative and executive personnel, including of course the officers of the military services.

While the expansion of educational facilities inevitably led to demands for broadening the base of native participation in colonial governance, the intrinsically European structure remained basically unaltered as long as colonialism lasted. Forced to live for the greater part on the political periphery of colonial states unwilling or unable to accommodate and absorb them, the new intelligentsias provided the main spokesmen for a total reform of colonialism if not for its outright abolition in the name of an increasingly radical nationalism.

The reasons for the prevalence of such radical tendencies must be sought in part in the nature of the outside intellectual influences encountered by the young student elites, especially abroad, but in part also in the intelligentsias' own characteristics and predilections. In both respects, the leaders of twentieth-century Burmese, Vietnamese, and

Indonesian nationalism differed rather markedly from Southeast Asia's first modern nationalists, the Filipinos.

When Rizal and his *ilustrado* friends started on their activities in the last quarter of the nineteenth century, liberalism was the most progressive and, in the restrictive Spanish environment, even the most revolutionary intellectual movement. Thus it was natural that the young Philippine patriots should have patterned their thoughts on contemporary Europe's most advanced political ideas; these ideas, moreover, happened to serve quite adequately the purposes of the Filipino and *mestizo* gentry—as they had served those of the gentries of North and Latin America—who clamored for political self-determination. The transition from Spanish to American liberalism was for this reason rendered relatively smooth, and the political elite of the *Nacionalista* Party found in the American intellectual orbit ample satisfaction for its social and ideological aspirations. More radical ideologies did of course reach the islands in the 1930s, but they remained, or were forced to remain, on the political periphery.

By the time young men from other parts of colonial Southeast Asia came to study abroad in larger numbers, liberalism, though far from discarded, was intellectually on the defensive in Western Europe (though not in the United States). The First World War, the Russian Revolution, and revolutionary changes in other parts of Europe had given currency to new ideological trends, socialist and other, that found ready acceptance among many Western intellectuals. The ferment also extended to a critical examination—by no means limited to Marxists and other socialists—of European imperialism and colonial practices. Such criticisms penetrated into some of the British and Continental universities which enrolled increasing numbers of colonial students. The same universities incidentally also helped train several latter-day colonial administrators and teachers who embarked on their Asian careers with a reformist zeal unknown to earlier generations.

To very many Burmese, Indonesians, and also Vietnamese studying in the West, this postliberal critical and radical intellectual climate must have appeared highly congenial. Even then, however, the number of those who came to identify with Western modes of thought, let alone to join foreign-led political movements, always remained rather limited. Many others merely borrowed, more or less consciously, elements of European ideologies and modified or syncretized them with native intellectual strands, as had so often happened in the past in the

course of the domestication of foreign cultural elements in Southeast
Asia. Some attempted to formulate syntheses between, for example,
Marxism and either Islamic or Buddhist social thought.

More generally, radical nationalism could obviously be nourished
by xenophobic, often religiously tinged aversion to foreign overlordship,
while even Marxism-Leninism, readily acceptable as the most sophisticated and "modern" critique of the capitalist system, may well have
struck responsive chords in the deep-seated traditional disdain for
private traders embedded in both "Indianized" and "Sinicized" cultures.
What, finally, rendered all these ideological tendencies so prevalent was
the fact that, unlike the Filipino *ilustrados,* and also unlike educated
Malay and Cambodian nobilities, most of these intelligentsias (with the
partial exception of bourgeois Cochinchinese) were in a very real
sense "outsiders"—people with no vested social and economic, and
hence psychological, stake in the modern colonial order.

Yet, though identification with foreign political ideologies was in
most cases partial rather than complete, the Western-educated (whether
trained at home or abroad) tended to form rather distinct groups with
marked preferences not only for life and work in the urban centers,
especially the colonial capitals, but also for Western modes of political
organization. There was, it is true, a broad division in the Burmese,
Indonesian, and Vietnamese urban political elites, some of whom decided to work for their ends within the institutional framework created
by the colonial authorities, while others, influenced by the Indian Congress, preferred to shun all participation in advisory or legislative bodies;
but most of the political parties founded by intellectuals of either
orientation were clearly closely patterned on those of the West. As we
shall presently see, this proclivity inhibited rather than enhanced their
effectiveness.

However, the new ideological currents, especially radical nationalism, were by no means limited to the few and numerically small urban-
ized groups of intellectuals. For one thing, political organizations of
all kinds, newspapers, magazines, and latterly also the radio helped in
the diffusion of the new political vocabulary among ever wider layers
of the population. For another, education in the colonies, especially in
vernacular—including religious—schools, was visibly gaining momentum
from the 1920s on. Their graduates came to form a secondary echelon
of potential political leadership, close enough to both modern and
native value systems to serve as intermediaries in the process of political
communication. It was, indeed, among these groups—still rather close

spatially, socially, and ideologically to the mass of the population—that radical ideologies of foreign origin found deeper roots than among the intelligentsias themselves who, for all their verbal radical proclivities, remained wedded to Western, even liberal, ways. Ideological syncretism, as we have already seen of great significance among the Western-schooled, played a still more prominent role among the vernacular-educated. And it was of course widespread among those segments of the public—tenant farmers, industrial and agricultural laborers, petty traders, and others—whom economic and social change had partly detached from traditional habitats and who yet lived on the fringes of modernity.

Most important of the foreign influences affecting the second-echelon elite group was doubtless Marxism-Leninism. It had been brought to colonial Southeast Asia by Western intermediaries, as happened in Indonesia where Dutch socialists on the eve of the First World War were instrumental in the founding of what became Asia's first Communist party proper. Contacts abroad provided another channel of communications, the most noticeable example being provided by the Vietnamese Nguyen Ai Quoc (better known in later years under the name of Ho Chi Minh): after years in relative obscurity in Paris, where he had joined the French Communist Party in 1921, he went to Russia and Asia, rising to prominence in the Communist International (or Comintern).

In the early 1920s the *Partai Komunis Indonesia* (pki, Indonesian Communist Party) shed its Dutch mentors, most of whom were in any case expelled from the Indies by the colonial government. For several years, the party was spectacularly successful in organizing strikes among urban workers, those in government employ in particular; but its leaders also vied for control of the mass membership, much of it rural, that had rallied under the banner of *Sarekat Islam*, both within that movement itself and against its central leadership. By the mid-1920s the uneasy alliance between *Sarekat* and pki was broken, the former abandoning much of its revolutionary stance in favor of a more decidedly Islamic orientation, while the Communists found themselves at the helm of the ebbing revolutionary expectations fanned for some years by Tjokroaminoto and his rural *ulama* following.

Its leadership divided and truncated—many prominent Communists had been exiled by the authorities—the party embarked upon a suicidal head-on collision with the colonial regime in late 1926 and early 1927, which, in addition to isolated acts of terrorism in the capital, involved large peasant followings in the western parts of Java and Sumatra. The poorly armed and inadequately prepared uprisings were ruthlessly quelled, and large-scale banishments decimated the PKI's lower-echelon leadership to the vanishing point. While this methodical repression extinguished the organized Communist movement, the rebellions doubtless formed the most vehement expression of widespread anticolonial sentiment.

Short-lived Communist successes were even more impressive in Vietnam, even though there, too, the party's existence was virtually destroyed in the end. The political climate in the French colony, far more restrictive than the relatively liberal attitude that prevailed in Dutch-ruled Indonesia until the mid-1920s, had tended to force political activities into conspiratorial channels. Working through an elaborate underground network, the Vietnamese Nationalist Party (VNQDD) planned a major uprising in the early 1930s, sparked by the premature outbreak of an anti-French mutiny among the native garrisons in Yen-Bay. The party's subsequent destruction left the field free for the Communists. Like the Nationalists, the Vietnamese Communists found ideological and organizational inspiration in adjacent China; in fact, the Communists' center of activities was in Canton, where Ho Chi Minh for years trained Vietnamese refugee youths at the Communist-led Whampoa Academy, founded there with Soviet help to train Chinese Nationalist as well as Communist cadres.

In 1930 Ho succeeded in forging a united Indochinese Communist Party out of mutually antagonistic smaller Marxist groupings. A year later, these young leaders, having slipped back into their homeland, launched strikes among factory workers at Benthuy in northern Annam, soon merging them with a far-flung series of peasant uprisings that spread through the Provinces of Nge Anh and Ha Tinh. For a while, the protectorate's organs of local government disintegrated under the violent onslaught of armed peasants whom the Communists hastily organized in the village soviets. But French retribution was swift and merciless, even employing aerial bombardments. As in Indonesia, executions and arrests decimated the most revolutionary anticolonial movement, though, more adept at underground organization, its infrastructure remained somewhat stronger in the French colony. After 1937, when metropolitan France under the aegis of the Popular Front allowed Communists greater leeway at home, Vietnamese Communists were again able to play a modest part in above-ground colonial—especially urban—politics on the eve of the Second World War.

While their actual strength was of course no match for the police power of colonial governments, the Communists had nonetheless proved to be remarkably adept organizers and ideologues in the potentially revolutionary climate of colonial Indonesia and Vietnam. (There was very little Communist activity in other parts of Southeast Asia at that time.) Their successes in rallying to their cause fairly large numbers had to all intents and purposes little to do with guidance, let alone financial support, from Soviet Russia. Liaison with the Comintern, it is true, existed—for Indonesia both via the Dutch party and by means of some few Indonesian emissaries to Moscow, for Vietnam on account of Ho's high standing in the international movement itself. But, unlike China, Southeast Asia was not then a central concern of Moscow, whose information on that part of the world was at best intermittent and sketchy. Indeed, the Russians unsuccessfully tried to dissuade the Indonesian party from embarking on its ill-fated, premature revolt, and it is unlikely that its Vietnamese counterpart was undertaken at the behest of the Soviet leadership.

But whatever significance these foreign ties may have had, it was above all the ability of native *cadres* to adapt foreign teachings to their own environments and to provide organizational and ideological leadership for the discontented and uprooted that accounted for Communist ascendancy. Doctrinal Marxism-Leninism obviously was less important for the movements' mass following than the syncretic fusion of traditional chiliastic expectations with revolutionary appeals for the attainment of a "classless" society; the subtle blending of antiforeignism with anticapitalism was similarly successful. It is in any case significant that the Indonesian Communists—in virtual defiance of the International's strictures—had succeeded in making common cause with, and had been supported by, a good many Islamic leaders in rural areas.

Such links with lower-class audiences, rural communities, and religious spokesmen in particular were not so easily established by the Western-schooled intelligentsias. Even those with avowed radical leanings and with awareness of the widespread restiveness among the victims of social change often found it difficult to perceive of meaningful political work outside their urban habitats. Most of them, moreover, were almost totally absorbed by the central political confrontation with colonialism; this tended to limit their attention to the capital cities, the seats of legislative and executive power as well as the centers of modern journalistic activities. At times, upheavals in the countryside thus bypassed urban intellectuals altogether; the Saya San Rebellion, for one, took the Rangoon nationalists, just then involved in the debate over the separation of Burma from India, by surprise. For, like their European colleagues, the professionally educated political leaders (including academic Marxists) quite often suffered from a congenital disdain for the "old fashioned" and "superstitious" countryside; they thus failed to see —perhaps even feared—its revolutionary potential.

Unquestionably, the urban elites possessed a degree of political sophistication unmatched by those farther removed from the Western intellectual orbit. They understood and formulated the idea and ideal of the nation-state far better than could or did religious leaders with their particularist (but in the case of Muslims also vaguely supranationalist, pan-Islamic) orientations. The Communists' allegiance to a worldwide revolutionary cause similarly precluded full comprehension of nationalism as a potent driving force. Intelligentsia politicians were, moreover, far better versed than their competitors in such things as parliamentary tactics and formal party organizations.

But these skills, however important in the longer run, actually restricted effective political action in the colonial setting to urban environs and to a relatively small clientele. Such a clientele was bound to be all the more limited since the largest number of better educated natives, the colonial bureaucrats, for reasons of prudence and self-interest barely allowed themselves to be drawn into agitational anticolonial movements and parties. Most of these parties were, in turn, patterned on Western models, liberal or socialist, and for this reason alone failed to serve as appropriate organizational nuclei in Southeast Asian societies, which were for the greater part still lacking in modern social stratifications. Divorced from identifiable classes or interest groups, intelligentsia politics thus tended toward the factionalism peculiar to small groups; in the often artificial environment of the larger cities it erupted in a plethora of growing or waning parties whose *raison d'être* was mostly determined by personal rather than ideological or other substantive factors.

The fragmentation of the Burmese, Indonesian, and Vietnamese nationalist movements was, of course, to an important extent also the direct result of the harsh realities of colonial rule. In Vietnam, the suppression of the revolts of the early 1930s was followed by the continuing, ruthless suppression of all signs of antigovernmental activities. Both nationalist and Communist ranks had in any case been decimated to such an extent that new political talent on anything approximating a truly nationwide level became extremely difficult to find. Deep-seated Vietnamese regionalism, strongly reinforced by the tripartite administrative division of the country, henceforth provided the only basis on which "cooperative" nonrevolutionary natives—most numerous among the "Gallicized" elite in Cochinchina—were carefully selected to occupy the few nominal positions assigned to Vietnamese on the various colonial councils. So unwilling were the French to make concessions to Vietnamese sentiment that they nullified the efforts to reinvigorate and modernize the "protected" monarchy of Annam launched by the young, French-educated emperor Bao Dai—with the assistance of such men as Pham Quynh and Ngo Dinh Diem—in the early 1930s. Ideologically camouflaged opposition to the government was perhaps best organized by the Cao Dai sect in Cochinchina; only toward the end of the colonial era did some few Marxists (Stalinist as well as Trotskyite) emerge in the elections for the Saigon city council. The collapse of Republican France, followed by the emergence of the Vichy regime, put an immediate end to this short-lived liberal interlude. Before long, suppression of native political life was resumed with ever greater vigor.

Indonesia's Communist-led revolts of the mid-1920s marked an even greater watershed in Dutch policies vis-à-vis native political life, inaugurating an era of severe and stifling repression which lasted until the end of Dutch colonial rule. The elimination of the PKI had deprived Indonesians of many talented political leaders, as for example the brilliant Tan Malaka (who, like Ho Chi Minh, occupied a high position in the Comintern's Asian affairs). But whereas in Vietnam no leader arose to equal the exile Ho's talents and stature, the most outstanding Indonesian political figure was not a Communist but a radical nationalist, Sukarno. Swiftly rising to prominence after the Communist debacle, Sukarno's sheer personal magnetism and uncanny oratorical gifts gave widest currency to the idea of an all-Indonesian nationalism to which, before long, most Indonesian groups, including even most Islamic ones, came to subscribe.

Ideologically, the Dutch-trained Sukarno—an omnivorous multilingual reader who obtained a degree from the Bandung Institute of Technology—attempted a conscious fusion of traditional Javanese, Islamic, Marxist, and other concepts, welding them together under the banner of national unity in the face of colonial exploitation. No less important than these intellectual attempts was Sukarno's ability to speak meaningfully to urban and rural mass audiences in the language and symbols of primordial utopianism. Like Tjokroaminoto before him (at whose house Sukarno had spent some years in his teens), Sukarno thus became a towering charismatic leader who drew vast crowds to the

gatherings of his *Partai Nasional Indonesia* (PNI, Indonesian Nationalist Party). The colonial authorities, having recently smashed the organizational apparatus of Communist cadres, lost little time in removing
Sukarno from the political scene in the early 1930s: twice arrested and
tried, he was finally exiled from his native Java until the end of Dutch
rule in Indonesia.

Sukarno's disappearance from Indonesian political life was soon
followed by the banishment of other nationalists, most notably of
Mohammad Hatta and Sutan Sjahrir, both Dutch-schooled Sumatrans
with socialist leanings who were in fact opposed to Sukarno's agitational approach to nationalism. With the removal of these men, intelligentsia politics tended to degenerate into the factionalism we have
already referred to above, Sukarno's absence also contributing to renewed
dissensions between religious and "secular" groups. The severe limitations imposed by the government induced more and more of the remaining leaders to abandon the path of noncooperation in favor of participation in legislative bodies, especially the central *Volksraad*, whose formation in 1918 has been described in Part One. Agitation for constitutional reforms continued, as did efforts to create unity among the
various Indonesian groupings. But they were of no avail in winning
concessions from the colonial authorities, even after the German invasion had forced the Dutch government into exile in London in mid-1940.

Compared to Vietnam and Indonesia, political life in Burma enjoyed relatively great freedom throughout the colonial era. Even though
the British executed Saya San and took harsh reprisals against the
leaders of urban race riots—the result of heightened anti-Indian sentiment fanned by the economic hardships of the depression—in the 1930s,
the colony's constitutional development allowed for rapidly increasing
native participation in government on a level only surpassed in the
Philippines. In the course of time, "cooperation" thus became far more
attractive to English-educated Burmese than it ever had been to Indonesians, let alone Vietnamese. In fact, the colonial masters did not so
much take Burmese nationalism into account as allow its proponents to
participate, on their own rather than on Burmese terms, in the country's
governance. For example, the British blandly ignored the overwhelming
Burmese vote (tactical rather than substantive as it was) opposing
Burma's severance from India, proceeding with separation in 1935.

From the late 1930s on, Burmese nationalists like Dr. Ba Maw—a
barrister who had risen to fame as Saya San's defense counsel—led
colonial cabinets; but unstable majorities caused by party factionalism,

combined with the necessity to govern with the support of European and foreign Asian (Indian and Chinese) parliamentary factions, made it virtually impossible to implement nationalist political aims. Their attainment was also thwarted by the reserved powers of the Crown which barred such major issues as continued and unrestricted Indian immigration from the cabinets' purview. Burma, in other words, remained almost as British as ever, and the gulf between rulers and ruled was barely narrowed by nationalist politicians who were torn between the lures of ministerial prestige and the actual impotence of office.

A student strike at Rangoon University in 1936 was the curtain raiser for the entry of the younger generation political intelligentsia into the Burmese scene. Homegrown in a volatile academic environment replete with the most variegated intellectual influences, these young men from all walks of life were far more prone to radical nationalism than their more sedate, British-educated elders. Where dominion status within the Empire appeared as the most desirable goal of the foreign-schooled, the new elite—who defiantly styled themselves *Thakins* ("Masters"), the respectful address demanded by Europeans of their native servants—stridently insisted on Burma's complete independence. Equally important, the students' leaders, such as Thakin Nu and Thakin Aung San (the victims and heroes of the strike), had a far clearer insight than the older politicians into the need of building political bridges toward the victims of the great depression: they started rather haphazard organizational activities among laborers and peasants, while they also sought to cooperate in a more or less systematic way with politically conscious *pongyis* (Buddhist monks). The *Thakins*, it is true, did not boycott elections, but their avowed aim was not to work within the parliamentary system so much as to wreck it from within the legislative chamber.

The outbreak of the war brought to the breaking point relations between the colonial administration and the young radicals, who had won Dr. Ba Maw and other nationalists and Buddhist groups to their side in the so-called Freedom Bloc in the fall of 1939. Since they refused to support Burma's entry into the war on the side of the British, they were arrested, as was Prime Minister U Saw who had taken a last-minute plea for Burmese independence, or at least full dominion status, to London. Aung San and several other *Thakins*, such as Ne Win, fled Burma to accept Japanese hospitality and military training on the island of Hainan in the expectation of winning from Britain by military means what they had failed to attain through political agitation.

V

In spite of the growing challenges it had encountered in several parts of the region, Western dominance in Southeast Asia appeared secure and firmly established on the eve of the Pacific War. Only the Americans had given clear proof of their willingness to liquidate their colonial relationship with the Philippines, which were to be granted full independence in 1946 after a ten-year transitional Commonwealth. Admittedly, there had been a marked devolution of governmental responsibilities in Burma, but as yet the colonial power had made no definite commitment to extend to her (or for that matter to British India) a constitutional status commensurate with that achieved by the self-governing "white" Dominions in the Commonwealth during the twentieth century.

No such devolution was envisaged either for the various parts of British Malaya, where, indeed, a highly complex racial communal pattern seemed to call for the well-nigh indefinite presence of a colonial arbiter. Constitutional innovations had been similarly kept to a minimum in the French protectorates of Laos and Cambodia, while in the rest of French Indochina administrative modernization had if anything helped in the ever firmer establishment of direct colonial control. The same was true in the Netherlands Indies, where the earlier cautious experimentation with limited codetermination for the native population suffered an abrupt halt after the political upheavals of the mid-1920s.

The many-faceted opposition to colonialism which we have reviewed in this chapter can leave no doubt that anticolonial sentiment was visibly gaining momentum as the century proceeded, especially with regard to organizational cohesion and ideological sophistication. It was least in evidence in French Laos and Cambodia, the latter country in particular benefiting from the French presence to ensure its territorial integrity vis-à-vis Vietnam and Thailand. Indirect rule was similarly conducive to relative tranquillity in both the Federated and Unfederated Malay states under British protection. (Minor tensions existed in the Straits Settlements, but they were limited to certain sectors of the urban Chinese, who had been drawn into agitational political action, whether under nationalist or communist aegis; demonstrations and strikes occurred in the early 1930s.)

In most of the directly ruled areas, it was peasant discontent inspired by traditional modes of thought and under religious leadership that was still the most widespread and almost universal vehicle of the opposition to colonialism. New influences from the outside, however, were steering it increasingly into new directions. At the same time, more modern-oriented groups were starting to mount urban-based attacks on the colonial regimes. But we have seen that none of the challengers to the status quo were ever able to cause the authorities more than temporary disarray. Possessed of a monopoly of armed might—and also, we should add, of the invincible belief in the beneficial legitimacy of colonial rule—these governments found it rather easy to quell even the most ambitious (not to say most foolhardy) rebellions launched against them. Nor were they slow in destroying structures or removing leaders that threatened to link the bulk of the rural population with nationwide political agitation.

It was the very strength of colonialism that not only physically subdued its most vociferous enemies but also psychologically disarmed most of its subjects and indeed many of its loudest critics. Indifference if not condescending aloofness toward its critics, so characteristic of the tone of latter-day French and Dutch colonial administration, dampened realistic hopes for substantive change in the foreseeable future. The seeming immutability of the colonial order acerbated the factionalism already prevalent among urban political intelligentsias, their ranks often deprived of talented leadership through imprisonment or exile.

Anticolonial movements also continued to suffer from internal cleavages, such as the ongoing controversy between Muslims and "secular" nationalist leaders in Indonesia; disunity yielded only spasmodically to tenuous unity forged by Sukarno's outstanding but even then short-lived political leadership. In addition, many of colonialism's beneficiaries—civil servants, entrepreneurs, and others—whether out of conviction or timidity failed to make common cause with political movements. Last but not least, some members of the older privileged classes, though they had mostly forfeited rank and status, remained hostile to the impatient younger harbingers of opposition and change. The colonial rulers, of course, knew how to exploit all these divisions to their advantage.

Unquestionably, Western colonialism had incurred widespread disaffection and hostility, and at best enjoyed no more than unwilling and lukewarm acceptance among broad layers of the native populations. But as long as its very existence remained unchallenged from the outside, the colonial order was by and large immune to the variegated, often contradictory, and invariably impotent attacks to which it had been subjected from within. When, in the months after Pearl Harbor, Japanese armed forces ended with swift strokes the era of Western dominance in Southeast Asia, they provided the catalyst for the eruption of the divergent forces that had been nurtured within the colonial realms for several decades.

The
Japanese Interregnum

Between December 1941 and April 1942, Imperial Japan in a series of striking military and naval victories brought the *Nampō* (as the Japanese called the Southern Regions) under one central political authority for the first time in history. The Japanese interregnum itself was short-lived, terminating with the Empire's surrender to the Allies in August 1945. If Japan had been able to retain her conquests for some decades, her military imperialism, so different in several respects from Western colonial rule, would in all likelihood have wrought far-reaching changes in many parts of Southeast Asia.

As it was, the very brevity of Nippon's rule, the harsh wartime demands made by the conquerors on the region's material and human resources, and finally the frantic efforts to involve Southeast Asians directly in the conduct of the war Japan was visibly losing, followed by her collapse—all these factors helped to set in motion a many-faceted process of decolonization. The coming of peace and the partial return to the area of the Atlantic powers could at best interrupt but in the end barely halt it. Triggered by new alien rulers, that process very soon started to follow native paths in the context of national states. In Part Three we shall see that there were only a few, though occasionally quite important, lasting effects from the Japanese era upon the further evolution of Southeast Asian life.

I

The Japanese conquest of Southeast Asia was the result of last-minute brilliant improvisation rather than of long-term military planning. It succeeded because of Japanese superiority in manpower as well as naval and aerial strength, all pitted in surprise attacks against small colonial forces never geared to large-scale combat and quite inadequately protected against seaborne invasions with massive support from the air. Nor could the Atlantic powers, engaged in desperate struggles against the Axis in Europe and northern Africa in 1941, divert troops and matériel to the defense of their colonial domains in Southeast Asia. The immobilization of the American Pacific Fleet at Pearl Harbor, followed by the sinking of the two British men-of-war, the *Repulse* and *Prince of Wales*, off the east coast of Malaya, and of the small Dutch navy in the Battle of the Java Sea, left the area wide open to the invader. By March 1942, what limited military resistance had taken place in the preceding weeks virtually ceased; only in Luzon did combined American and Filipino forces heroically but fruitlessly try to hold out for some agonizing months, while most of the islands, and Manila itself, were already occupied.

Even before the lightning campaigns got underway, Japan had already succeeded in pressuring the French authorities in Indochina and their Vichy superiors into large-scale concessions which placed the colony's military facilities and natural resources at Nippon's disposal. Yielding to these demands, the French managed to preserve their administration intact, albeit under increasing Japanese surveillance, until March 1945. By then, the liberation of metropolitan France made the Japanese, fearful of an American attack from the already liberated Philippines, suspicious of continued collaboration with French colonial officials; they decided to end the unique and privileged position which the French, alone among all European administrators in Southeast Asia, had occupied for so long.

Japan's forward thrust was similarly facilitated by Thai cooperation. Siam's military rulers, attuned to the changing equilibrium of forces in Europe and Asia and increasingly espousing a militant nationalism of their own, had accepted Japanese diplomatic support in forcing the weakened French to agree to the cession of some Cambodian territories. Once the Japanese military advance started, the Thai willingly opened their country as Nippon's staging area. Thailand's alliance with Japan was rewarded in due course with the retrocession of the four northernmost Malay States which had been ceded to the British in 1909.

Exceptional as the positions of French Indochina and Thailand were, it must not be assumed that direct military administration of the rest of Southeast Asia produced anything like a single, standard pattern of Japanese rule. For one thing, the area as a whole was divided into two major parts, one administered by the army, the other by the navy. For another, military governments *per se* differed from area to area in the course of time, two of them—in Burma and the Philippines— actually being replaced by nominally independent native regimes in 1943. No simple explanation can be proffered for the varieties of Japanese rule, for which no all-embracing, monolithic, carefully prepared blueprint seems to have existed.

Only very broad and general principles had been worked out in Tokyo, leaving military administrations on the spot with wide discretionary powers. But military and civilian authorities, both at the center and in the occupied territories, quite often held divergent views concerning policies and their implementation. Moreover, since military commanders as well as high-ranking civilians seldom remained in any one place for long, policies tended to change with the arrival on the scene of new key personnel. Last but not least, regional commanders did not always exercise complete control over all Japanese agencies or individuals—"Ugly Japanese" as well as less attractive figures among them, some with direct links to Tokyo—in their areas of jurisdiction.

As for the major division, the army was assigned the most densely populated and culturally more advanced regions—Burma, Malaya, Sumatra, Java, and the Philippines—while the navy exercised control in the sparsely peopled and relatively underdeveloped islands of the former Dutch empire—Borneo, Celebes, the Moluccas and lesser Sundas, as well as New Guinea. Whether this division was intended to have long-term significance or was primarily created to assuage the stubborn inter-service rivalry between army and navy—a rivalry that had, as both sides realized and admitted, impeded smooth cooperation in the China theater—is hard to know. In all likelihood, however, naval administrations were established in regions destined for permanent incorporation into Greater Japan, while army rule was envisaged as gradually leading to a political evolution with varying degrees of native codetermination or even autonomy. The trend of overall policies was, finally, dependent on the course of the Pacific War; as the early victories gave way to stalemate and before long to impending defeat, original plans were considerably modified.

It is therefore difficult to generalize about the course and effects of the Japanese interregnum in Southeast Asian history; still, some broad general trends can be discerned. One of these, the partial redrawing of the region's political map, has already received passing mention in connection with Thailand's territorial gains with Japanese support. In the Malayo-Indonesian world, the new overlords redrew the artificial boundaries born of historical accident and diplomatic bargaining between Dutch and British. Malaya (including all Federated Malay States, Johore, and the Straits Settlements) was joined to Sumatra, with Singapore as the seat of an army command. Java constituted a separate military administration, while the other islands of the archipelago came under loosely centralized naval control.

Arbitrary as the new divisions were, they were not devoid of a certain intrinsic ethnic and sociological merit, especially with regard to the Malayo-Sumatran arrangement; in 1943 Sumatra actually became a separate army command, although still linked to Singapore. Had it not been for the virtual cessation of inter-island communications, this reordering might have had longer lasting effects. But the very perturbance of political boundaries created by Western fiat constituted a first step in decolonization, pointing the way to border disputes and a fluidity reminiscent of the precolonial state of affairs.

While these territorial changes were geographically limited, other concomitants of the Japanese conquest impinged on almost all of Southeast Asia. Above all, the abrupt cutting of ties with Europe and America had far-reaching material and psychological effects. We have seen that for decades, and in some instances for centuries, the colonial possessions (and to a large extent also Thailand) had been integrated into the Atlantic power system, an integration particularly noticeable in the region's modern economic life and in the administrative structures introduced by the West. We should also recall that the links forged between metropole and colonial dependency had led to the gradual transfer of specific British, American, French, and Dutch modes and behavior patterns, as well as of Western languages, superimposing foreign distinguishing characteristics on Southeast Asian diversities. Suddenly, these Western imprints were willfully swept away by yet another foreign master bent on forging an Asian commonwealth—the Greater East Asia Co-Prosperity Sphere—with Japan at its center.

The Japanese, that is to say, were not content to wrest Southeast Asia from its former overlords; they also sought to erase Western legacies and to substitute a new value system, their own, for them. The interregnum was, of course, far too short to effect a complete revaluation and to spread Japanese indoctrination—unevenly attempted as it was— far enough. Yet the very fervor with which the old colonial order was being attacked and innovations instituted and propagated did much to undermine the prewar order. One of the culturally most significant and lasting effects was the bolstering of Southeast Asian national languages which went hand-in-hand with less successful Japanese efforts to spread their own tongue in the occupied countries. Burmese, Indonesian, and Tagalog were the main beneficiaries of this wartime measure.

The change, moreover, was not merely one of masters but one of purpose. We saw how Western colonialism had been basically geared to the maintenance and functioning of a capitalist economy. The occupation was, by contrast, a wartime expedient in which economic desiderata were subordinated to the exigencies of Japan's far-flung military ambitions and needs. Southeast Asia's export economy, barely recovered from the ravages of the great depression, was, almost at one stroke, decreed unessential if not out of existence; only commodities of immediate strategic importance, like tin, bauxite, rubber, and oil, received attention and support, as did of course rice and other foodstuffs. Indeed, acreages previously devoted to sugar, coffee, tea, and other export crops were turned to food production for military consumption in Southeast Asia theaters and beyond. At the same time, the flow of imported goods ceased and was not replaced by Japanese merchandise, due to shipping shortages and wartime economic stringency in the homeland.

Taken together, these damages betokened the virtual collapse of the modern economic superstructure introduced in colonial times; and even though Japanese concerns, headed by the "Big Four" *Zaibatsu* financial and industrial combines, moved into the places vacated by Western enterprises, Southeast Asian economic life receded from modernity. Interstitial small-scale commercial and occasional industrial entrepreneurship partly started to fill the void, aided by Japanese policies that tended toward regional and local economic self-sufficiency. A steady worsening of sea transportation as well as of the road and rail systems pushed the economy even further toward an isolation and autarchy that harked back to precolonial times. Growing inflation caused by the injection of ever larger amounts of military scrip further eroded the monetized sector of the economy.

Equally startling was the switch from government by reasonably well-trained civilian bureaucrats to the rigors of military administration proper. Thus much of the modern economy as well as a good deal of the Western administrative apparatus ceased to be meaningful, though in places it continued to exist vestigially, side by side with the new, overarching network of military governance. The two structures were at best precariously linked together, being kept apart by different operational procedures no less than by linguistic barriers. As important as this technical dichotomy was the difference in what, for want of a better term, we might call "style." Where Western administrations had become routinized and rationalized in the service of economic and administrative efficiency, the Japanese relied far more heavily on improvisation, *esprit*, daring, and, of course, the sheer force of military commands.

It is hard to exaggerate the far-reaching changes that the Japanese "New Order" brought in its wake, but we should beware of ascribing them *in toto* to a conscious Japanese desire to upset the entire existing order of things in Southeast Asia. It is true that Japanese propaganda loudly proclaimed the destruction of the Western imperialist superstructure and the creation of the Co-Prosperity Sphere to be revolutionary goals. Undeniably, too, the economic and administrative problems we have just discussed were fraught with large-scale perturbances of the colonial status quo. But as far as overall policies were concerned, the Japanese were basically intent on moving with the utmost caution lest undue haste and insistence on premature change jeopardize the attainment of their short-term military and economic objectives. Wherever possible, military commanders were enjoined, existing institutions were to be preserved, native customs and mores respected. In all probability it was this ambivalence between the desire to preserve and the need to innovate that, combined with the vicissitudes of local conditions, caused many inconsistencies which in the end yielded unplanned if not also unexpected results, cumulatively hastening the tide of change.

What, then, were the effects of these Japanese policies on Southeast Asian societies? The "plural" colonial order was, to begin with, deprived of its Western entrepreneurial and administrative top layer, Japanese military, bureaucratic, and economic personnel taking up many but not all of the positions and amenities from which Europeans and Americans had been forcefully ejected. With the exception of Axis and neutral nationals, Westerners (including women and children) were interned shortly after military administrations had been established. Many Eurasians, especially the sizeable Indo-European group of Dutch descent in Indonesia, shared the harsh lot of the Europeans proper.

Other alien segments of the "plural" pyramid were dealt with more leniently, a good indication of innate Japanese conservatism which, though not oblivious of native resentments, recognized the importance of Chinese, Indians, and others to the smooth functioning of the economy. The Chinese communities, suspect on account of their loyalties to Chiang Kai-shek's Nationalist regime (if not also to Mao Tse-tung's Communist movement), experienced harassment, increased tax burdens, and strict political surveillance, coupled with concerted efforts to win them over to the rival *Kuomintang* government established by Wang Ching-wei under Japanese sponsorship. There was only one area, Malaya and Singapore, where the Japanese launched a frontal assault on the sizeable group of Chinese residents long intimately tied to mainland causes. The exodus of substantial numbers of urban Chinese to remote rural areas and the creation of a Communist-led anti-Japanese guerilla movement were among the results of Japanese brutality. In most other occupied areas, however, the Chinese minorities were by and large allowed to maintain their livelihoods and positions.

Japanese leniency toward the Indian minorities in Malaya (marred by initially ruthless exploitation of plantation labor) and in Burma (where their numbers had been drastically reduced by voluntary evacuations on the eve of the Japanese invasion) was dictated by impelling political considerations. Subhas Chandra Bose, a militant Indian nationalist leader of a stature rivaling that of Gandhi's closest lieutenant, Jawaharlal Nehru, had left India and, after some years in Germany, proceeded to Southeast Asia in mid-1943. Already before his arrival a beginning had been made with the recruitment of an Indian National Army, with Japanese support. Under Bose's leadership it became a fairly impressive fighting force, recruited from among British-Indian prisoners of war and the resident Indian minorities. He also proclaimed a Provisional Government of *Azad Hind* (Free India), which was welcomed by the Japanese as a member of the Co-Prosperity Sphere and which they expected to facilitate the planned invasion and "liberation" of the Indian subcontinent. The Japanese attack on Imphal in 1944, in which Bose's contingents participated, ended in dismal failure; but the heightened political consciousness of Southeast Asia's Indians survived this military debacle and Bose's death.

It was native Southeast Asians, however, especially Burmese, Javanese, and in the latter stages of the war also Vietnamese, who were most profoundly affected by the interregnum. To many of them, the occupation caused untold hardship, loss of livelihood and even of life itself. There were those who, rendered jobless by the shutdown of Western enterprises and plantations, returned home, only to aggravate an already impoverished village economy drained by persistent military requisitionings of rice and other victuals. And there were thousands, hundreds of thousands perhaps, whom the Japanese drafted into slave labor battalions (*rōmusha*) forced to work at home or abroad, often under abominable conditions, as for example on the notorious Burma-Thailand railroad.

Countless Southeast Asian peasants must have suffered a serious decline in living standards that had barely sufficed for survival in late colonial times. Here and there rural poverty assumed grave proportions, and in some districts extreme malnutrition, hunger, and near-starvation resulted from Japanese exactions and indifference, malfunctioning administration, and disrupted communications. Migrants to towns and cities swelled the ranks of the impoverished urban semiproletariats for whom little gainful employment was provided by the new rulers. And all segments of society experienced the arbitrariness and brutality of harsh military regimes, in many respects so unlike the impersonal, bureaucratic ways of the Western colonial powers. The Military Police (*Kempeitai*), in particular, cast its ominous and ubiquitous shadow over all the occupied countries.

But these woefully negative aspects were counterbalanced to some extent by the partial restructuring of native societies, planned or accidental, that took place under the Japanese aegis. In general—and again reflecting the conservative aspect of overall occupation policies—indigenous officialdom, especially that in charge of regional and territorial administration, was confirmed in office. Tenuously linked to the Japanese administration, it was yet entrusted with onerous and vexatious responsibilities. Indeed, many government officials experienced rapid promotions to positions vacated by Europeans; admittedly, under the circumstances these brought prestige and higher incomes rather than real power, yet they were prized by the new beneficiaries. Not unexpectedly, native officials executing Japanese orders could not always escape the wrath of the population which came to hold them responsible for the increasing burdens imposed on the people by the wartime governments.

If the retention of much of the structure of the former territorial administration was dictated by common sense and the relative paucity of trained Japanese officials (most of them were transferred to Southeast Asia from Taiwan, Korea, and Japan-occupied China), it only constituted one facet of the Japanese endeavor to win acquiescence in, and wherever possible support for, the new order. To obtain it, military administrations—particularly those in the army zones of occupation—sought the active cooperation of elite groups and potential leaders who, in contrast to the colonial civil servants, either had opposed or at best had remained on the periphery of the colonial establishments.

While hesitant and reluctant to make nationalist intelligentsias and Muslim or Buddhist spokesmen true partners in the occupation regimes and in the Co-Prosperity Sphere, the new rulers departed quite markedly from Western colonial practices in drawing these men—several of them freed by the Japanese from imprisonment or exile—into public life and officially sanctioned positions of prestige, if not of actual power. And with very few exceptions, Japanese overtures received an overwhelmingly positive response, even from intellectuals who in colonial times had professed socialist leanings and actually had shown themselves critical of Japanese imperialism. Excluded from the range of native cooperators were, of course, known Communists and those suspected of Communist leanings, since the Japanese, with their bitter experience of fighting Communism in China, were intent on suppressing it throughout the Co-Prosperity Sphere.

Did the cooptation of these native elites mean that Japan was willing to champion the cause of Southeast Asian nationalism? And obversely, was the almost universal readiness of political and religious leaders to "collaborate" with Nippon proof of their loyalty to Japanese goals and ideals? The Japanese were obviously and knowingly taking a calculated risk in rallying to their side Western-schooled intellectuals. True enough, most of them were imbued with a fierce dislike of Western overlordship, yet at the same time they had been reared in oppositional politics with an unmistakably Western-derived ideological bias.

Mobilizing religious sentiments, too, was a double-edged proposition, especially among Muslims in whose eyes the Japanese were not just *kafirs* (unbelievers) but indeed idolaters. Once aroused, religious fanaticism might prove difficult to control. But the military authorities must have felt that on balance the advantages outweighed the dangers. They needed urban intellectuals to aid their organizational efforts and political propaganda, and they may also have wished to neutralize the best-educated and politically most sophisticated group of natives lest they subvert military rule. The Japanese must have similarly recognized that their ruthless exploitation of the rural population might lead to peasant unrest, and that to forestall it *ulama* and Buddhist monks, the usual leaders of such unrest, should be given a stake in the *Pax Nipponica.*

Doubtless, then, a good deal of calculated pragmatism lay behind the gamble of making alliances with Southeast Asia's religious and political elites, and the Japanese were careful to circumscribe their allies' scope of action, if need be by recourse to subtle or not so subtle threats of sanctions against the recalcitrant. As seen from Tokyo, nationalist movements were not to be overtly encouraged as such, unless their utilization could serve an immediate Japanese purpose, as happened to be the case in Burma and the Philippines. In Java, for example, military administrators were instructed to use individual leaders rather than organized movements, the better to manipulate them in serving Japanese long-term interests.

Japanese imperialism—its idealistic projection of Nippon as the light, the savior, and the liberator of all Asia notwithstanding—could not bring itself to espouse honestly the cause of Southeast Asian national or religious aspirations. Japanese national pride, often verging on arrogance, as well as fanatical belief in the innate superiority of Shintō over other faiths, rendered sincere cooperation almost impossible; yet there were individual Japanese who genuinely identified themselves with Southeast Asian goals, at times not without risks to their own careers.

We have equally good reasons to doubt that willingness to "collaborate" with the Japanese necessarily signified the native leaders' wholehearted loyalty to the cause of the Co-Prosperity Sphere. That very many of them were swept off their feet by the breathtaking victory that Asian Japan had inflicted on their erstwhile Western overlords is understandable: the spontaneous welcome accorded the invaders almost everywhere in Southeast Asia was as manifest among the literate as among the mass of the population which believed that age-old prophecies of deliverance from the white man's rule had at long last suddenly come true. That such early enthusiasm eventually evaporated into disappointment and restiveness—isolated outbursts of peasants' revolts did occur here and there—can be deduced from what we have said about economic deterioration and Japanese ambivalence vis-à-vis national and religious expectations. Yet, whatever their second thoughts may have been, for a long time few Southeast Asian leaders were able or willing to turn against the new masters in whose designs most of them had by then become quite deeply implicated.

In any case, in making common cause with Japan, neither political nor religious leaders necessarily betrayed their own ideals and convictions, let alone their countries. Invidious comparisons with collaborators in Nazi-occupied Europe are for this reason altogether misplaced. Few of them, as we saw, had a stake in the colonial order, and a good many who used to espouse Western-derived political doctrines may have found it relatively easy to make at least tactical or nominal adjustments to Japanese ideological dictates; to some Southeast Asians, moreover, Japanese values were probably quite attractive. Whatever their preferences, nationalist and religious spokesmen in fact had few alternatives. The new order was, to all appearances, firmly established. To resist it may have seemed hopeless if not dangerous. Outside the Philippines and perhaps Malaya, the return of the former colonial powers was unlikely to evoke enthusiastic expectations; it must also have appeared a remote possibility to people dependent on the highly censored Japanese accounts of the progress of the war.

While Japanese propaganda may only have won a small number of true political or religious converts, it is easy to see that many more may well have admired the disciplined might of Dai Nippon and the Asian renascence expressed in the idea of the Greater East Asian Co-Prosperity Sphere. Be that as it may, members of the elites were quick to grasp the new opportunities which the occupation offered to the realization of their goals. Cooperation with military governments admittedly was not without serious risks. Yet Japanese willingness to accord some kind of recognition and support—not to mention considerable personal privileges and rewards—to nationalist and religious spokesmen contrasted so sharply with what most of them had recently experienced that few were willing to ignore their new sponsors. Many found themselves for the first time at or near the centers of public life, where hitherto they had been forced to exist on its periphery, if not in exile or prisons. Circumscribed though they were by Japanese vigilance and interference, they had now at their disposal unprecedented facilities for communicating with hundreds of thousands of their countrymen, such as officially sanctioned newspapers, public appearances, and the radio, using, as we said, national rather than Western languages.

There were, then, ample reasons why a wartime marriage of convenience was contracted between so many Southeast Asian leaders and their Japanese masters. Almost until the very end of the occupation, however, it remained a marriage of unequals, one partner possessing well-nigh undisputed power to impose his will on the other. Nor was this all. Little unity existed, it may be remembered, among Southeast Asian elite groups, few of them boasting anything approaching organized mass followings. Military governments hardly required Machiavellian techniques to exploit these weaknesses and ready-made dissensions.

Thus, playing off groups or individuals against each other was not so much part of a premeditated policy of "divide and rule" as the outcome of unceasing rivalries among a host of different Japanese agencies, each of them jockeying for influence, and in the process often attaching to itself a clientele of native leaders of its own. A highly intricate pattern of overt and behind-the-scenes competition on both sides was the inevitable result. It was only from late 1943 on, when the occupation authorities, because of Japan's declining military fortunes, came to grant ever wider concessions, that Southeast Asian leaders were able to manipulate this complex situation to their increasing advantage.

Up to this point our attention has been exclusively focused on the interplay between Japanese and already existing indigenous elites. But these, however prominent, were not the sole beneficiaries of the Japanese interregnum, for the wartime regimes also called into being entirely new groups. These were primarily recruited from among the younger generation of Southeast Asians. Few of the reservations the Japanese might have held concerning either Western-trained intellectuals or religious leaders applied to the young. Here, surely, were Southeast Asians unencumbered by prewar habits and ideas, who, for that very reason, could more easily be molded in the Japanese image. And indeed, no other segment of the population experienced the "New Order" with similar excitement and exuberance, none proved more pliable in absorbing Japanese ways and what we have called Japanese "style."

To understand their positive reaction to the occupation regimes we must keep in mind how little use colonialism had had for the young, how little challenge they had experienced not only in colonial but also in traditional native cultures. All of a sudden, a clarion call to action was directed to school children, high school and college students, and to youths in general, urging them to become the builders of the "New Asia." It was well-nigh irresistible, the more so since the Japanese also knew how to channel youthful enthusiasm into a multitude of organizations that were mushrooming all over the occupied territories. They ranged all the way from imitations of uniformed boy and girl scouts

through air raid associations, from auxiliary police corps and paramilitary combat forces with primitive arms to the establishment of
some embryonic national armies. Thousands of youngsters moreover
found employment in various branches of the military administrations.
All of them were almost constantly exposed to a broad range of propaganda appeals, to parades, rallies, and demonstrations, and to the excitement generated by organized mass movements.

The mobilization of youth was without doubt the most radical
innovation wrought by the Japanese in wartime Southeast Asia. Where
in colonial times upward social mobility had been limited to those of
aristocratic birth or those with more or less advanced secular or religious
education, the ranks of the new elite were now thrown open to young
people with the right *élan* and daring, with organizational skills, and
with military or at least militant bearings. Impatient with their elders,
prone to direct action rather than given to intellectual disputation or
religious speculation, these young men (and women) constituted the
potentially most revolutionary legacy that Japanese rule was to bequeath
to the decolonization process in many parts of Southeast Asia.

This does not mean, however, that indoctrination invariably succeeded in turning the area's youths into uncritical admirers and obedient
adjuncts of the Japanese. It was, in fact, the Japanese way of approaching and handling problems, rather than Japanese values as such, that the
younger generation so eagerly imbibed and emulated. Far from being
mere tools, many adopted only what they instinctively felt appropriate
to their own needs. It is true that the new emphasis on the young in
many ways ran counter to age-old Southeast Asian social norms and
mores. But not all Japanese innovations proved by that token alone unassimilable: the *bushido* warriors' code, for one, extolling the virtues of
the legendary *samurai*, could be linked to the *ksatriya* ideal embedded in
the "Indianized" lore of Southeast Asian aristocrats and commoners
alike. Far fewer youths could be won over to Shintō or the veneration
of the Japanese emperor, let alone to beliefs in Nippon's innate superiority—beliefs all too often translated into haughty and disdainful behavior toward indigenous disciples.

The occupiers' short-sighted innovating radicalism thus in the end
begot its own challengers. Side by side with those still under the spell
of Dai Nippon, the numerous new organizations also counted thousands
of youngsters burning with a fierce national pride of their own, incul-
cated by native rather than Japanese propaganda. Clandestine anti-
Japanese organizations, some of them with distinct Marxist and Com-

munist proclivities, started to sprout as the rigors of the occupation mounted. When, under the threat of Allied reconquests, the Japanese girded themselves and their "wards" for pitched defense, agitation increased among many youth groups and guerilla bands. It was a moot question against whom they would use the skills they had so recently acquired should their countries become actual battlefields; as we shall see, in one instance, at any rate, a national army did turn against its Asian mentors.

II

Not all the countries of Southeast Asia experienced the full impact of the various factors we have discussed in the foregoing survey. With only one exception—Vietnam—the occupation era left its severest marks where prewar conditions had already shown more or less clear signs of internal perturbance, while those on the fringes of colonial modernization survived the Japanese interlude fairly intact. This apparent congruence is due only in part to the fact that the Japanese singled out for intensive administrative care the very same areas that had attracted the most prolonged Western attention. In part, too, it was the conduct of the war itself that made some countries, Burma and the Philippines in particular, the focus of heightened Japanese activities.

To begin with those parts of Southeast Asia least affected by the war, Laos and Cambodia seem to have enjoyed virtual isolation, both but little touched by incipient modernization and marginal to Japanese designs. This was less true of the former Dutch islands of Indonesia under Japanese naval administration, but while these experienced a sharp economic decline and also some especially brutal repressions, Borneo, Celebes, and the island chains to the east do not seem to have been subjected to large-scale changes. The navy, at any rate, was far less addicted than the army to experiment with ambitious organizational innovations.

That Thailand, Southeast Asia's sole sovereign state on the eve of the war, escaped practically all Japanese influences was of course due to the fact that it was not an occupied country at all but rather an ally that permitted itself to be used as a staging area for the Japanese war effort. She owed this fortunate status to the skill with which the country's leaders had, in time-honored tradition, adjusted to Japan's growing diplomatic and military stature in Asia, benefiting, as we already saw, from Japanese support to obtain the retrocession of territories once lost to Britain and France. Granting Japan access to Thai military facilities and ample food supplies, the government was only asked to accede to the Co-Prosperity Sphere and to declare war against the Allies—a small price to pay for the retention of national sovereignty. Siamese military authoritarianism, on the rise since the 1930s, also required but little conscious recasting to accord with the prevailing Japanese temper.

In turn, the blessings of independence aided Thailand in gently severing her alliance with Japan when changing fortunes rendered this desirable. Far better aware of the course of the war than Southeast Asian leaders in truly occupied countries, the Thai military, who had identified with Nippon's temporary dominance (headed by Field Marshal Phibun Songkhram), peacefully withdrew from the political stage in late 1944. A civilian regime took over under the leadership of Nai Pridi (Pradit Manutham), a French-educated political figure who had played a key role in and immediately after the 1932 *coup*. Forced into political retirement by the military in subsequent years, he now emerged as the ideal leader to seek a *rapprochement* with the approaching victorious Allies. Another timely switch thus again preserved Thai freedom, albeit at the cost of restoring the recently annexed territories to their returned Western suzerains.

In terms of sheer physical destruction and violent exploitation, the Philippines under Japanese rule offer the starkest conceivable contrast to the placidity of wartime Thailand. Yet to a surprisingly high degree, a great deal remained unchanged in spite of the fact that heavy fighting and bombing marked both the beginning and the end of the Japanese era; Manila itself was twice heavily punished. This was, moreover, the only colonial domain in which the armed struggle was not limited to Westerners and Japanese; the small Commonwealth Filipino army, developed on the advice of General Douglas MacArthur, shared with American forces the heroism and humiliation of Bataan and Corregidor; and Philippine guerillas prepared the way for the Americans' triumphal return, from the landings in Leyte in October 1944 to their reentry into Manila in February 1945.

The presence of considerable anti-Japanese guerilla forces was facilitated by geographical factors. For the Japanese at no time had enough manpower at their disposal to occupy and effectively control the far-flung Philippine islands. They focused their administration on key areas, leaving outlying parts to fend for themselves, and thereby provided American and Filipino military escapees with ample operational bases. The anti-Japanese cause attracted large numbers of Filipinos who ere long had good reason to fear and hate the new masters' harsh demands for food supplies. As a matter of fact, it was in Central Luzon— for decades, as we already noted, in the grip of a deep agrarian *malaise* —that the resistance to Japanese exactions became most widespread and also best organized in the *Hukbalahap* (an abbreviation for the Tagalog name *Hukbong Bayan Laban sa Hapon*, or People's Anti-Japanese Army) movement. Led among others by Communist leaders like Luis Taruc, the Huks succeeded not only in training well-indoctrinated guerilla forces able to harass the enemy, but also in setting up a virtually autonomous rebel government beyond the reach of Japanese reprisals.

More than a grave challenge to the occupying power, the *Hukbalahap* also threatened to undermine the inequitable social order, particularly in the sugar-rich Pampanga Province, which served as the Huks' center of operations. While fighting the external foe, the Huks at the same time set about to abolish some of the worst abuses of the rural status quo, most prominent among their wartime measures being the distribution of the land to the tillers themselves; this was the more easily accomplished since most landowners had sought safety in Manila at the beginning of the occupation. Haves and have-nots thus started to confront each other in an incipient social revolution, fanned by an energetic leadership of modern, predominantly leftist elements.

The Japanese conquest posed a dilemma to the Filipino political elite, tied as it was politically, ideologically, but also economically to the United States. On American urgings, Commonwealth President Quezon and a small entourage left their beleaguered country and by way of Australia came to Washington. Quezon himself, in ill health for several years, died in the American capital before the end of the war. Before leaving, he had enjoined his cabinet colleagues—and thereby the entire country—to accommodate themselves to the Japanese as best they could.

In fact Filipinos, like other Southeast Asians, were given little real choice in the matter of cooperating with their new masters. The Japanese, for their part, obviously realized that here they were dealing with an entrenched social class of considerable wealth and influence which it might be difficult and perhaps hazardous to ignore or bypass. They were aware, too, of the fact that this class was "Western" in education, orientation, and living style to an extent unparalleled among Southeast Asian leaders elsewhere. Therefore they sought to attract Filipino *ilustrados* by holding out to them retention of their possessions and privileged positions, while promising even larger political concessions than the Philippines had enjoyed under American aegis, on condition that Filipinos cooperate with Japan and embrace a more genuinely "Asian" orientation as members of the Co-Prosperity Sphere.

Japanese overtures yielded, at least on the surface, almost total success, prominent Filipinos with only few though notable exceptions accepting official positions under the occupation. A "Central Administrative Organization" was established within a month after the fall of Manila; headed by an Executive Commission, it functioned alongside the Japanese Military Administration, with Japanese "advisers" attached to its various departments. A new political movement, *Kalibapi*, inspired or sanctioned by the Japanese, took the place of all former parties, and the Japanese gave clear indications that they intended to grant the Philippines independence even before 1946, the date envisaged in the American legislation establishing the Commonwealth in 1935. This Japanese-sponsored Republic was inaugurated on October 14, 1943, with José P. Laurel (Secretary of Justice in Quezon's cabinet) as president.

Were Filipino leaders taken in by Japanese benevolence? It is hard to say, though in all likelihood their actions were prompted by pragmatic rather than ideological considerations. But whether *ilustrados* were primarily motivated by the desire to retain status and possessions at almost any cost (as their detractors claimed) or by the belief that "collaboration" was their only way of protecting the country against even greater Japanese depredations (as they themselves asserted), the fact remains that elite continuity prevailed. True enough, the collaboration issue loomed large in the eyes of Americans and their Filipino allies in Washington. But quite soon after the expulsion of the Japanese and the restoration of the Commonwealth it lost all significance. Only some few, lesser "collaborators" were brought to trial, while practically all wartime leaders were allowed to resume public offices after a brief interval; even Laurel, who had fled to Japan and been imprisoned there by the Americans, returned to the political arena in due course. Quickly adjusting to Philippine political realities, on July 4, 1946, the United States made good on the prewar promise to grant independence to their former Asian colony. Once again, Filipinos were ahead of their Southeast Asian neighbors, those of their leaders who had emerged before and during the war remaining as a group at the helm of the state.

What also remained, apart from wartime destruction, was the rift between the Central Luzonese peasantry and the Manila elite, deepened further by the return of landlords, under armed protection, to their latifundia. Actually, the *Hukbalahap* (now renamed "People's Liberation Army") leaders had switched for a time to open political action. Having successfully contested elections in several regions, they soon found themselves barred from the political arena by frightened *ilustrados*. They then returned to their rural strongholds, from whence they resumed armed rebellions against the powers-that-were, increasingly identifying the returned Americans in place of the departed Japanese as the true enemies of the Filipino underdog. For several years, the new republic was thus saddled with the wartime legacy of widespread revolutionary peasant unrest, as were some other countries once decolonization got underway.

If Japanese rule in the Philippines had been instrumental in accelerating class conflicts in the autochthonous population, in the former British Malaya it primarily accentuated and exacerbated racial division between Malays, Chinese, and Indians. The interregnum thus produced yet another combination of continuity and change in an entirely different setting. Change was most pronounced among the Chinese and Indian communities, whose fate under Japanese military administration we have briefly described. By contrast, the Malays were once again privileged to enjoy relative tranquillity. Interestingly enough, original Japanese plans had envisaged depriving the Malay rulers of practically all the residual powers still allowed them by Britain. Had these plans been put into effect, they might have caused widespread opposition. (British proposals for similar constitutional changes in postwar Malaya produced, as we shall see later, a very violent reaction.) Instead, the new rulers soon chose to perpetuate the "indirect rule" practiced by their colonial predecessors with so much sagacity and success.

In spite of growing economic deterioration, the Malays therefore remained for the greater part more sheltered than others from the ravages of the Pacific War. It was only when in the final stages of the occupation British counterattacks threatened them, that the Japanese, now anxious to mobilize rather than placate the Malays, turned for support to the numerically small Malay intelligentsia. In contrast to the British-educated nobility which had enjoyed the sheltered benefits of the colonial order, these were commoners schooled in vernacular schools, especially in the country's only college for the training of Malay teachers. From the 1930s on, these young men had become increasingly attracted to the radical nationalism preached and practiced in neighboring Indonesia. But shortly before the war in the Pacific broke out, the British colonial authorities jailed the leaders of the *Kesatuan Melayu Muda* (Union of Malayan Youths) which had been founded in 1938. Freed by the invaders and given limited organizational support for some years, these were the men whom the Japanese at the eleventh hour encouraged to seek contacts with Indonesian leaders. Nippon surrendered, however, before plans for a Greater Indonesia incorporating Malaya—in all probability hatched by Japanese civilian advisers—had gone beyond the stage of preliminary discussions.

The Malay intelligentsia's ephemeral appearance on the political scene created no significant obstacles to British efforts to restore the status quo with broad Malay cooperation; some *Kesatuan* leaders actually sought refuge in Indonesia at war's end. Far more serious was the challenge posed by the guerilla forces that had been recruited almost in their entirety from the harassed Chinese population by the Chinese leadership of the Malayan Communist Party. Avowedly an anti-Japanese underground movement that had received British supplies during the war, it had in fact avoided head-on collisions with the occupation army, readying itself instead for the revolutionary takeover of the country in the vacuum which was expected to follow Japan's defeat. Emerging from the jungle, they made an open bid for power, until the arrival of sufficient British troops temporarily quelled the insurrection. The ensuing breathing spell was to be short-lived: Malaya had to pass through an era of violence before its intrinsically conservative pattern could form a reasonably stable basis for the decolonization process.

Neither in Burma nor in Indonesia did the remnants of prewar stability survive the impact of Japanese rule; and in Vietnam it was only the artificial Franco-Japanese *entente* which, until March 1945, prevented the consummation of the country's revolutionary potential. Wartime changes in all three countries led to eruptions of such magnitude that neither British, Dutch, nor French colonial rule could again be foisted upon them without bloodshed on a large scale. To avoid it, Britain surrendered her sovereignty over Burma. Risking it in costly and agonizing colonial wars, France and the Netherlands lost their Asian empires.

Most dramatic were the Burmese developments. It may be recalled that, alone among all Southeast Asian nationalists, some *Thakins* had fled their country to find succor from Japan even before the Pacific War began. Indeed, their escape had more than mere symbolic significance, for it marked the birth of colonial Southeast Asia's first national army. Under the tutelage of a devoted Japanese officer, a Colonel Suzuki, the *Thakin* escapees underwent rigorous military training which transformed the former student agitators into a military elite. The "Thirty Comrades"—the name under which the group became famous—accompanied the Japanese invaders into their homeland. The routing of the rapidly retreating and disintegrating colonial garrisons, though primarily the handiwork of Nipponese soldiers, also involved the haphazardly recruited Burma Independence Army; its ranks were swelled by enthusiastic volunteers as the campaign went on, amidst the jubilation of the population which mistook their own army for the real "liberators" of Burma.

Once the occupation was accomplished, the Japanese authorities proceeded to trim the Burmese army down to token size and to restrict its operational independence. But despite these humiliating setbacks, the young officers, *Bogyoke* (General) Aung San in the lead, had already won both political stature and a bargaining position that ultimately assured *Thakin* ascendancy over all other political forces. As in the Philippines, the Japanese established at the outset a native civilian authority that was to act as auxiliary to their own military administration of Burma. To staff it, they drew on a wide spectrum of prominent Burmese, by no means limited to the youthful *Thakins*, whether in or out of uniform.

Overshadowing them throughout the interregnum was the veteran politician and former prime minister, Dr. Ba Maw. An ambitious and forceful leader, he became in due course the architect and head of the independent Burmese state which ostensibly replaced the Japanese administration in August 1943, three months before Japan granted independence to the Philippines. The new state's constitution, in accord with both Burma's precolonial political tradition and contemporary Japanese designs, placed virtually all powers in the hands of the executive. Ba Maw not only adopted the title of *Adipadi* (head of state) rather than that of president, he also received support from the Buddhist monkhood and surrounded himself with some of the pomp and regalia of Burmese kingship.

Needless to say, Burma's independence, joyously welcomed though it was, remained as narrowly circumscribed by the Japanese army's total control of the country as was that of the Philippines. In fact, it had very likely been bestowed upon Burmese leaders not so much in recognition of their own political maturity as on account of Burma's proximity to British India, a prime target of planned Japanese attacks (with *Azad Hind* support) in 1943 and 1944. There was little the Burmese authorities could do to mitigate, let alone stop, Japan's ruthless exploitation of native resources and manpower. Thousands upon thousands died on the infamous "death railway" the Japanese were constructing, at fantastic human cost, to connect Burma and Siam. Its victims included not only Southeast Asians and Japanese, but also European prisoners of war. The Japanese also bypassed Ba Maw's cabinet in creating a variety of youth and other organizations under their own control. But these positive and negative interferences by the foreigner only enhanced the *Thakins'* drawing power and prestige, and lent growing strength to their organizational network, part of it clandestine.

While Ba Maw's government, in spite of increasing difficulties, continued to "collaborate" with the Japanese command, its *Thakin* members, together with their military and civilian colleagues outside the cabinet, decided to turn against their sponsors once the British, having foiled the invasion of Bengal, reentered Burma. Determination to retain Burma's independence, rather than ideological considerations, led to their founding of a new, broadly based coalition movement, the Anti-Fascist People's Freedom League (AFPFL), whose leadership also included some Communist elements in touch with, and supported by, Allied counterintelligence. (Their firm opposition to Japan no less than their proven talents in underground activities made the Communists attractive recipients of Allied support, and hence prominent in anti-Japanese guerilla movements, in most of the occupied territories during the latter stages of the war.)

The occupation ended almost as strikingly as it had started, with British and Japanese forces exchanging roles, and the Burmese once again allying themselves with the winner. Actually Aung San's disciplined army played a far more decisive role in hastening the British reconquest of Rangoon than it had done in assisting the capital's capture by the Japanese a few years before. In the interval, Burmese nationalism had soared to unknown heights. At the crucial moment, it presented the returning colonial power with a virtually united front under the now undisputed leadership of *Bogyoke* Aung San. (Ba Maw, like José Laurel, fled to Japan in fear of Allied reprisals; both returned to their homelands, free, before long; Bose, revered as a patriotic hero in India after the war, died in an airplane crash on his way to Tokyo.)

For some time, British opinion was sharply divided on what to do with liberated Burma, most of the returning prewar officials favoring the reimposition of strict colonial rule and the punishment of the *Thakins* for their wartime alliance with the enemy. In the end a new government in London heeded the advice of the highest military commander on the scene, Admiral Lord Louis Mountbatten. It recognized

Aung San's true stature as the only legitimate spokesman for Burmese aspirations and accepted him as prime minister. The road was thus opened to amicable decolonization, rough as it proved to be once independence had been won for the second time.

Less conspicuous at the outset, Indonesian developments were also retarded by the division of the archipelago into distinct military zones of occupation, which until almost the end of the war kept the islands isolated from each other. But even though wartime changes lacked coherence and unity, those in Java, in particular, generated a momentum toward the end which eluded Japanese control; indeed, Nippon's surrender could neither halt nor prevent it from spreading to the other islands.

It is a moot question whether some Indonesians, nationalists as well as religious figures, had been in touch with Japanese agents before the outbreak of the war in Asia; what little specific evidence there is points only to an active pro-Japanese movement among the Achinese in northern Sumatra which came to the support of the invaders. No advance preparations of similar scope existed in Java. The island's population, it is true, greeted the Japanese with enthusiasm, and very many among the bewildered political leaders were quick to proffer their cooperation to the new rulers. But unlike the situation in Burma, the liberation from the Western yoke owed nothing to native initiative in Java.

Indonesia was at one and the same time farthest removed from likely future battle zones, richest in vital raw materials, and also the least advanced politically under Western rule—three important considerations that had doubtless helped in shaping a Japanese policy geared to a high degree of economic exploitation combined with a modicum of political concessions. By comparison with Burma and the Philippines, political evolution was, as we have said in passing, to proceed quite slowly even in highly developed Java, at a lesser speed in Sumatra, and barely at all in the naval zone of operations.

What made it even easier to implement this cautious guideline was the fact—as previously mentioned—that for several years before the invasion, Indonesian political life had been in serious disarray, because the Dutch had removed Sukarno, Hatta, Sjahrir, and other prominent nationalists from the scene. Where in Burma the nucleus of a national army shared in the triumph of liberation, where in the Philippines the occupation army was face to face with an entrenched elite exercising considerable power in an already semi-independent polity, in Indonesia it was the Japanese who actually freed the most gifted nationalist spokesmen from colonial oblivion and disgrace. It would take time, and indeed changes in Japan's fortunes of war, to redress this symbolic imbalance.

Japanese initiative and bargaining strength notwithstanding, Indonesians in Java started to gain organizational benefits once Sukarno had been returned to Java from his Sumatran exile and had assumed, with Hatta as a close second, the leadership of the first officially sanctioned intelligentsia movement, *Putera* (an acronym formed from the Indonesian *Pusat Tenaga Rakjat*, or Center of the People's Strength). This movement seems to have been restricted as to membership and scope; the omission of "Indonesian" from its name clearly suggested Japanese hesitation to recognize and utilize Indonesian nationalism—which by definition would not be limitable to Java alone—as a driving force at that time.

For almost two years, in fact, the military authorities appeared more willing to encourage Islamic rather than nationalist activities; why Japan should have expended such considerable energy on enlisting Muslim support—especially but not exclusively in Java—while, as far as is known, far less was systematically done among the Burmese Buddhist clergy or that of the Independent Philippine Church, for example, is hard to ascertain. Whatever the reason, the occupation forces included a small but energetic contingent of Japanese Muslims (whether true believers or mere propagandists we cannot tell) who established the requisite contacts with leaders of both the traditionalist and modernist wings of the Islamic movement.

In addition to forging a federative body, *Masjumi* (*Madjelis Sjuro Muslimin Indonesia*, or Consultative Council of Indonesian Muslims), that brought together the major associations, *Muhammadiyah* and *Nahdatul Ulama*, as well as some lesser groupings in late 1943, the Japanese also conducted a major recruiting campaign among unaffiliated individual *ulama*, urging them to join the new federation. *Masjumi* was increasingly entrusted with the administration of religious affairs, the first field from which the Japanese started to withdraw most of their own supervisory personnel from early 1944 on. A paramilitary force, the *Hizbullah* (Allah's Army), came into being under the federation's own jurisdiction.

These unprecedented opportunities provided Muslim leaders with enhanced stature and bargaining strength vis-à-vis other elite groups in Java; in parts of Sumatra, too, Islamic communities benefited from the occupation. Their differences temporarily muted, traditionalists and reformists combined to steer into religious channels the increasingly turbulent movement toward independence that emerged in the last year of the Japanese interregnum. Their demands to make Indonesia a Muslim state largely contributed to the bitter political dissensions that were to mark the decolonization process for many years.

Side by side with organizational support to Islam, the Japanese created in 1944 a new mass movement best known by its Japanese title, *Djawa Hōkōkai* (Java Service Association). Intelligentsia leaders as well as other prominent natives staffed its elaborate structure; Sukarno, however, had to share leadership for several months with high-ranking Japanese administrators. Japanese control, also evident in the various representative advisory assemblies that had come to replace the Dutch-created bodies, was lessened only after a change of government took place in Japan in the fall of 1944, in response to the empire's worsening military situation. The new prime minister for the first time committed Japan publicly to the ultimate independence of Java, if not of Indonesia, thus setting in motion a gradually accelerating process of "Indonesian-ization" in the island's institutional life. Before long, nationalist agitation started to sweep everything before it, Sukarno's oratory in mass meetings and on the radio creating an atmosphere of growing expectations and excitement.

Tensions mounted in anticipation of independence, heightened by awareness that in all probability it would have to be defended in the face of expected Allied landings. The Japanese, that is to say, had skill-fully timed their promised gift of freedom so as to use it as a major spur in mobilizing Indonesian enthusiasm in support of their own defense effort. This not only broadened the organizational scope of the intelli-gentsia politicians, it also infused Muslim groups, especially *Hizbullah*, with the anticipatory fever of waging a "Holy War" against the "infidel" Western powers. At least equally important, the increasingly martial environment brought to the fore the officers of *Peta*, Java's Japanese-trained defense corps founded in 1943. (Similar but smaller nuclei of armies later came into existence in Sumatra and Malaya.) Militancy also increased among all kinds of youth groups, and a few months before their surrender, the Japanese set up a network of guerilla youth corps whose guidance and ideological training were entrusted to the nationalist leadership.

As the official independence preparations got underway in the spring of 1945, the Japanese finally took steps to terminate the isolation of Java from the rest of Indonesia; as we saw, they permitted Sukarno and his lieutenants to establish contacts not only with their colleagues in the other islands but also with leaders of the Malay intelligentsia. But at the same time much was happening behind the backs of the military authorities. Many of the officially sponsored youth groups had been infiltrated by anti-Japanese elements, including some few Communists. (These were new recruits, most prewar members having left or been exiled.) Other groups that had kept aloof from all things Japanese—such as an underground movement headed by the socialist leader, Sutan Sjahrir—started to exert growing influence on the course of events.

With Japan's impending defeat a certainty in the minds of most literate Indonesians, internal differences of opinion came to divide cautious members of the intelligentsia unwilling to move without Japanese fiat from militant youths eager to dissociate their country's freedom from the compromising goodwill of Dai Nippon. Almost anticlimactically, under pressure from the younger generation, Sukarno and Hatta proclaimed Indonesian independence on August 17, two days after Japan had capitulated to the Allies. Although the war was officially over, the consummation of the Indonesian Revolution was to take five more years, involving the shedding of much Asian and Western blood, followed by agonizing internal conflicts among the various Indonesian elements which the occupation had forcefully drawn into political life.

The outward tranquillity that prevailed in wartime Vietnam until the spring of 1945 was yet replete with paradoxes which, in combination, created even graver complexities and dangers than elsewhere in Southeast Asia. The first of these, the tenuous Franco-Japanese "condominium," has already been briefly alluded to. Japanese tolerance of and cooperation with the continuing French colonial regime belied Japan's anticolonial pretensions. True enough, some Japanese agencies did pursue anti-French policies of their own, even while officially amicable relations with the Vichy-directed French authorities continued; thus the Cao Dai sect as well as members of the Dai Viet Party received clandestine Japanese organizational and financial support. Yet on the whole, the French were left to look after internal affairs, and the Japanese apparently saw little reason to interfere in the repression of Vietnamese anticolonial groups, particularly those of leftwing orientations. In fact, however, a good many Communist cadres had escaped from Vietnam to China on the eve of the Japanese invasion.

While these repressive policies formed a continuation of prewar French practices, the wartime administration headed by Governor-

General Admiral Jean Decoux did not restrict itself to such negative measures. Anxious to safeguard French sovereignty under the threatening pan-Asian shadow of the Japanese military presence, Decoux instituted a policy without precedent in Southeast Asian colonial practice, thereby precipitating the second major paradox. Ironically enough, his mobilization of young Vietnamese in a variety of sports and other organizations was almost identical with similar innovations sparked, as we have seen, by the Japanese in most other Southeast Asian countries. And, just as the Japanese were to all appearances far more successful in breeding self-confidence and self-discipline among their young native wards than in rearing obedient Nipponese puppets, Decoux, far from winning native youths to the cause of continued French rule, merely readied a young generation of Vietnamese for organized, revolutionary resistance.

The third, and perhaps most fateful, paradox arose when powerful generals of the Chinese Nationalist wartime government, planning to revive age-old Chinese territorial ambitions in Vietnam, decided to use some Vietnamese Communists for their plans. This is how Ho Chi Minh finally returned to his native country (it was at that time that he actually assumed his pseudonym) from China, whither he had fled and where he had been kept captive until 1944. Chinese schemes also included non-Communist Vietnamese refugees, but these *Kuomintang*-influenced nationalists were mostly older men who had long since lost contact with their homeland and who, moreover, possessed no organizational or ideological experience to equal that of the Communists. The Chinese, of course, were quite confident that they could utilize Ho's services for their own ends and control him and the other Vietnamese patriots by playing one side against the other. Freeing Ho and allowing him to reactivate Communist cells in Tonkin proved, like Imperial Germany's gambit with Lenin in 1917, to be the beginning of a local Communist revolution rather than the fulfillment of the foreign anti-Communists' aspirations.

Vietnamese developments, so long artificially dammed up, erupted after the Japanese abruptly terminated their collaboration with the French authorities in early March 1945. French military garrisons and civilian officials were forced to surrender to the Japanese, who thereupon prevailed upon Emperor Bao Dai to proclaim Vietnamese independence. (It may be recalled that Bao Dai had led a shadowy existence at the court of Hué ever since his return from France in the early 1930s.) Japan's surrender came only six months later, followed by the Chinese occupation of the northern part of the country and that of combined British and French forces of the south, in accordance with prior Allied decisions.

Even before then, the Japanese had started to withdraw from outlying northern areas into which Ho's cadres now penetrated, their advance facilitated by acclaim from thousands of peasants struck by disastrous floodings of the Red River delta that caused widespread famine and death. While still in China, the Communists had formed a multiparty front organization, the *Viet-Nam Doc-Lap Dong Minh Hoi*, or Revolutionary League for the Independence of Vietnam, best known under its abbreviated name, *Viet Minh*. It was this front, controlled by Communists, which emerged as the only well organized and determined bidder for political power in the chaotic confusion of the immediate postwar period. With the Japanese in retreat, the Chinese occupation forces pursuing their own interests, and the interned French garrisons still immobilized, Bao Dai's weak government melted away, the emperor himself abdicating in favor of the *Viet Minh*. Revolutionary forces temporarily gained control in Saigon, and on September 2, Ho Chi Minh, amidst wild public enthusiasm, proclaimed in Hanoi the first independent Vietnamese state, the "Democratic Republic of Vietnam."

The consummation of Vietnamese national aspirations thus differed quite markedly from the independence struggles in Burma and Indonesia, both of which were led by members of nationalist intelligentsias, civilian or military, who had risen to prominence with the help of their erstwhile Japanese masters. In Vietnam, power fell to sworn adversaries of Japanese imperialism who had assembled their forces abroad and who also, like underground movements elsewhere, had received considerable military support from British and American counterintelligence agencies. The *Viet Minh* thus enjoyed the advantage of being untainted by "collaboration" (even though after the surrender, several Japanese aided them). This, combined with the virtual absence of sufficiently organized competing groups, assured them of victory. (The Communists, be it noted, ruthlessly destroyed in subsequent months some of their real or potential adversaries, notably Trotskyites in the South and Vietnamese pro-*Kuomintang* nationalists in the North.)

Consolidating his power, Ho Chi Minh became to all intents and purposes the representative and symbol of Vietnamese independence, with claims to national fame reaching back to the late colonial era. For

some years, his Communist-style "people's democracy" remained camouflaged behind the screen of the *Viet Minh* coalition—the Communists
even disbanded their own party for tactical reasons in late 1945—but it
had already developed the tools by which it could hope to remain in
power—most importantly, a guerilla army recruited in part among
minority tribes for the first time actively drawn into wider national
political activities. In the spring of 1946 the Chinese occupation forces
at long last abandoned northern Vietnam, leaving Ho in undisputed
control, while in the South the French returned in strength, quickly
reasserting their authority at the expense of the revolutionary administration. When drawn-out negotiations between France and the Democratic Republic failed to create a new *modus vivendi*—radical elements
had gained the upper hand in both camps—the colonial power, here as
in Indonesia, decided to regain its colony by military means. The ensuing conflict, in which the issues of colonialism, nationalism, and Communism were inextricably intertwined, raged for many, bitter years,
ultimately engulfing the major world powers.

III

When in August 1945, its navy and air force almost annihilated,
much of its home territory devastated by incendiary and other bombings,
and its will to resist finally broken by the atomic destruction of Hiro-
shima and Nagasaki, the Japanese Empire capitulated to the victorious
Allied powers, only Burma and the Philippines had been freed from
Japanese occupation. At the time of the surrender the Allies were unpre-
pared and inadequately equipped to undertake the rapid reoccupation
of those parts of Southeast Asia still under Japanese control. Only four
months had elapsed since the end of the war in Europe, with too little
time available for the redeployment of naval and other military forces
to Asia. Allied strategic plans for the reconquest of Southeast Asia had,
furthermore, undergone last-minute changes, accompanied by a good
deal of acrimonious discussions between British and American military
authorities. A newly created Southeast Asia Command under Admiral
Mountbatten, with headquarters in Ceylon, was still without adequate
manpower and naval strength, let alone clear planning, when the Pacific War ended.

Under such circumstances, it proved utterly impossible to restore
anything resembling the prewar status quo by military means. A veritable
power vacuum ensued in many parts of Southeast Asia as the Japanese

abandoned all interest in the local situations they had done so much to create. Though entrusted by Mountbatten with continued responsibility for the maintenance of order and the safeguarding of Allied internees, Japanese garrisons as a rule concerned themselves with their own safety more than with these thankless policing duties. Stunned and shamed by defeat, most Japanese commanders simply let matters slide. Few were willing to turn the reins over to European administrators in Japanese prison camps, but few, too, wished to run the risk of transferring arms and authority to Southeast Asian leaders (though some individual lower-rank Japanese military or civilians, disobeying orders, did just that, and some even joined nationalist groups).

The hiatus of power was especially agonizing in Indonesia, where the Dutch, possessing neither troops nor shipping of their own in Asia, were unable to free hundreds of thousands of Europeans in prisoner-of-war or civilian internment camps in the immediate postwar weeks. Left to their own momentum, wartime developments quickly gathered strength; as we have seen, seizures of power were in fact attempted in most of the countries of Southeast Asia, though in Malaya and the Philippines they were quickly subdued. Could timely and sizeable Allied landings have prevented the success of the revolutionary movements elsewhere, too? Doubtless they might have forced them militarily at least to a temporary standstill. But it is highly questionable that colonial control proper could ever have been foisted again upon those Southeast Asian countries where the violent postwar eruptions merely constituted the consummation of a many-faceted process of over half-a-century's duration.

The meticulously worked out plans which wartime colonial administrations in exile—those for Burma and the Netherlands Indies in particular—had prepared for their Southeast Asian dependencies show quite clearly that reimposition of unfettered colonial authority had indeed been intended. Devised by former colonial administrators and approved by home governments far too preoccupied with domestic, European affairs, these plans dealt exclusively with economic reconstruction and administrative rehabilitation—with the restoration, that is to say, of the apolitical structures of prewar days. Admittedly, Southeast Asia after 1945 stood in dire need of firm measures, and of European expertise, to repair the fantastic ravages caused by armed conflict and heedless Japanese exploitation. But exclusive preoccupation with these very real and pressing needs only betrayed Western officialdom's almost total blindness to the powerful forces released in most Southeast Asian societies by the Japanese interregnum. For better or worse, it had unloosed a political avalanche that could not be forced back into the artificiality of the old colonial order. Tragically, both Dutchmen and Frenchmen ignored or failed to understand the dimensions of the vast changes wrought in their colonies in four short years. Their attempts to turn the clock back, by force of arms, had to be paid for dearly long after the Co-Prosperity Sphere had been buried by the Allied victory in World War II.

PART THREE

Decolonization

PART THREE

Decolonization

Southeast Asia
Since World War II

Only twenty-odd years have elapsed since Japan's sudden surrender to the Allied powers dramatically inaugurated the most recent chapter in Southeast Asian history. The decolonization process has, historically speaking, barely begun, and it is therefore difficult to know what on the swiftly changing scene is ephemeral and what destined to perdure. In such countries as Burma, Indonesia, and Vietnam, postwar changes have, moreover, borne many of the hallmarks of political and incipient social revolutions; and these almost certainly have not yet run their full course. What has up to now emerged may, then, be no more than surface phenomena shrouding hidden factors and forces that may still emerge.

Postwar developments in Southeast Asia are, however, only one facet of the new power relationships in Asia as a whole, just as the area's incorporation into the Atlantic state system had been part of a larger historical process. The rise of the West in Asia had culminated in the subjugation of the Indian subcontinent by Britain in the late eighteenth century, followed by the virtual disintegration of the Chinese empire in the second half of the nineteenth. Though the great powers continued to pay lip service to her "territorial integrity," China ceased to be a truly independent country. Moreover, Japan, at that time Asia's only modernizing state, had become a partner in the Atlantic system from about the turn of the twentieth century: she owed this spectacular ascendancy to her victories over China in 1894-95 and over Tsarist Russia in 1904-5, as well as to her participation in World War I on the side of the victorious Allies.

Japan's contracting out of the Atlantic system by making war on the Western colonial powers in 1941 and the lightning speed with which she made herself master of the *Nampō* mark the beginnings of the de-colonization process in Southeast Asia. Ironically, this process was immensely accelerated by the collapse of Japan as a world power in 1945. Nippon's withdrawal from China (large parts of which she had occupied since the 1930s) and from Southeast Asia occurred before either the Western Allies or the Soviet Union could decisively fill the suddenly vacated Asian space.

In South Asia, Britain voluntarily liquidated her Indian empire, granting independence to India and Pakistan in 1947 (and shortly thereafter to Burma and Ceylon). Russian power in East Asia only sufficed to install a Communist government in the northern part of Korea, since 1910 a Japanese colony; the Soviets apparently also pro-vided some military aid to the Chinese Communists, for decades em-broiled in a civil war with Chiang Kai-shek's Nationalist government. American intervention protected South Korea, but could not prevent the ejection of Chiang from the Chinese mainland to Taiwan (Formosa) in 1949. The consolidation of Communist rule marked the end of a century's foreign dominance over China. A decolonized India and Pakistan, a united China freed from alien control, and a prostrated Japan—these provide the larger Asian setting for Southeast Asian history since 1945.

In turn, that history all of a sudden shed its parochial limitations. Gone was the confining seclusion, the virtual isolation, which the Westerners had imposed on Southeast Asians in colonial times. Gone, too, was Japanese overlordship which, for all the internal upheavals it had caused, had after all kept them more tightly insulated from the rest of the world than ever before. Henceforth, Southeast Asian develop-ments, more volatile than ever before, were destined to be increasingly influenced by political events from the outside. At times, indigenous leaders would seek to involve foreign powers in their domestic affairs, but more frequently still intervention would be injected into the region without local prompting. The global confrontation between two, and latterly three, world powers inevitably came to impinge upon the South-east Asian scene, the area's internal developments often affecting the course of international affairs.

I

Even though Southeast Asia's history has become increasingly dominated by the emergence of independent nation states, Western power has not been altogether eliminated from Southeast Asia. As a matter of fact, the first postwar decade witnessed Dutch and French attempts at restoring colonial rule in Indonesia and Indochina, albeit with some belated concessions to nationalist aspirations. The Dutch staged two military campaigns, euphemistically labeled "police actions," against the Indonesian revolutionaries in 1947 and 1948; although they were partly successful militarily, the Dutch finally abandoned these attempts, under considerable international pressure, and transferred sovereignty to Indonesia (with the exception of West New Guinea) in December 1949. French efforts to impose their domination upon the Communist-controlled *Viet Minh* government of Vietnam led to a shattering military defeat at Dien Bien Phu in 1954, followed by France's withdrawal, not only from Vietnam but also from her former protectorates of Laos and Cambodia.

We already noted that the Philippines received their independence from the United States on July 4, 1946, and that the British relinquished Burma in 1948. In Malaya, however, British power was restored without encountering lasting native (as distinct from Chinese-led, Communist) opposition; even there, however, colonial rule ended with the creation of the independent Federation of Malaya in 1957. This left only Singapore and the northern fringes of Borneo—Sarawak, Sabah, and Brunei —under various kinds of colonial and protectorate ties to Britain, and Western New Guinea (Irian Barat, in Indonesian) under Dutch, Eastern New Guinea and Papua under Australian rule. Singapore and the Bornean territories, with the exception of Brunei, merged with Malaya into a wider Malaysian Federation in 1963, Dutch Irian Barat having been incorporated into Indonesia the year before. By the mid-1960s, the Australian-governed territories and the eastern half of the tiny island of Timor—like Goa in India (until the 1960s) and Macao in China, a minuscule but stubborn remnant of Portugal's erstwhile far-flung Asian realm—were all that survived as colonial dependencies in Southeast Asia.

Area-wide national independence did not mean, however, that the Atlantic powers had lost all influence in postwar Southeast Asia. The disappearance of direct French and Dutch military and political control was, indeed, unique, for Britain not only retained the use of her naval base in Singapore, but independent Malaya, and later Malaysia, remained within the Commonwealth, some countries of which, in turn, provided military personnel for the new state's internal and external defense. The Philippines likewise allowed the continued presence of American ground and naval forces in accordance with a treaty ratified simultaneously with the transfer of sovereignty.

Before long, moreover, the United States—a major Pacific power after World War II, with bases spread over a wide arc from Japan, Okinawa, South Korea, Taiwan, to several Pacific islands—moved into the vacuum created by the French withdrawal from Indochina. Laos and South Vietnam—the country had been temporarily divided by an international agreement in 1954—thus remained within the Western orbit. At the same time, Soviet and Chinese support was injected into North Vietnam, though on a far less massive scale. America's deepening military involvement in mainland Southeast Asia also brought Thailand, the area's only independent state throughout modern history, into a military alliance with the United States with ever larger contingents of American military and other personnel stationed on her soil.

Military involvement to one side, Western economic interests regained a strong position in several parts of Southeast Asia. Thus tin and rubber companies, most of them British, as well as many other enterprises returned in full strength to postwar Malaya, while American business was granted far-reaching privileges in the Philippines. French entrepreneurs continued to play an important role in the Cambodian and, on a diminishing scale, in the South Vietnamese economy after 1954. Thailand in fact granted wider facilities to foreign, notably American, economic interests than they had enjoyed before the war. Economic nationalism, it is true, placed increasing restrictions on the foreigners' economic activities; most governments now levied taxes on aliens and some made the operation of foreign-owned enterprises conditional on their employment of indigenous executive personnel. While such measures undeniably restrict the activities of outside investors, the Western economic superstructure created during the colonial era continued to function in these new nation states.

In those countries, however, where decolonization assumed a revolutionary momentum—Burma, North Vietnam, and Indonesia—most European economic interests were liquidated in the course of the first postwar decade. North Vietnam, like all Communist polities, nationalized all foreign capitalist concerns outright. In Indonesia the process passed through several stages, affecting Dutch concerns in the first place, followed by British ones in the early 1960s; though these measures practically eliminated Western holdings, some firms, especially American oil and rubber companies, survived the general onslaught. Nationalizations came to a halt—whether temporary or more permanent remains to be seen—when Indonesian politics took a sharp turn in late 1965. By contrast, a succession of Burmese governments took over all foreign-owned enterprises, including British concerns as well as Communist Chinese banks.

The temptation may be strong to discern a causal relationship between military and economic power. Some might argue that the West's continued economic interests demand a similarly continuing military presence. Others might even insist that the retention of economic predominance is one of the real, "neocolonialist" motives for the deployment of Western military might in Southeast Asia. This kind of interpretation, dear to Marxists of all hues, should not be dismissed out of hand: what exactly the interplay between economic interest groups and policy makers in the leading Western countries with a stake in Southeast Asia is, is very hard to know. But it is highly unlikely that such private pressures as are doubtless brought to bear on Western governments are given as great, let alone greater, weight than are economic and above all political and strategic considerations of a higher—i.e., national or even international—order. The very limited size of Western investments in Southeast Asia as a whole makes it unlikely that private and corporate interests are allowed a decisive voice in the formulation of foreign policies affecting this part of the world. But be that as it may, a good case can be made for viewing the fate of Western economic enterprise primarily in the internal context of the decolonization process in the different countries. It will be examined in some detail later.

II

We should begin, however, with some general factors that pertain to practically all of Southeast Asia, albeit to different degrees. In the first place, the uneven pattern of the West's residual influence in postwar Southeast Asia suggests that the political boundaries that existed before World War II may not survive progressive decolonization. Drawn in the nineteenth century, many of these borders, as we know, resulted from arbitrary arrangements among the Western powers. The crumbling of the colonial regimes during the war and the only partial rehabilitation of Western control since 1945 caused a fluidity in interstate relations unknown for almost a century. One result of such fluidity was that illicit trade or "smuggling"—in fact, the prevailing maritime relations in precolonial times—revived, especially in island Southeast Asia, where local naval patrols lacked adequate strength to interdict it.

Another result was the resurgence of interstate rivalries, some of them of very old standing. We have already seen in Part Two how Thailand had sought to benefit from the West's temporary weakness by regaining several "lost" vassal territories, only to find herself forced to restore them to the victorious French and British after the war. But when France withdrew from mainland Southeast Asia after 1954, Siamese territorial ambitions vis-à-vis Laos and Cambodia were re-kindled. (One border dispute between Thailand and Cambodia was actually settled by the International Court of Justice.) The latter-day Thai-American alliance may, moreover, provide the Thai with a con-venient anti-Communist rationale for the pursuit of their aims. North Vietnam's intervention in Laotian affairs provides a further instance of intervention, under a "national liberation" label, resulting from interna-tional boundaries in the former French Indochina.

A more complicated example, likewise already briefly dealt with, is furnished by Indonesia and Malaya. From the 1930s some Malays, in opposition to the colonial status quo, and certainly some Indonesians, too, had been thinking in terms of a Greater Indonesia that would unite Dutch and British possessions. Briefly encouraged by the Japanese toward the close of the occupation, these vague hopes were dashed by the Allied victory. But they cropped up again once decolonization got under way.

Shortly after the Federation of Malaysia came into being in 1963, Indonesian leaders mounted a vigorous campaign, including guerilla units, against the new state. Officially, the Indonesian government's attack was directed against "neocolonialism," but there were quite a few spokesmen—both in Indonesia, where they enjoyed at least tacit governmental support, and in Malaysia, where they suffered arrest—who agitated for the abolition of the separateness imposed upon the area by European fiat. At any rate, overt hostility between the two countries ceased in 1966, and it is an open question if and in what form such ideas may develop and gain ground in the years to come. On a far less but apparently increasingly acrimonious scale, the Philippine govern-ment has contested the formation of Malaysia, claiming residual rights, as successors to the Sultanate of Sulu, to Sabah (British North Borneo).

If interstate boundaries are thus at least potentially in a state of flux, the frontiers between the countries in mainland Southeast Asia and China may also be subject to future instability. Many of these borders were, after all, determined and imposed on an impotent Chinese imperial government by the colonial powers in the nineteenth century. Though not yet as violent as the border dispute between China and India which led to armed clashes in the early 1960s, Peking's relations with Burma started to deteriorate a few years later. (Those with Pakistan have, by contrast, so far remained amicable.) Even so, militant Chinese and anti-Chinese rhetoric apart, nothing definite is known regarding China's ultimate territorial ambitions in the adjacent Southeast Asian lands. The forced pace and vast scale of mainland China's modernization programs tend to point inward rather than outward, and the convulsions of the "Great Cultural Revolution" similarly militate against expansion across China's borders. In any case, American military might renders territorial adventurism hazardous.

Some aspects of the boundary question are intimately connected with the second problematical legacy of the colonial era, the minority problem. No less than intercolony frontiers, many of the colonial states themselves were artificial creations devoid of ethnic, religious, or cultural homogeneity. In precolonial times, various ethnic groups had coexisted, martially more often than peacefully, in geographic spaces without clearly demarcated frontiers. The rise and fall of political structures was determined by individual rulers or dynasties rather than by "national" criteria; political integration of different ethnic groups was practically unknown in these polities. Relations were particularly weak and intermittent where communities were kept apart not only by linguistic and cultural divisions, but also by ecological ones, of which those separating sedentary lowland cultivators from highland shifting agriculturists were the most important. Colonial boundaries all too often cut across such "natural" divisions, however: in modern times, some groups thus found themselves on either side of the new frontiers; others, more fortunate if perhaps no less bewildered, were *in toto* incorporated into colonial states, together with other peoples with whom they had had nothing in common in the past.

Whatever the case, the colonial rulers felt little need to forge closer bonds among these various groups; almost nothing was done to integrate minorities into larger entities. Worse still, separateness was in many instances preserved by the application of indirect rule to minority peoples; this even happened in colonies whose ethnic majorities were administered under direct rule. Ethnic barriers were sometimes reinforced by religious ones. For example, Christian missionaries were far more successful in winning converts among "heathen" minorities than among Buddhist and Muslim Southeast Asians. Tensions were thus understandably acerbated between Buddhist Burmans and Protestant Karens in British Burma, but also between the Christianized Ambonese, Timorese, Minahassans, and Batak minorities and the Islamic majority in the Dutch East Indies; and these are certainly not the only examples.

Progressive decolonization has, not unexpectedly, tended to bring these latent divisions into the open. Many minorities have become either passive onlookers or helpless pawns in the "nation building" of political leaders, most of whom are recruited from ethnic majorities and are primarily responsive to their wishes. We shall later see how difficult it is to forge a national consensus even among relatively well-integrated majority populations; but the problems which ethnic heterogeneity poses are far more stubborn and harder to solve. They are especially grave where international boundaries separate ethnic groups.

Nowhere is the pattern more intricate than in mainland Southeast Asia, as a comparison between an ethnic and a political map of that part of the area will readily reveal. Only Cambodia is unencumbered by sizable, restive minorities. By contrast, the Lao political elite since the French departure tried, without success, to generate a sense of national identity among the country's diverse ethnic groups. The Lao themselves constitute only a minority (many Lao actually live in Thailand); other ethnic groups of the kingdom also straddle national boundaries.

Relations between majorities and minorities, difficult here as they are in many other parts of the world (analogies with central and eastern Europe come readily and unhappily to mind), are further aggravated by the uneven levels of political development among continental Southeast Asia's various communities. Most of the lowland civilizations, we know, had attained rather high levels of sophistication long before the modern era, partly on account of their century-long contacts with other cultures—contacts which rarely reached their mountain cousins. The sedentary areas, moreover, experienced a far more thoroughgoing modernization in colonial times than was true of the remoter upland regions. Old distinctions were thus further accentuated. Traditionally, little love was lost between the more highly civilized and the more backward peoples, and hardly anything has happened in the past half-century or so to narrow the gap. No wonder that pent-up animosities, here and there already heightened during the war, came to bedevil the newly independent states. For even where political leaders had the will to accommodate minority aspirations—as only few of them did—they still lacked the requisite understanding and skills to build multi-ethnic national states. As a result, many minority groups have failed to identify, or have been prevented from identifying, with the countries of their domicile.

Minority disaffection has been a serious enough problem in such countries as Burma which, though constitutionally a quasi-federal union, was nonetheless plagued by chronic rebellions (not all of them of ethnic origin, it is true) as soon as independence was achieved. But it can become more perplexing wherever minorities can expect succor from the outside. Thus there are some groups in northeastern Thailand whose vaguely articulated political sympathies appear to lie in Laos rather than in Thailand proper; and the Muslims of Malay extraction in the southern part of that country feel closer to their Islamic brethren in Malaysia than to the Buddhist monarchy in Bangkok. Since neither the Laotian nor the Malaysian government has encouraged these minorities in Thailand, their dissident aspirations have not yet proved dangerous. Minority irredentism, however, is a potent weapon in the armory of inter-state relations. Merely dormant now, its potential dangers should not be underrated.

Some minority groups in mainland Southeast Asia have, moreover, become potentially more intractable as a result of Communist indoctrination and training. These groups have learned new loyalties and acquired modern skills on a scale which some of the national governments find it hard to match. This is a direct reversal of a centuries old imbalance between lowland majorities favored by outside influences and hill-dwelling minorities living beyond the periphery of such influences. The Communist regime of North Vietnam has managed to accord some of its ethnic minorities a distinct, if not even a distinguished, place in both military and civilian affairs. (By contrast, South Vietnam's *montagnard* minorities have not yet received a comparable recognition of their political ambitions.)

It takes little imagination to realize how easily such well organized and well indoctrinated ethnic nuclei can serve as magnets, attracting their kinsmen from across international boundaries. This is particularly the case when minorities harbor grievances, whether real or imagined ones, against national governments which they do not consider to be really their own. Conditions are far from stable or clear in many areas, but Communist-inspired minority insurrections, probably abetted and supported by North Vietnam and China, have already occurred in northern Laos and northeastern Thailand. Such a state of affairs, in turn, is increasing the chances for stepped-up Western military involvement in those regions threatened by Communist agitation and subversion.

Though far from negligible, island Southeast Asia's minority problems differ in kind and extent from those on the mainland. Ethnic heterogeneity is there less sharply marked and only rarely accentuated by deep-seated religious cleavages. Thus while Indonesia, for example, was shaken by rebellions in the mid-1950s, they stemmed from regional and economic, rather than from primarily ethnic causes; few if any of the dissenters chose to forsake the common Indonesian identity cemented by revolutionary nationalism. Communism in Indonesia, powerful and well organized until 1965, has played practically no role fomenting minority grievances; on the contrary, the Communist Party has drawn the bulk of its supporters from among the Javanese majority, and not from the ethnic minorities. In Philippine political life, too, ethnic cleavages have rarely been in evidence: the *Moros*, the largest distinct group, are a religious minority. Philippine Communism, proscribed as it is, has regionally flourished because of social, rather than distinctly ethnic, grievances.

There are some indications that the Malaysian federation may yet come to be plagued by minority problems from non-Malay, Bornean peoples; they were unknown in the peninsula, where for decades a fairly homogeneous Malay community has been preoccupied with the presence of foreign racial groups rather than indigenous minorities. As we saw, the very large size of these immigrant communities had caused a vocal minority of Malays to seek close ties if not outright union with Indonesia. Similarly, postwar stirrings among Philippine *Moros* point to the probable rise of irredentist sentiments—until 1966 occasionally fanned by Djakarta—toward the Islamic majority in nearby Indonesia.

Decolonization has, then, impinged on Southeast Asia's diverse native minority groups in a variety of ways. At the same time, it has deeply, and on the whole adversely, affected the region's Indian and Chinese minorities. Almost everywhere in twentieth-century Southeast Asia, it may be recalled, these aliens had come to play well-nigh indispensable roles in the modern economy. Their economic prominence, coupled with the racial separatism peculiar to the colonial "plural" societies, had usually earned them the wrath and envy of the indigenous population in Thailand as well as in the colonial countries. Anti-Indian or anti-Chinese sentiments had thus been deeply woven into the fabric of Southeast Asian nationalisms, exploding at times into serious race riots, as happened in Burma in the 1930s.

The Japanese interregnum had deepened these antagonisms. Almost everywhere, chaotic wartime conditions impoverished the mass of the natives while it visibly enriched the conspicuous if small group of Indian and Chinese businessmen and moneylenders. (It should not be forgotten, however, that thousands of Indian and Chinese petty traders, artisans, and laborers suffered great hardships during the war, and that many native Southeast Asians became *nouveaux riches* as a result of the occupation.)

In Burma, which became the center of Bose's Indian Independence League, the Indians enjoyed special privileges from the Japanese. And though Malaya's large Chinese community had suffered badly from Japanese oppression, hostilities between Malays and Chinese grew apace; if anything, they were exacerbated by the Chinese-led Communist insurgency, with its inevitable racial overtones and repercussions. Rightly or wrongly accused of wartime profiteering, of racial and national separateness, if not also of partiality for the colonial regimes—an accusation especially leveled at the Indonesian Chinese—the foreign minorities thus were in a highly precarious position when decolonization got under way.

Indeed, while most Southeast Asian governments have done little to solve their most pressing internal problems, almost all of them have moved against the foreign minorities in their midst. It was perhaps unavoidable that nationalism triumphant would turn against one of the colonial era's most woeful social and economic legacies. But the racial minorities have in all probability been made the scapegoats for the exaggerated yet disappointed hopes generated by the attainment of independence, with or without prompting from above. As so often happens when racial sentiments get inflamed—it was, after all, a king of Siam who wrote an anti-Chinese brochure in the 1910s which he almost prophetically entitled *The Jews of the East*—entire communities have had to pay for the presumed or real sins of a few of their members.

By the mid-1960s, most Indians had been forcibly repatriated from Burma; several hundreds of thousands of Chinese in Indonesia had been expelled from many rural areas and small towns, while increasing numbers were forced to return to mainland China, with the fate of the entire community in grave jeopardy; the Philippines had passed laws barring foreigners—in fact, Chinese—from retail trade; and anti-Chinese laws had also been promulgated, though barely translated into fact, in South Vietnam. Only in Malaysia and, to a lesser extent, in Thailand has the position of the Chinese not—not yet?—been endangered by repressive legislation. Their sheer numerical and economic strength in the former, and the strong assimilationist record, coupled with Thai political protection for big Chinese enterprises, in the latter, are doubtless responsible for this state of affairs.

Even though legal measures occasionally do distinguish between those who have acquired their host country's citizenship and foreign subjects, in practice these distinctions are all too often blurred. Anti-Chinese measures thus affect those with long roots in Southeast Asia, many of them for generations cut off from Chinese language and culture, as well as the more recent, and nationally conscious, immigrants with their separate schools and social life. Equally important, the Chinese policies of Southeast Asian governments have shown little variation regardless of which of the "Two Chinas" they recognize; nor has either Peking or Taiwan effectively intervened when Chinese minorities overtly loyal to them were subjected to discrimination and persecutions. Yet some Southeast Asian governments have used accusations of political subversion on the part of their Chinese inhabitants as a major explanation (or rationalization) of racial discrimination.

III

The political and constitutional constellations that have emerged during the first two decades of the decolonization process in Southeast Asia are as varied as the area itself. Different cultural foundations and historical experiences have produced a broad spectrum of political structures, ranging all the way from democratic governments in Malaysia and the Philippines, through military rule in Burma and Indonesia, to the Communist dictatorship in North Vietnam. The international alignments of the various states likewise run the gamut from Western to neutralist and Communist orientations. Neither of these criteria, however, suffices for a meaningful analysis of decolonization in its wider, sociological ramifications. In the first place, they do inadequate justice to the subtle differences that separate even seemingly similar states and to the nuances in their foreign policies. Second, and more important, political institutions as well as international affairs are subject to change;

short though the era of independent nationhood has been, actually it has already provided several instances of abrupt reversals.

The historical developments which we have traced in the preceding chapters suggest the possibility of analyzing the decolonization era in terms of both elite composition and what might be called social and political mobilization. Viewed from such a vantage point, Southeast Asian polities fall into two broad categories. First, there are states with a marked degree of elite continuity: in addition to Thailand (not a "decolonized" country, properly speaking) they comprise Cambodia, Malaysia, and the Philippines. In all these countries political power in the postwar years has come to be wielded by groups which had already been well established and socially prominent before 1942. Burma, Indonesia, and Vietnam constitute the second category. In these three states, power accrued to political elites who had started to move from peripheral and in the main oppositional places in colonial times toward the centers of political power during the Japanese occupation. These basic elite differences are in large measure accompanied by disparate levels of social dislocation and political awareness among wider segments of the general population: Southeast Asians in the first category have, on the whole, enjoyed internal stability while those in the second have been poised on the brink of incipient social upheaval.

Politically, decolonization has resulted in national independence for all former dependencies. Not only was the transfer of sovereignty in Cambodia, Malaysia, and the Philippines peaceful, but the attainment of independence practically constituted the sum-total of significant change. It was otherwise in Burma, Indonesia, and Vietnam, where independence was won through threatened or actual violence, and where, furthermore, the severing of political ties with the metropolitan country, though crucially important, merely opened the way to large-scale internal changes. It stands to reason that the "conservative" aristocratic or gentry elites who have inherited functioning social orders in the former countries should find the tasks of "nation building" far easier than do the "revolutionary" intelligentsias in the latter; newcomers to power, they also confront a decades' old legacy of social perturbances. "Conservative" and "revolutionary," however, derive their significance primarily from sociological, rather than from political or ideological, criteria. Generally speaking, it may well be true that established elites tend toward social and political conservatism while intelligentsia-leaders espouse radical or rather "populist" courses; indeed, their respective political vocabularies often enough reflect such divergent orientations. But it does not follow—nor has it followed—that established elites invariably shun modernization, or that, conversely, intelligentsias always attempt it. Political labels and rhetoric are poor guides to the complexities of decolonization in Southeast Asia. Turning now to a discussion of the course it has taken in each individual country, we shall attempt to place it in historical perspective.

Thailand

Least affected by Western dominance and the Japanese interregnum, Thailand, alone among Southeast Asian countries, emerged virtually intact in the postwar world. It will be recalled that military officers had gained the upper hand after the *coup* of 1932, at the expense of civil servants who had before then been allied with them. In turn, the military had yielded to civilians when the Thai-Japanese alliance drew to a close during the final stages of the Pacific War. This, however, proved to be only a transitional adjustment to the needs of presenting a government acceptable to the victorious Allies. In November 1947, the civilian cabinet headed by Pridi was overthrown and the wartime premier, Field Marshal Phibum Songkhram, usurped power. The return of the military —Phibum was subsequently ousted, only to be followed by other officers as premier—was not only indicative of the firm hold the post-1932 elite had on the instrumentalities of political power, it also once again clearly demonstrated the country's pragmatic approach to the international situation.

With the United States emerging as the dominant power in the Pacific, Thailand sought ever closer ties with her; apprehensive lest the turmoil in neighboring Indochina affect her security, Thailand became, next to the Philippines, the sole Southeast Asian country to enter the Southeast Asia Treaty Organization (SEATO), created under Western auspices after the French withdrawal from the peninsula in 1954. As the Vietnamese civil war grew into a major arena of international conflict, involving hundreds of thousands of American troops, Thailand became a staging area (a role not dissimilar to that she had played in the Second World War, it may be recalled), permitting the construction of military facilities and the stationing of large American ground and air contingents on her soil.

In addition to involving Siam more or less directly in the affairs of the peninsula—Thai forces were actually deployed in Vietnam and Laos in the late 1960s—the towering American military presence also had internal ramifications. True enough, the Thai ethnic majority, the beneficiary of social stability and increased economic prosperity, gave little cause for concern. (With the export economy of postwar Burma and Vietnam in disarray, Thailand actually became Southeast Asia's major rice supplier for an expanding world market.) Even the capital's educated groups, though occasionally stirred by yearnings for democratization, could be counted loyal to king and country. But some long neglected minority groups, especially the sizable Lao community in the economically backward northeast of the country, caused growing apprehension in Bangkok. Fear of Communist subversion in that area led the government to seek American advice and technical-military support, leading in turn to joint actions whose final ramifications cannot be foreseen.

Cambodia

Thailand's neighbor, Cambodia, enjoyed a smooth transition from colonial dependency to independent state. Heir to the proud Khmer dynastic tradition, the Cambodian kingdom became, as we have seen, a protectorate of France in the 1860s. But though France assumed virtually total political, administrative, and military control, depriving the "Indianized" monarch of all real power, she also safeguarded Cambodia against the perennial ambitions and pressures of her more powerful would-be-suzerains, Vietnam and Thailand. French protection thus provided dynastic continuity and internal peace. The country's rural economy, moreover, did not attract French investors, so that the peasantry was spared the upheavals that were so prominent a part of the colonial experience of Vietnam and Burma, for example. In short, Cambodia formed a classic case of "indirect rule," with a bare modicum of attempted modernization. French education only benefited some select few members of the court and the nobility; in fact, higher education was available only in Vietnam (and very occasionally in France), but not in Cambodia itself. It was foreigners—Chinese as well as Vietnamese—rather than natives who performed the ancillary services in the minuscule modernized sectors of the administration and the economy.

The sudden collapse of French authority at the hands of Japan in March 1945 had no far-reaching repercussions, even though the Japanese prevailed upon the young king, Norodom Sihanouk, to proclaim

Cambodian independence. The immediate postwar era did witness a good deal of political strife in the capital, fomented by antagonistic factions supported either by Thailand or by Vietnamese Communists (the latter being especially active among the small resident Vietnamese community); but Sihanouk was able to outmaneuver both. With astute and patient diplomacy, he secured Cambodia's independence from France, at the same time winning, through stubborn bargaining, recognition by the Communist powers of his country's neutrality at the Geneva Conference in 1954. It was the rapid growth of American military power in the region, in particular American patronage of Cambodia's traditional rivals, Thailand and South Vietnam, that in Sihanouk's eyes constituted grave dangers to Cambodian neutrality. Having for some years accepted both American and Chinese aid, he finally broke off diplomatic relations with the United States. This, however, by no means closed all doors to Western contacts. Relations with France have remained cordial in recent years. Cultural ties between the two countries are actually far stronger now than ever before, with ever increasing numbers of Cambodian students studying in France. Even diplomatically Sihanouk has leaned heavily on French support in the 1960s.

The keystone of Cambodian internal politics has been the survival and strength of the monarchical traditions, buttressed by the Buddhist monkhood, which in turn is closely allied with and dependent upon the monarchy. Paradoxically enough, Sihanouk abdicated as king in order to become the actual political leader of his country (the throne is presently vacant); but it is exactly the sacral aura of traditional kingship, combined with Sihanouk's personal magnetism and manipulative skills, that have proved such a strong anchorage for independent Cambodia.

After a brief experiment with the forms of constitutional democracy had foundered on the rocks of factional politicking, Sihanouk first created a national front, the *Sangkum Reastr Niyum* (People's Socialist Community), and shortly thereafter embarked on an increasingly personalized form and style of government. Given the low level of political development, the former king's assumption of virtually complete and authoritarian power has met with relatively little opposition. Yet the growing number of young Cambodians returning from study in France —they are no longer exclusively drawn from the most privileged class in the country—is giving rise to intergenerational frictions and tensions not unknown to other parts of Southeast Asia. It may be some time, however, before these younger elements can successfully challenge Sihanouk and his close associates.

The Philippines

In the Philippines, planned decolonization antedated the storms of the Pacific War. American colonial rule had no sooner become firmly established in the first decade of the twentieth century, than the process of devolving power to Filipinos was set in motion. Before long, the executive and judicial branches of government were similarly "decolonized," until in 1935 the Philippine Commonwealth became colonial Southeast Asia's first self-governing state headed by an indigenous president. The remaining American prerogatives—foreign relations, finances, immigration, and the governance of minority groups—were surrendered when the Philippines became independent, for the third time, in 1946.

Nationhood was attained while the country was still bleeding from the manifold wounds of a cruel war. While the political system could be fairly quickly consolidated, some wartime legacies, especially widespread corruption, continued to plague the Philippines for many years. The return to political stability was greatly facilitated by the presence and cohesion of the *ilustrado* ruling class. For a short time the collaboration issue divided it, but it was the "collaborators," under Manuel Roxas, rather than their opponents, led by Sergio Osmeña (Quezon's successor to the Commonwealth presidency in Washington during the war), who emerged victorious in the republic's first general elections in 1946.

Though collaboration ceased to be a meaningful issue, the *Nacionalista* Party could not contain all the politically ambitious, as it had done in the days of the Commonwealth. The death of Manuel Quezon had deprived the party, and the country, of a truly national figure around whom all political forces could have rallied in the immediate post-independence period. A two-party system soon took shape and has dominated Philippine politics ever since. Power has tended to alternate between the Nationalists and the Liberals, who are more divided by personalities and local sources of influence than by substantive or ideological cleavages. (Every now and then third-party groups emerge, only to coalesce with either of the two major parties in the end.) After a slow start, the electoral process became reasonably clean, politicians and the public having learned to abide by the rules of constitutional democracy (in large measure fashioned after the American model).

Both parties derive their financial resources as well as the bulk of their leadership from the small *ilustrado* elite which directly or indirectly commands most of the country's wealth and power. The peculiar combination of democracy and oligarchy—somewhat reminiscent of post-

1867 Britain—is, however, not a static phenomenon. An emergent urban middle and professional class has started to affect the near-monopoly of the landed ruling class. The influence of this new class was largely responsible for the election of Ramon Magsaysay, a "commoner," to the presidency of the republic in 1953. Magsaysay, who had gained national prominence as defense secretary, in the space of a few years transformed the style of Philippine politics by vigorously campaigning among the peasantry, drawing them for the first time into active political participation. Yet the dynamic president encountered stiff opposition to his ambitious reform programs from the vested interests that dominated the Philippine Congress; his premature death in an airplane crash in 1957 led to a virtual return—only once since then interrupted—to the old political pattern of outright *ilustrado* dominance.

The only major threat to that dominance was the Communist-led *Hukbalahap* movement, which at the end of the Second World War emerged entrenched as a state within the state in parts of Central Luzon. At the outset, the *Huks* sought to attain political power through the electoral process; they successfully contested several provincial and national offices in the republic's first elections of 1946, only to have their elected candidates, including *Huk* leader Luis Taruc, barred from taking office. From the late 1940s until the early 1950s, the Communists reverted to guerilla warfare from their rural bases in Central Luzon, at times coming dangerously close to threatening Manila itself.

It was only when Defense Secretary Magsaysay was placed in charge of the anti-*Huk* campaign that the tide started to turn in favor of the government. Magsaysay achieved success by reorganizing and revitalizing the Philippine army, but he also used a highly imaginative political approach to the peasants in the *Huk* areas, promising relief and reforms. Magsaysay furthermore promised fair treatment and resettlement to surrendering *Huks*. (In all his actions he enjoyed considerable American support.) Taruc's surrender and arrest signaled the end of large-scale guerilla war, and to all intents and purposes ended the threat of revolution, geographically limited as it had been, in the Philippines. But very little has yet been done, certainly far less than Magsaysay had been able, let alone had hoped, to achieve, by way of ameliorating the social conditions that had nurtured the *Hukbalahap* movement.

For understandable reasons the Philippine Republic's foreign policy orientation has heavily leaned on alliance with the former colonial power. Apart from the fact that the country's political elite had been American-educated, the economic ties with the United States favored a continuation of close Philippine-American relations; it must not be forgotten that Filipino landowners and exporters had for decades reaped the benefits of a protected American market. Protection was extended into the post-independence era by the United States, albeit on a declining scale; it is to expire in 1971. At the same time, the young republic had to extend so-called "parity" rights to American firms which allowed these unfettered operations on Philippine soil, identical with those enjoyed by local enterprises. In addition, the Philippines also granted territorial leases for American bases, originally for a 99-year period, but recently reduced to a far shorter term.

Though Philippine-American relations seem to be safely anchored, latter-day Filipino nationalists have smarted under "parity" and the leases (especially since the latter involve the issue of extraterritoriality), interpreting them as vestiges of colonial inequality. Such sentiments have become particularly prevalent among the urban professional and intellectual groups and among the swelling student population. Many of these younger people have been increasingly affected by the turbulence of events in adjacent Southeast Asian countries if not in the entire Afro-Asian world. The search for a new, "Asian" identity has thus gained some prominence among the very elements which would like to steer Philippine politics in a more truly democratic, socially conscious direction. Though they suffered a serious eclipse after Magsaysay's death, the influence of these groups has by no means ceased. In the years ahead, it may well lead to a gradual transformation of Philippine political life, rather than to a dramatic break with the past.

Malaysia

The near anarchy that reigned in Malaya in the immediate postwar years stood in stark contrast to the relative tranquillity of the country's earlier evolution under British rule. The Malayan Communist Party, led by and recruited almost exclusively among peninsular Chinese, made an initial bid for power in the vacuum that followed the Japanese surrender. The Communists attempted to work through the trade unions to capture control. Thwarted in their major designs by the quick restoration of British authority, the Communists in Malaya—as in some other countries of South and Southeast Asia—in 1948 resorted to protracted terror tactics and guerilla warfare from jungle retreats prepared during the war. It took a sizeable military effort by combined Commonwealth contingents, coupled with the forced resettlement of Chinese squatters who had supported the guerillas from the edges of the jungle, to subdue this second Communist challenge. The "Emergency" (the official name for the insurrection) only ended in 1960, three years after Malaya had become an independent state. Progress toward independent nationhood had actually proceeded apace while danger still loomed large, in an endeavor to counter the Communists' propaganda appeals to be fighting for the liberation of the country from British colonialism.

Curiously enough, British wartime plans for the future of her Malayan possessions had departed rather markedly from the colonial pattern. Considerations of rapid economic reconstruction, reinforced by the desire to simplify, centralize, and modernize the cumbersome administrative machineries for the Straits Settlements, the Federated and Unfederated Malay States, as well as belated willingness to grant citizenship to large numbers of non-Malays—all these apparently combined to lead colonial officers in London to urge a unitary structure for postwar Malaya. The plan which they had devised did away with the separate constitutional entities; they were to be incorporated (with the exception of Singapore) into a tightly knit, centralized Malayan Union. The Malay sultans, though doomed to forfeiture of their remaining powers under the new constitutional plan, gave their reluctant (if not forced) approval to the Union.

But almost at once opposition was aroused. In Britain, former colonial administrators waged a successful campaign against such a brusque departure from the hallowed principles of indirect rule for and through the Malay rulers. More important still was the reaction among Malays in the peninsula itself, where nationalism, long dormant, suddenly solidified in the face of the threat to Malay interests. We saw that before the war nationalist agitation had for all practical purposes been limited to members of the nonaristocratic intelligentsia; now it suddenly found vigorous spokesmen and leaders among the British-educated upper class. Significantly, the creation of the United Malays National Organization (UMNO) in 1946 was was the handiwork of Dato Onn bin Ja'afar from Johore, the most independent and most viable of the former Unfederated States. The new movement forged a close political link between rulers and subjects never before achieved. It generated an excited Malay public opinion which, together with the surprising political apathy of the Malayan Union's Chinese and Indian would-be beneficiaries, led to Britain's abandonment of the radical Union scheme.

Two years later was born the Federation of Malaya, which reflected a clear victory for Malay interests. As its very name suggests, the new constitutional arrangement largely reverted to the basic pattern of prewar colonial rule. It was squarely built on the supremacy of the individual Malay states (all of them entered the new Federation, which also contained the two Straits Settlements, without Singapore); Malay rights and privileges were safeguarded, especially with regard to such key issues as land ownership, citizenship, access to political offices, and for that matter the national language as well as religion. (Islam was made the state religion, with adherents of other faiths being guaranteed freedom of worship.) The traditional rulers and sultans thus retained their prerogatives, while their English-educated descendants came to occupy positions of authority at the center, which was being progressively decolonized. In August 1957 the Federation of Malaya, the West's last major dependency in Southeast Asia, attained independence in a peaceful transfer of power.

The federation involved a constitutional monarchy patterned after the British model, with the various rulers rotating on an elective arrangement between themselves in the office of the *Yang di-Pertuan Agong* (supreme head). Also of British origin was the institution of a cabinet responsible to the totally elective lower house of the bicameral legislature; the upper house was semi-appointive. Uniquely Malayan was the political underpinning that made the successful operation of constitutional democracy possible in a multiracial state. For, though Malay interests were to remain constitutionally guaranteed for quite some time, large segments of the resident Chinese, and also Indian, populations were actively drawn into the political process.

The basic compromise that made such a solution possible depended on the leaders of the two major communities. Tungku Abdul Rahman, Chief Minister before and Prime Minister after independence, a scion of the royal house of Kedah, and a British-trained lawyer (he succeeded Dato Onn as president of UMNO in 1951), and Tan Cheng-Lock, founder of the Malayan Chinese Association (MCA) in 1949, laid the groundwork for the Alliance Party, a tripartite coalition joined by the Malayan Indian Congress (MIC); it has been the governing majority party since the early 1950s. The leadership obviously represents the intrinsically conservative elements of both communities, the Malay aristocracy and the well established Chinese commercial middle class, the beneficiaries —the one political, the other economic—of British rule in the peninsula. Retention of close ties with Britain and the Commonwealth and a favorable climate for foreign investments are other aspects of the gradual nature of decolonization in Malaya.

In 1963, the Federation was expanded to include the remaining British colonial enclaves of Singapore and the Bornean territories of Sarawak and Sabah (British North Borneo); the sultanate of Brunei chose to remain outside the federation of Malaysia. Yet only two years after its founding, Singapore "seceded" (or was forced to leave) the federation, to become an independent republic in its own right. The short history of Malaysia shows that the economic and political advantages to be derived from merger into a larger entity may be offset by centrifugal tendencies born of the divergences between peninsular Malaya and the other components. The incorporation and subsequent ejection of Singapore, in particular, highlighted the difficulties of accommodating the volatile and ambitious Chinese political leadership of the city-state's ruling People's Action Party (PAP) in the carefully balanced political system that had developed in mainland Malaya.

The creation of the larger federation for some years also led to near explosive tensions with neighboring Indonesia and the Philippines. The former alleged to see in Malaysia a "neo-colonialist" threat to its own security, while the latter objected to the inclusion of North Borneo, claiming residual sovereignty over that area arising from the Sulu "cession" in 1878. Indonesia's "Confrontation" vis-à-vis Malaysia led to armed conflict, but a change of political regime in Djakarta in 1965–66 brought a relaxation and resumption of friendly relations; in the Philippines, too, a new administration quietly dropped Filipino claims in the mid-1960s, similarly opening the road to diplomatic normalization. Outside dangers have thus subsided if not entirely disappeared, but the separation of Singapore, and to a lesser extent the continuing political problems in Sabah and especially Sarawak, have injected an element of instability and potential economic disarray, which have been acerbated by racial tensions in the region.

Even peninsular Malaya itself is not entirely free from the threat of internal instability. The fiscal base for the Alliance governments' vigorous welfare policies is, of course, the export economy; and unlike tin, natural rubber has fared uncertainly on world markets in the 1960s. But though a precondition for the smooth functioning of the political equilibrium, economic prosperity is not necessarily a guaranty for its viability in the future. Like all compromises, it is in constant and perhaps growing danger of falling victim to racial extremists, dissatisfied with the status quo, at either end. The nicely balanced arrangement by which Malay political predominance is matched with Chinese (and to a lesser extent Indian) economic supremacy has been worked out by men reared in the British tradition.

We saw that even in prewar Malaya there were others, particularly among the Malay-educated urban intellectuals, who were heavily influenced by more radical political ideals. There were also staunch adherents to strict Muslim values among the rural groups, especially on the economically less developed east coast of the peninsula. Both these groups have come to form elites opposed to UMNO, and even within that Malay-dominated party—dedicated as it is to an essentially secular state in cooperation with non-Muslims—religious pressures have increased. The Pan-Malayan Islamic Party (PMIP) has scored electorally on the east coast, forming the government in one of the states and temporarily holding power in another. The Socialist Front, on the other hand, constitutes an intercommunal effort of younger leaders of socialist leanings who seek support on the basis of class sentiments, most notably among the urban populations.

For the time being, neither of these (and other) opposition parties —let alone the still proscribed Communist Party—have come close to challenging the dominance of the Alliance Party. But as elsewhere in postcolonial Southeast Asia, a new generation is entering the political scene in Malaysia, largely through the rapidly expanding educational institutions. Presumably these young men and women will be far less imbued with British values than the present elite; whether they will be able and willing to perpetuate the give-and-take that has marked the first decade of independence must remain a moot point. The logic of the situation—the presence of diverse and unevenly endowed racial groups—would dictate the necessity of continued cooperation; but old parochialisms infused with youthful impatience may yet imperil the region's most successful and economically most prosperous democratic state.

Laos

Laos, which leaped from colonial obscurity into the limelight of international conflict in the 1950s, does not readily fit into either of our two main categories. If anything, her case shows that neither indirect colonial rule nor rural peace necessarily is a harbinger of continued stability. Arbitrarily carved out of a variety of lesser principalities by French caprice in the late nineteenth century, Laos in modern times remained a geographical rather than a political reality. Unlike Cambodia and Vietnam, the fifth *pays* of the former French Indochina lacked historical cohesion and a sense of national unity. The French protectorate stilled, but did not obliterate, quarrels among either dynastic families or personal rivals. Equally important, we saw that the lowland-dwelling Lao only form a minority in the country (a sizeable number of Lao actually live in Thailand), while the different hill peoples were barely touched by the administration of the French-created kingdom.

Even before France relinquished her protectorate in 1954, Laos' neighbors, Vietnam and Thailand, had covertly started to exploit the unfolding elite rivalries in the country; the entry into the area of the United States further complicated and acerbated these rivalries. Since independence, the king himself has only played a minor role, three princely brothers being the chief *dramatis personae* in Laotian politics. One of them relied on American-Thai, the other on North Vietnamese, support. The third, Souvannaphouma—Prime Minister in the 1950s and again in the 1960s—has sought to steer a precarious middle course between "right" and "left." The political scene has been further complicated by competing factions in the armed forces.

For some years now, an uneasy coalition has held the three major groups together, but the Communist-led *Neo Lao Hak Xat* (NLHX—Patriotic Laotian Front), with a solid territorial and military base in the north, appears to be the best organized of the three. With North Vietnamese inspiration, if not guidance, the Communists have in that part of Laos attracted some discontented minority groups to their cause. In all but name, Laos—whose neutrality was once again confirmed by the Second Geneva Conference in 1962—is a divided country. American influence is strongest in the south, that of the Communists in the north. This reality overshadows the meagerly developed institutionalized political process as well as practically all other problems.

IV

Change has been the hallmark of the decolonization process in Burma, Indonesia, and Vietnam. Subjected to direct colonial rule, all three countries, as we have seen, had had their traditional political systems destroyed. Potentially new leaders, the intelligentsias, had started to come to the fore from the 1930s. But it was only during the Second World War that these men officially assumed places of public leadership in Burma and Indonesia, albeit under close Japanese control; in Vietnam they emerged only after the Japanese surrender. We also saw that religious leaders, both rural and urban, had become increasingly involved in the political developments of the late colonial era. Once again, this trend was accelerated by Japanese policies toward religious groups in parts of the area. Last but not least, protracted economic interference by Westerners had wrought significant changes among Burmese, Indonesian (especially Javanese and Sumatran), and Vietnamese peasants; it will be recalled that their situation had further deteriorated during the Second World War.

Japan's surrender in August 1945 abruptly released the pent-up energies and ambitions of political and religious leaders, as it kindled the peasants' expectations for release from their harsh wartime burdens. Open warfare had commenced with the British reentry into Burma in 1944, while Dutch and French troops attempted colonial reconquests in Indonesia and Vietnam as soon as the war ended. The struggle for independence thus sparked the violence of steadily inflamed revolutionary expectations. As long as it lasted, elite and rural masses appeared united by common goals. Yet the attainment of independence in both Burma and Indonesia provided no more than a breathing spell, soon to be followed by further upheavals; Vietnam barely enjoyed even such momentary internal peace.

Rotation of national leadership has been the most conspicuous feature in these new states. With the exception of North Vietnam, whose Communist ruling group has so far remained intact and united, none of the leaders under whom independence had been won is still in power in the 1960s. Far from being a purely personal phenomenon, the displacement of these leaders—men of considerable stature and charisma —signifies a further change in the elite pattern. However important the towering individual was in rallying the country to the struggle for independence, he proved inadequate to the burdensome tasks of "nation building." Disillusionment with such leaders has tended further to discredit the political intelligentsias from whom they had sprung. Most of the men who have taken over power in the second decolonization decade belong to the military establishments created during the war. They represent not only a younger but also a decidedly less educated generation of Southeast Asians.

The transition from civilian to military regimes has usually been accompanied by marked constitutional changes. Strong anti-Western strains in their nationalist thinking notwithstanding, most intelligentsia-leaders were beholden to Western political forms. To all but the doctrinaire Communists, Western democracies were patently the most modern, and, after the Allied victories in the Second World War, once again the most successful states in the world. It is therefore not surprising that both Burma and Indonesia (and to some extent even Vietnam) after independence adopted constitutions derived from Western models. Whether such liberal-democratic systems could have operated successfully in these Southeast Asian countries even under optimal conditions is highly doubtful. While fairly clean elections were held in Burma and Indonesia (though not in either Vietnam), they demonstrably encouraged ideological, ethnic, and other fissures, rather than promoting national unity. Be that as it may, the military for the greater part professed dislike for parliamentary democracy; once in power, they replaced it by authoritarian regimes while retaining the rhetoric of revolution, even of revolutionary socialism.

The emergence of military regimes is no accident in Southeast Asian history. Unquestionably, the military are the most cohesive and best disciplined social group in the formerly directly ruled countries (just as the Communist party constitutes such a tightly structured group in North Vietnam). More than that, the coercive physical power at their command practically guarantees the military services' supremacy vis-à-vis civilian competitors; the Thai example clearly demonstrated such a supremacy thirty-odd years ago. The military takeovers have been the more easily accomplished, since civilian politicians usually possess neither firm roots nor organizational strength. In all likelihood, however, the political evolution of these countries has only reached a temporary halt. For one thing, theirs are young armies born of revolution and anticolonial war rather than professional bodies with traditions of military discipline: unavoidably, officers as well as rank and file reflect the same social and political tensions and cleavages that exist among their civilian compatriots. For another, the military are almost totally lacking in political, economic, and administrative expertise and experience.

The faltering performances of the military elites, especially in the economic field, have compounded the progressive social and political dislocation in Burma, Indonesia, and South Vietnam. The suppression of civilian organizations, the silencing of opposition leaders, the impatient clamoring of high school and college students, and, last but certainly not least, continually declining rural welfare coupled with high birth rates—all these are indices of latent instability rather than of semipermanent new orders. Nor must it be forgotten that, like most other Southeast Asia states, the military *juntas* in these countries are beset by ethnic as well as racial minority problems; the fact that Burma and Indonesia have taken extremely severe measures against their Indian and Chinese residents, respectively, may serve as one indicator of the frustrations the new governments have experienced since they assumed control.

Burma

The opening phase of decolonization in Burma looked promising enough. Toward the end of the Japanese occupation, the Anti-Fascist People's Freedom League (AFPFL), a broadly based nationalist front, came, as we saw, to dominate the political scene. The League's leaders included civilian politicians—most of them *Thakins* with left-wing leanings—and army officers. When the Second World War ended, these leaders were strong enough to displace the older generation of British-educated, professional men like Burmese wartime Chief of State, Dr. Ba Maw. In turn, Britain's newly elected Labor government proved willing to surrender sovereignty to the AFPFL leadership. The transition to independence was thus smooth and bloodless, the new Union of Burma being born in early 1948. But even before its birth, the country came face to face with a major tragedy in the brutal assassination of Aung San; student-turned-national hero, founder and leader of the AFPFL, well-nigh legendary commander of the Burmese army, it was Aung San who as prime minister had brought negotiations with London to the brink of success. (Plotted by U Saw, one of Burma's best known prewar politicians, the murder occurred in the cabinet chamber, six other ministers being killed at the same time.)

No sooner was independence proclaimed than quarrels over ideologies and personalities came to the fore. Communist factions, among others, broke away from the AFPFL, at least one of them going underground and waging war against the emasculated governmental coalition. Armed bands mushroomed, some formed by Karens, others by demobilized veterans, and others still by bandits out to gain advantage from the anarchy that was spreading all over the land. It took several years before the government, since Aung San's death headed by his old comrade U Nu, managed to restore a semblance of order and to breathe new life into civil government. The AFPFL, true to its avowed left-wing orientation, then embarked on the implementation of an ambitious welfare program, but apart from nationalizing foreign-owned enterprises, it did little to promote real economic and social progress.

Though law and order did improve, creeping corruption eroded confidence in and patience with the AFPFL and with constitutional government. (It will be recalled that the colonial constitution of 1935, which had granted a high degree of self-government, never enjoyed widespread prestige or popularity either.) What brought matters to a head was disunity within the loosely structured AFPFL, in which the small Socialist Party had provided the steering element. Up to the late 1950s, the League had virtually dominated the political scene with a network of rural branches as well as associated workers', peasants', and youth associations. But once independence had been achieved and the most important rebellious dissidents either subdued or accommodated, the coalition leaders could no longer hide their personal animosities from the public. In 1958, when these fissures erupted into the open, the AFPFL split into two warring groups.

It was at that point that the army under Colonel (later General) Ne Win intervened in the political process. Though many of its officers who originally had been members of the *Thakin*-intelligentsia continued to share with civilian politicians certain ideological orientations, the army as a whole had developed a separate identity. Increasingly disdainful of and impatient with their nonmilitary colleagues, the military was yet unwilling to bring about a complete break in 1960. After consultations with the political leaders, they created an army caretaker government. As a matter of fact, the officers lived up to their promise of holding new national elections. These were duly held in 1960, with U Nu's AFPFL faction winning a sweeping victory, a tribute to its leader's vast popularity.

The restoration of constitutional government proved, however, to be quite short-lived: two years later, Ne Win and his men abruptly abrogated it, this time with no promise or prospect of surrendering power again to civilians. Large numbers of politicians, U Nu among them, were confined to detention camps, while army officers assumed most executive and administrative posts. In the place of the prohibited political parties, the military created a single national front under rigid governmental control, the leadership of the nation being exercised by a Revolutionary Council under the presidency of Ne Win. The Council's "Burmese Road to Socialism" has become the only officially sanctioned political ideology. So far, however, the eviction of Burma's Indian minority has been the new government's most signal achievement. Partly as a result of it, agricultural production has continued to fall, while neither inflation nor corruption has been halted by the imposition of ever-tighter governmental controls.

If Burma has barely progressed economically and politically under military rule—the regime, for example, subdued vocal student opposition by brutal reprisals—it must not be forgotten that Ne Win and his colleagues inherited a far from orderly or prosperous country. Though U Nu's personal character, as well as his commitment to democratic values, were above reproach, his performance as prime minister had aroused deep misgivings. Impatient with the minutiae of administration, U Nu had alienated even close associates by his arbitrary mode of governing. His increasing partiality for religious elements, culminating in the proclamation of Buddhism as the official state religion, antagonized many Burmans; moreover, it heightened tensions between Buddhist majority and non-Buddhist minorities.

At the same time, U Nu was willing to grant such far-reaching concessions to favored minority groups, the Shans in particular, that the unity of the state appeared to some, the military above all, in jeopardy. The economy, too, floundered because of maladministration. To win popular support, U Nu had instituted a government-financed rural credit system which lent itself to widespread abuse without yielding incentives for increased rice deliveries; rice exports could, in fact, have furnished sorely needed foreign exchange for capital investments, as they have done in neighboring Thailand since 1945. In any case, Ne Win seems to have coped successfully if forcefully with several pressing political and security problems. Though politically dictatorial and inept economically, he has skillfully endeavored to safeguard Burma's neutral position—at the cost, it may be said, of reverting to a xenophobic seclusion from the world that harks back to precolonial days—amid the international entanglements that have come to engulf mainland Southeast Asia in the 1960s. Recent tensions with China threaten to disrupt Ne Win's efforts, however.

Indonesia

Indonesia's transition from parliamentary democracy to military dictatorship has been slower and more complex than Burma's. On one hand, the Netherlands' attempt to regain Indonesia through two military campaigns in the late 1940s helped to unite the heterogenous forces at work within Indonesian society. On the other, the drawn-out struggle with the Dutch imbued political life generally with a radicalism and potential violence that proved difficult to contain. Animosity toward the Dutch temporarily abated after the transfer of sovereignty, steadily gaining momentum again in the late 1950s, until Holland relinquished New Guinea (Irian Barat) in 1962. Almost at once, militancy was once more on the upsurge, this time directed against the federation of Malaysia. Nor was violence limited to external foes. In some parts of the archipelago, the Indonesian Revolution itself had unleashed bloody social revolutions. Simmering beneath the surface, violence sporadically flared in later years, sparked by extremist dissidents of both right and left. In the mid-1950s abortive regional revolts threatened the state with dismemberment, but a decade later mass killings on an undreamt-of scale swept the entire country. Coming to power after so many convulsions in the mid-1960s, the army—itself deeply involved in many of these events—certainly faced formidable problems.

We have seen that, unlike in Burma, no single, all-embracing nationalist front arose in Indonesia during the war. Not only was the country administratively fragmented during the Japanese occupation, but even in Java, the center of national political activities, two major groupings, Muslims (centered in the *Masjumi*) and nonreligious nationalists (centered in the *Hōkōkai*), had kept their separate ideological and organizational identities. Each of these major groups contained in turn a host of subdivisions, cliques, and factions. And here, as elsewhere, younger men were starting to exert pressure on a political process gradually emerging from tight Japanese tutelage. Some of these were allied to one or the other parent group, but others, notably the army officers, kept consciously separate. Just before and immediately after the Japanese surrender, these antagonistic forces clashed openly: Muslims demanded that independent Indonesia become an Islamic State, but had to yield on this crucial issue to the "secular" leaders. The young activists, restive and reckless, tried to snatch independence in an act of anti-Japanese defiance, and were only with difficulty restrained by their elders. In the end, the older intelligentsia-leaders did proclaim the Indonesian Republic, with halfhearted Japanese concurrence, in August 1945.

The centrifugal tendencies in Indonesia were held in check by two major factors, one external the other internal. From the outside, mounting Dutch pressures, culminating in open warfare in the late 1940s, united all contending groups under the banner of militant nationalism. Among Indonesians, Sukarno, the most prominent nationalist before and during the war and already proclaimed president of the new republic, acted as the major rallying point for his beleaguered people. For several years after the transfer of sovereignty, the charismatic president continued to stand head and shoulders above other persons and factions. But here, as in Burma, independence brought in its wake a weakening of national consensus and the resurgence of irreconcilable internal cleavages.

The democratic system, patterned after that of Holland, acerbated rather than mitigated the sharpening of Indonesia's political crisis. For the first few years of independence, the country functioned under two successive provisional constitutions; the parliaments consisted of appointive, not elected, representatives. But with the approach of the oft-delayed general elections, the political parties embarked on increasingly intensive campaigns. Inevitably, the electoral contest came to focus on ideological commitments to mutually exclusive value systems. The elections of the mid-1950s clearly revealed a pattern of intrinsic disunity: the Indonesian voters had ranged themselves into four major—and a host of smaller—political camps, two of them Islamic (reflecting the prewar split between traditionalist and reformist Muslims), one nationalist, and one Communist. More ominously, the voters at either extreme not only represented ideological, but also regional, ethnic, and urban-rural rivalries. Even before the elections, some of these antagonisms, especially that between Muslims and Communists, had occasionally flared into violence. In subsequent years, they progressively inhibited the functioning of tenuously constructed coalition governments. The split between Muslims and their opponents also deadlocked the Constituent Assembly, chosen in 1955 to write a definitive constitutional charter for the republic. The outbreak of regional rebellions with ideological overtones in several parts of the archipelago brought Indonesia to the brink of civil war and dismemberment in the late 1950s.

Though many of these regional revolts were sparked by military commanders outside Java, the central army leadership saved national unity, as was the case in Burma. Its prestige vastly enhanced by swift and practically bloodless victories against the rebels, the army from the late 1950s moved ever closer to the center of political power; mobilization against the continuance of Dutch rule in New Guinea, as well as the takeover by army administrators of confiscated Dutch corporations and estates, added to the prestige and strength of the military. It was the army, too, that played a vital part in the step-by-step dismantling of Indonesia's liberal-democratic constitutional structure. But President Sukarno, not the army, was its major grave-digger. Unlike many other Western-schooled Indonesians, he had never admired liberal democracy; in fact, he had tolerated rather than promoted the political system that had developed, with considerable intelligentsia-pressure, since the transfer of sovereignty. Casting off the restrictive limitations imposed on him as constitutional chief executive, Sukarno now stepped forth to denounce the party system as the cause of Indonesia's paralyzing political ills. In its stead, he proposed to introduce a "Guided Democracy" of his own.

Originally this new system rested on close understanding and co-operation between president and armed forces. Far more authoritarian than its predecessor, "Guided Democracy" arbitrarily reduced the number of parties, dissolving those deemed most inimical to national harmony, most notably the reformist-Islamic *Masjumi* and the small but influential, intelligentsia-led Socialist Party. Rigid censorship appeared side by side with increasingly strident indoctrination. Ignoring Indonesia's progressive economic deterioration, Sukarno was primarily interested in generating a militant national consensus directed against real or imaginary foreign enemies.

The growing agitation largely stemmed from the third major element in the new system, the Communist Party of Indonesia (PKI). The party, it may be recalled, had played a conspicuous part in the opposition to Dutch rule, placing itself at the helm of the rebellion of the 1920s. Though practically destroyed by the Dutch and proscribed by the Japanese, Communism nonetheless reappeared even before the war ended. Its growth in the immediate postwar era came to a disastrous halt when the party launched an attack on the republic at the height of the struggle against the Netherlands in the late 1940s. It failed, and several leaders were executed. (The almost simultaneous eruption of Communist violence in so many Southeast Asian countries in the late 1940s points to external, central direction; but the evidence has so far remained circumstantial rather than definitive.)

Surprisingly, a new PKI leadership, recruited from among the wartime generation, succeeded so well in blotting out the party's tarnished recent past as to gain an impressive electoral victory less than a decade later. Under "Guided Democracy" the PKI increasingly allied itself with the president in the name of national unity. In turn, Sukarno came to place ever greater reliance on the Communists in an effort to counterbalance the entrenched power of the military. In the 1960s, the PKI claimed the largest membership of any Communist party outside the socialist bloc, with additional millions of youths, laborers, farmers, and women enrolled in PKI-dominated front organizations.

The Communists' growing importance in internal politics was also reflected in Indonesia's abandonment of her original, neutralist orientation in international affairs in favor of ever-closer relations with the Communist powers; interestingly enough, it was the Soviet Union that furnished the sizeable military equipment for the armed forces while the PKI allied itself with the Chinese. As the hostile confrontation with Malaysia gained momentum, Indonesia defiantly left the United Nations Organization.

Sukarno's efforts to balance the army against the PKI, though outwardly successful, encountered mounting restiveness, the more so since the economy's downward bend continued unabated. Political tensions increased, isolated clashes, particularly between Communists and Muslims, flaring up from time to time. Suddenly, the entire edifice of "Guided Democracy" came crumbling down in a series of dramatic events that started in the fall of 1965. Ostensibly sparked by a junior officers' revolt against the General Staff, in which six senior officers were brutally murdered, it soon became clear that others—notably high-ranking air force officers as well as leading elements of the PKI—had been involved in the attempted *coup*. But in a matter of hours the truncated army command regained complete control. In the following months it used that control to destroy its main enemy and consolidate its power. A systematic purge of the Communist Party was set in motion, in the course of which most of its leaders, thousands of cadres, and uncounted numbers of members and sympathizers were killed; Muslim youths appear to have played a key role in the fratricidal bloodbath, unparalleled in Indonesia's modern history.

Having decimated the PKI, the army proceeded to whittle down Sukarno's powers. At first divested of his life tenure as president, he was a few months later forced to resign his office in favor of the army's new leader, General Suharto. Virtually all Sukarno's principal advisers were brought to trial on charges of complicity in the *coup*, and voices were even raised to bring the former president himself, whose involvement in the events of late 1965 has remained unclear, into the dock. In the meantime, military men were placed in almost all important regional and even local administrative positions, thus guaranteeing de facto army rule—albeit with individual civilians' cooperation—in what has come to be called "The New Order." No new constitutional and political edifice has yet been constructed, but it is fairly clear that the old political parties, heavily tarnished by their collaboration with Sukarno's regime, may be relegated to a secondary place; *Masjumi*, incidentally, has not been allowed to reemerge. In the immediate post-*coup* months, youth and student groups in Djakarta took a lead in the anti-Sukarno drive; but it remains to be seen whether, and in what form, the young generation will find an institutionalized place in the "New Order."

On the positive side, some freedom of the press has been reestablished and political life generally has become far freer than it had been under "Guided Democracy"; pro-Marxist groups and all advocates of the "Old Order" are, of course, strictly barred from public life. New elections have been promised, but it is unlikely that they will be held in the late 1960s, as originally envisaged. A very slow beginning has also been made with economic and fiscal rehabilitation, aided by cautious support from Indonesia's main foreign creditor nations. Equally important, confrontation with Malaysia was officially ended, and cooperation between the two sister nations augurs well for the future. Indonesia has also reentered the United Nations. But even under optimal conditions, Indonesia's recovery from the profound shocks of the recent past may take decades. Unless the leaders of the "New Order" can, in fact, attend to the country's pressing social and economic ills—and there are as yet very few indications that they can—further political radicalization may be unavoidable. The destruction of the PKI constitutes no solution of these problems; indeed, it was they—e.g., the official torpor in implementing much-needed land reforms—which in the first place had provided the Communists with their vast following. Tensions between the military and civilian politicians, a sharpening of cleavages between Muslims and their opponents, and the growing restlessness of the highly politicized younger generation all contribute to political uncertainty.

Vietnam

Vietnam's tortuous path toward decolonization has traversed drawn-out war with the former colonial power and partitioning of the country, followed by renewed fighting which has come to involve the United States and, indirectly so far, the Soviet Union and Communist China. The defeat of the French at Dien Bien Phu (near the Laotian border) by Ho Chi Minh's forces in 1954 was the signal for the liquidation of the French empire in Southeast Asia. The Geneva Conference, convened in that year to discuss armistices for both Korea and Indochina, resulted in the temporary division of Vietnam along the seventeenth parallel. French and Communist forces were to be regrouped on either side of the dividing line, pending the gradual withdrawal of the French, with nationwide elections looking toward unification scheduled after two years.

As it turned out, France relinquished South Vietnam very quickly, leaving behind a weak and inadequately organized, quasi-autonomous government under Chief of State Bao Dai, with Ngo Dinh Diem as premier. Both men had, in fact, been absent from the country for long stretches of time, the former emperor (who, it will be recalled, had abdicated in 1945) in France, his future prime minister in the United States. It was strong American support, now channeled directly to the Vietnamese rather than to the French, that kept the authorities in the south functioning. With this support, Diem felt strong enough to oust Bao Dai in a referendum which simultaneously made him president, and to turn the armistice line into a permanent, hermetically sealed, political boundary. Diem, whose government, then still autonomous rather than independent, had not signed the Geneva accords, furthermore postponed the planned all-Vietnam elections *sine die*. Henceforth, there would be two Vietnams, Ho Chi Minh's "Democratic Republic" in the north, Diem's "Republic of Vietnam" in the south.

True enough, significant regional differences exist between North, Central, and South Vietnam, and in the past the country has been more often divided than united; in fact, it was only under the Nguyen dynasty that Vietnam had been brought under unified control at the turn of the nineteenth century. But the 1954 division not only arbitrarily cut Central Vietnam (Annam) in two, it also disrupted the economic equilibrium attained in colonial times by severing the overpopulated north from the Cochinchinese "rice bowl" while simultaneously denying the south the mineral products, especially coal, of the north. (One inevitable concomitant was to make Ho heavily dependent on rice deliveries from China, Diem equally dependent for most of his supplies on the United States.)

Equally important, while French colonial policy had in several respects purposely accentuated regional separation, modern economic and educational life under colonial rule had fostered a good deal of mobility across the boundaries of the three *pays*. Twentieth-century nationalism had, in any case, started to transcend regional sentiments. More than any other modern group, the Communists, though undeniably stronger in the north—as had been all political movements before them—had created a nationwide organization with an all-Vietnamese appeal. Like the anticolonial struggles in Burma and Indonesia, for example, the *Viet Minh's* tenacious and ultimately successful war against France had generated a truly national sense of unity, cohesion, and exhilaration. Cutting the country in two was, therefore, a retrogressive denial of Vietnamese nationalism, and it is doubtful that the seventeenth parallel can obscure, let alone erase, Ho's stature as the "father" of independent Vietnam. This Communist-led nationalism may undeniably be anathema to sizeable numbers of Vietnamese; the post-Geneva exodus from the north of over 800,000 refugees (most of them members of the Catholic minority) certainly proves the point. But even the most deep-seated antagonism does not necessarily provide positive alternatives.

Indeed, partition has reinforced the peculiar paradoxes which we have previously observed at work in modern Vietnamese history. Under it, a tightly knit, totalitarian regime has remained entrenched in those parts of Vietnam where the fabric of society had least suffered from disruption, while the far more amorphous southern regions have been left suspended in a structureless void. It may be recalled that Cochinchina, Vietnam's frontier region, had only started to integrate with the rest of the country when the French conquest began a hundred or so years ago. Firmly established in Annam and Tonkin, the Confucian monarchy had not had time to strike deep roots in the south; as a matter of fact, the imperial bureaucracy was withdrawn from Cochinchina once French supremacy had become a fact. Similarly, Vietnamese Buddhism was far more flourishing at the center than in the south; as a result, a plethora of heterodox religious sects, most notably the Cao Dai and the Hoa Hao, had begun to proliferate in Cochinchina in modern times. Moreover, in no other part of Vietnam had French influence been as pervasively felt. Peculiar to the south was not only the "Gallicized" gentry, but also the large latifundia and plantations with their agricultural laborers and tenants. These factors were further acerbated and complicated by French political manipulations since the end of the Second World War.

In contrast to the high degree of cultural, religious, and social homogeneity that prevails in Annam and Tonkin, twentieth-century Cochinchina has, then, come to present a mosaic of discrete and mutually exclusive, if not antagonistic, forces. Divided by social, religious, and territorial, as well as ethnic cleavages, modern South Vietnam has lacked a common will and common loyalties. Not surprisingly, modern political movements originated in the north rather than the south. This is also true of the Communists, the most resolutely modern and supraparochial of these movements; they, however, succeeded in recruiting a nucleus of dedicated followers in Cochinchina. Furthermore, the Communists in the south, always weaker there than elsewhere in Vietnam, since 1946 experienced continued French harassment. In accordance with the Geneva agreements, the Communists had consented to withdraw their military personnel north of the seventeenth parallel; but they left an infrastructure behind. Communist power actually remained to all intents and purposes intact even after partition, particularly in the delta lands of the extreme south. When large-scale insurrections started up again in the early 1960s, local cells were thus ready to mount attacks against the Saigon government; in due course they were reinforced by returning cadres, and later still by contingents of North Vietnamese "volunteers" and army regulars.

Developments in the "Democratic Republic" have generally followed the standard pattern of Communist regimes elsewhere. The "united front" had been shed even before partition, the *Viet Minh* being disbanded in 1951. The process of establishing a full-fledged monolithic party dictatorship culminated in a new (though still transitional) constitution, adopted after a "unanimous" referendum in 1960. Perhaps in deference to Ho's stature, that constitution vests far greater powers in the president than is usual in Communist states. Ho Chi Minh is, indeed, not only the Communist world's ranking "Old Bolshevik" still at the helm of his country, so far he has also succeeded in holding his battle-hardened comrades together. Though there have been shifts in the party's high command—some of them presumably reflecting the waxing and waning of individuals or factions favoring Moscow or Peking—no public purges have yet taken place. In spite of the fact that the army bore the major brunt of the victorious war against France, it has to all appearances not challenged party hegemony. North Vietnam may also have avoided the intergenerational challenges so common to non-Communist states: several young men have been coopted and allowed to rise to party prominence.

From the outset, the "building of socialism" was taken resolutely and ruthlessly in hand. Its twin goals were the collectivization of agriculture and the laying of an industrial base. Of these, industrialization was indubitably far more successfully achieved. Blessed with mineral resources far in excess of those available in other parts of Southeast Asia, aided by an industrial base established under French rule, but above all supported by large-scale financial, technical, and manpower assistance from the Soviet Union, Eastern Europe, and China, the Democratic Republic forged to undisputed industrial primacy in the entire region. But American bombing in the mid-1960s appears to have destroyed most if not all of North Vietnam's plants and factories.

By contrast, the Democratic Republic's record in agriculture has at best been uneven; in the immediate postpartition years it was, in fact, disastrous. As in China, the Communists decreed a rural revolution involving large-scale redistribution and confiscation, only to reap the whirlwind of peasant defiance. Hardest hit at the outset were the Catholics, only about one-third, approximately 650,000, of whom had gone south immediately after Geneva. The regime's assurances of religious toleration notwithstanding, Catholics were an easy target for the Communists' "agrarian reform." The worst oppressions and the most violent reactions, however, occurred in the mid-1950s in the Central Vietnamese province of Nge-Anh, of old an area of peasant restiveness. This is not only the very locale where the Communists had staged their most conspicuous anti-French revolt in the early 1930s, but also—another irony!— the very birthplace of President Ho himself. Only with the help of vast rice imports from Burma (financed by the Soviets) was widespread famine averted in the wake of these upheavals. A 'correction campaign' was then instituted among cadres to erase some of the worst consequences of the early measures; but socialization of agriculture has continued apace, peasant cooperatives rather than more ambitious rural organizations based on either the Russian or Chinese models being the rule. As yet, however, agrarian output—the Achilles' heel of most Communist states—has failed to live up to the Hanoi planners' exhortations and expectations. Rice, always inadequate in the overcrowded north, and unavailable from the south since 1954, thus continues to form a basic import commodity.

Ho Chi Minh and his colleagues apparently have been more adroit in devising intelligent policies toward the non-Vietnamese minorities, numbering over 2½ million, in the north. We saw that the Viet Minh's first wartime base of operations had been located in montagnard country and that Ho had won some tribal groups to his side at that time. Expelled from Hanoi and other towns in the beginning of the Franco-Vietnamese war, the Viet Minh again retreated among the hill peoples. In fact, to this day several North Vietnamese divisions, including their officers, consist of montagnards. Politically, too, the minorities have been rewarded, three "autonomous areas" having been set up within the Democratic Republic. For sure, monolithic and centralized Party control is incompatible with political autonomy; but the Communists' willingness to recruit members of these minorities into the Party structure, as well as their pioneering cultural work among the tribal communities, deviate sharply from past relations between Vietnamese and montagnards. The leaders of South Vietnam have not yet displayed similar ingenuity in coping with minority problems.

Finally, North Vietnam's Communists have successfully steered a middle course between Soviet Russia and China—no small achievement at a time when the split between the two Communist giants threatens to reach a breaking point. Ho's small state could not have achieved industrialization without support from both, nor could it have armed its troops and its southern allies, let alone faced the massive American aerial onslaught, without the sophisticated weaponry and defensive equipment supplied from abroad. In turn, it seems obvious that neither Russians nor Chinese can afford to let the Democratic Republic go under; though bitterly accusing each other of defaulting from their commitments, both have continued to send supplies and technicians, without forcing Ho Chi Minh to choose sides.

The tasks of "nation building" which confronted Ngo Dinh Diem in the south, already complicated in view of the area's manifold social problems, were rendered more formidable still by the almost total void in which they had to be undertaken. In the years before Geneva, the French had barely permitted Bao Dai to create a skeletal and shadowy "autonomous" Vietnamese administration. In 1954 his government wielded less power than did a host of groups and armed sects; some of these, like the Cao Dai for example, actually possessed territorial bases of their own. Neither Bao Dai nor any of these self-seeking cliques commanded general respect or loyalty. It must be remembered that the *Viet Minh* had won the war against France, endowing Ho Chi Minh with an aura of well-nigh legendary prestige. Diem, a relatively little-known repatriate, could not hope to match, let alone surpass, Ho's stature. Moreover, the war had caused widespread destruction and economic decline, while a flood of refugees added to Saigon's preoccupations. And Communist nuclei continued to exist in many parts of the south, albeit temporarily submerged.

After a deceptively promising start amid improving economic conditions, Diem actually proved more adept at emulating some of North Vietnam's most reprehensible practices than at generating anything approximating Ho's organizational and ideological *élan*. Rigid censorship and the imprisonment of real or presumed opponents antagonized the urban sectors, while in the villages Diem abolished the traditional election of local officials. His dictatorial, family-centered regime in the end rested atop discordant if evenly muzzled groups—intelligentsia, political factions, and the Buddhists. Backed by the armed forces, Diem drew his only political support proper from the Catholic minority, particularly from the northern refugees whom he had settled on confiscated Crown lands.

In spite of rapidly mounting American aid, personnel, and advice, the president remained unwilling to placate political or religious opponents by widening the base of his government. He proved equally incapable of coping with the restlessness in the countryside, on the rise since the Communists returned to open insurgency in the late 1950s. Since Diem depended on the Cochinchinese landowners, he had difficulty in competing with the Communists' land reform program; rural resettlement programs, designed to deny the enemy access to villages, actually played into the hands of his enemies. Furthermore, before long the "Viet Cong" (as the Communists came to be called in the south) opened a political offensive. They created a "democratic" anti-Diem coalition, the National Liberation Front; though clearly under their control, the Front nonetheless attracted dissident non-Communists. In 1963, after the bloody suppression of Buddhist riots that attracted worldwide attention, Diem was ousted and killed by a group of senior army officers.

While South Vietnam's transition from civilian to military rule apparently paralleled the developments in Burma and Indonesia, the similarity is more apparent than real. For whereas the Burmese and Indonesian armies, and for that matter also that of North Vietnam, were born and tested in revolution and anticolonial war, the majority of South Vietnam's officers corps had served in the French colonial army. They consequently lacked the fierce ideological commitment to national independence and also the *esprit de corps* of their revolutionary counterparts. Though briefly united in opposition to Diem, military leaders succumbed to factionalisms and rivalries as soon as they assumed control of the government. Several army *coups* occurred after 1963, with the highest political offices changing hands.

The liberalization of South Vietnam's political scene after Diem's downfall lasted only for a short while. The military *juntas* soon appeared to fall back on many of their predecessor's policies and practices. They continued to alienate the most vocal urban elements, in particular resurrecting the repression of the militant Buddhist minority, without affecting substantial constitutional reforms. Their military performance proper did not show marked improvements over previous years either. American military power, grown from a few hundred "advisers" in the mid-1950s to over half-a-million combatants a decade later, was increasingly called upon to wage the relentless war against Communist guerillas, reinforced by political cadres and regular troops infiltrated from the north. Even "pacification" of the countryside, hitherto entrusted to the

South Vietnamese armed forces, progressively became an American responsibility.

Somber as the governmental record of South Vietnam is, her protracted agony has been caused only in part by the idiosyncrasies and shortcomings of the leaders who have come and gone since 1954. More was certainly needed than Diem's near-paranoid megalomania or his quaint Catholic-Confucian political philosophy; more, too, than the selfish ambitions of politically inexperienced and quarreling military men, most of them, moreover, northerners rather than natives of the south. Yet the generic problems besetting the infant state might have perplexed and defied even the most honest and dedicated leadership.

At the core of all its difficulties lies, as we said, the very texture of a divided society, kept apart by separate, parochial loyalties. Easy as it is to decry the absence of a truly elected parliament, the Indonesian precedent suggests that proper elections in South Vietnam would yield a legislature composed of factions representing mutually incompatible minorities: Catholics, Buddhists, Cao Daists, and *montagnards*, not to speak of the myriad of urban parties and intelligentsia-cliques. This at least would be the likely result as long as elections were to be confined to areas under Saigon's reasonably firm control, as has been the case with the pseudo-elections that have taken place in the past. It is quite probable, however, that the National Liberation Front, dominant in several parts of South Vietnam for years and presumably strong though clandestine in many others, might well emerge as the real victor in countrywide, open elections. In a very real sense the Front has, after all, passed a kind of electoral test by its sheer ability to survive, with little loss of territory or total manpower, in spite of the gruelling military and particularly aerial punishments to which it has been subjected by the Americans.

Unquestionably the Communists in the south are heavily dependent on material and human supplies from the north. Tactical guidance, if not more, may well come from Hanoi. It is true, too, that selective and brutal terror is one—but only one—of the Communists' chosen means of controlling the peasants. But none of these factors should obscure three perturbing facts: first, the bulk of Communist cadres, guerillas, and civilian auxiliaries is of local, southern origin (as are the ostensible leaders of the National Liberation Front, not all of them Communists); in the second place, the Communists' discipline, commitment to their cause, and endurance are without parallels among other segments of

South Vietnam's population; and third, the Communists have been accepted, or at least tolerated, by the population at large: only in very rare cases are the Viet Cong betrayed to their enemies.

South Vietnam's Communists thus enjoy a combination of internal and external advantages that render them far more formidable antagonists than those of other Southeast Asian countries. Whereas their Filipino and Malayan counterparts, for example, only represent small and distinct sectional or racial minorities, the Viet Cong have a seemingly national appeal. More than that, unlike in South Vietnam, the Communists in both the Philippines and Malaya were face to face with well functioning societies and established as well as resolute political elites. To take a different example, the Indonesian party was a colossus with almost nationwide representation; yet by its very growth the PKI generated widespread opposition, not only among the army leadership but also among millions of Muslims and other Indonesians with a vested interest in containing Communism. And finally, only in South Vietnam have Communists had access to a "fraternal" regime of compatriots across the border, not to speak of "sanctuaries" in, and support from, an adjacent Communist world power.

In most of Southeast Asia, Communism has ceased to be the "wave of the future." Significantly, its defeats were almost without exception accomplished by indigenous forces; only in Malaysia, with a minuscule army of its own, did foreign troops bear the brunt of the counterguerilla war, but even there with overwhelming local support. By contrast, the Vietnamese Communists have for years been able to withstand the armed might of the United States and its allies (besides South Vietnamese, they also include smaller contingents of Australian, New Zealand, South Korean, Thai, and Filipino forces). The people of South Vietnam, for twenty years embroiled in a war that has grown ever deadlier with the passage of time, seem to be hopelessly caught between terrorism on the land and destruction from the air.

V

Looking back, we can briefly summarize the key factors of the decolonization process in Southeast Asia as a whole. In our survey, we divided the region into two groups of countries, the first comprising Thailand, Cambodia, the Philippines, and Malaysia, the second Burma, Indonesia, and Vietnam; Laos occupied a place midway between the two groups. It will be recalled that the composition of national elites as well as degrees of general social stability were the two major criteria for this basic division. These criteria could be supplemented by a third, the role of religious elements in social and political life; in fact, it is closely related to the other two.

Elite continuity has been as apparent in the first group of countries as its absence has distinguished those in the second. Thailand's military oligarchy has now exercised power for over thirty-five years; it has, moreover, done so in the framework of a centuries old, gradually modernized, Buddhist monarchy. The Philippine *ilustrado* class, with deep roots in land ownership, preserved its social preeminence through Spanish, American, and Japanese rule into the era of decolonization. Political power accrued to the *ilustrados* from the second decade of the present century; it has been barely dented since the attainment of Philippine independence. In Cambodia as well as Malaysia, indirect colonial rule stabilized and partly strengthened indigenous monarchical institutions. The near-monopoly on modern education which royal and noble children enjoyed provided both countries with elite personnel that combined traditionally sanctioned status with modern political skills.

Though to different degrees, the countries in the first category have on the whole enjoyed fairly high levels of internal stability. The rice cultivators of Thailand and Cambodia, having been spared the dislocations caused by intensive outside interference, have continued to prosper in the postwar years. A similar situation has prevailed among the bulk of the Malay peasantry, especially in the eastern part of the peninsula; true enough, Malaysia experienced a drawn-out Communist-led insurgency, but as we saw it did not involve the bulk of the indigenous population, but only a small segment of the Chinese immigrant minority. In the Philippines, too, the *Hukbalahap's* revolutionary appeal was limited in the main to Pampanga, the sole region with acute rural unrest born of the dissolution of old social and economic bonds.

The prevalence of leadership continuity and social equilibrium has been paralleled by the predominantly conservative role played by religious elites in these four countries. The Buddhist monkhood has retained the firm place in Thailand's social fabric which the royal modernizers of that country had secured for it a century or more ago. The Buddhist *sangha* has occupied a comparable if less conspicuous place in modern Cambodian history. We have seen that British rule in the Malay States had provided the impetus for the establishment of a Muslim hierarchy closely attached to the peninsular sultanates. If anything, Islamic leaders have gained even greater prominence as purveyors of Malay national sentiment since independence. Finally, the Catholic Church in the Philippines, having weathered the Philippine Revolution, soon regained its dominant place as a national institution in the islands.

Generally favorable as the balance sheet for these four countries is, they do face a variety of problems, as we have seen. Only Cambodia, blessed with ethnic homogeneity and long sheltered from the turmoils of modernity, appears reasonably free from most of the internal vexations present elsewhere. Thus Thailand is still plagued by minority problems, now compounded by outside intervention, while Malaysia's communal tensions between the different racial communities show few signs of abating. Nor is this all. In all these states, expanded educational facilities and increased social mobility have brought to the fore younger people from a variety of social backgrounds, impatient to share in, if not to usurp, the fruits of political power hitherto monopolized by established elites. The spread of rural education, but also improved communications—not least in the form of the transistor radio—are making progressive inroads into the isolation of the countryside. At the same time, the continually rising population numbers have generally not been matched by commensurate economic development. These factors will doubtless affect the pace and direction in which these states will move in the future.

The countries in our second category, Burma, Indonesia, and Vietnam, clearly share with those just discussed the manifold problems relating to ethnic and racial minorities, as well as those stemming from intergenerational frictions, widening communications, population increase, and inadequate economic growth. Such problems, however, are in these three nations vastly compounded by intrinsic political instability at the top and large-scale social dislocation among wider sectors of the population. Though avowedly "conservative" and ruled by traditional political elites, the countries in the first group have, in fact, advanced along the road of incipient political and administrative modernization to an extent unparalleled in those of the second, with the notable exception of North Vietnam.

Direct colonial rule had virtually destroyed the traditional political systems of Burma, Indonesia, and Vietnam. New elites that had emerged in the 1930s came to dominate the political scene during these countries' struggle for independence. Governed by intelligentsias at the outset, all passed under military regimes in the second postwar decade, with the exception of North Vietnam, whose Communist leadership has provided the only element of political continuity in these states. The transition from civilian to military elites has, moreover, involved the abandonment of Western-style constitutional governments in favor of various kinds of dictatorship, none of which has been, so far, more successful in modernizing the political and economic structures than their predecessors.

In contrast to the countries in the first category, those in the second have, furthermore, suffered from a fairly widespread social *malaise* in the rural sector, the woeful legacy of decades of change induced by foreigners. Particularly acute in overcrowded Java, Lower Burma, and in those parts of South Vietnam affected by landlordism, unrest has also appeared in other regions, not least among urban dwellers who have suffered acutely from economic deterioration. Not surprisingly, such social discontent has provided fertile soil for political agitation and organized endeavors. Communist movements, usually restricted to specific groups or sections in the countries of the first category, have had a far wider appeal in those of the second; in fact, Communist activities were already strongly in evidence there in colonial times. In postwar Burma, the Communists' efficacy was admittedly inhibited by serious factional disputes, but in Indonesia they were the largest and best-led political party before their virtual destruction in the mid-1960s. South Vietnam's Communists have managed to hold their own in the face of concerted military attacks, albeit with growing support from the north.

The Communists, however, are not the only beneficiaries of the uncertainty and restlessness which have attended the early phases of decolonization in these three nation-states. Religious elements, always closely associated with political protest in colonial Southeast Asia, have regained importance since the Second World War. While religious elites in the countries in our first category have, as we said, tended to support the powers-that-be, such elites have played a far less conservative role in Burma, Indonesia, and Vietnam. The Buddhist *sangha* has been one of independent Burma's most significant political actors, as was witnessed by U Nu's design for a Buddhist state. Some of Indonesia's Muslims have similarly aspired toward a religiously based state; in several parts of the country Islamic dissidents went into open rebellion against the secular republic in the 1950s. Indeed, next to the army, the Islamic groups have been the most determined foes of Indonesia's Communists, having played a prominent part in their opponents' recent decimation. Finally, the low level of national integration among Vietnamese in the south has endowed the competing religious groupings there with even greater significance than they possess in the other two states. In spite of the appeals of Communism, or more probably side by side with such appeals, religious identifications have actually provided the major ideological and organizational foci for the bulk of the peasant population. In the 1960s, the Buddhists—a distinct minority in Vietnam, in contrast to the situation in neighboring Theravada Buddhist lands—emerged as a militant political element, harassed by successive regimes. Other religious minorities include, next to the Catholics, such sects as the Cao Dai and Hoa Hao, all of them involved to varying degrees in the political process.

In conclusion, we should once again remind ourselves that the decolonization era has barely begun. The contours of the future, of the immediate future even, can by no means be clearly discerned from the welter of the many-faceted, sometimes contradictory developments which we have discussed in the preceding pages. Quite apart from the innate complexities which beset each country's internal developments, outside intervention and interference will doubtless impinge upon and further complicate the future course of Southeast Asian affairs. Vietnam and partly also Laos are the first but almost certainly not the last parts of the region in which interference, from whichever of the major powers, may spell death and destruction on a frightening scale. The danger thus exists that the end of colonial dominance may but connote the onset of an era in which Southeast Asian countries may once again become mere pawns of outsiders. The chances of such intervention are the greater since independence has not, or not yet, endowed most of the new states with political strength, national harmony, or determined economic growth.

We have noted earlier in this book how the imposition of separate colonial administrations had accentuated the centripetal tendencies inherent in the Southeast Asian region. This latter-day separateness, coupled with the resurgence of many traditional animosities, has not only caused a great deal of instability, but has also opened the doors to additional foreign intrusion, which, in turn, further undermines the fragile equilibrium in the area. Regional cooperation, an obvious means for the attainment of collective strength, is even by most optimistic assessments in its infancy. The so-called Southeast Asia Treaty Organization (SEATO), founded in the middle of the 1950s, in fact includes only two Southeast Asian members, Thailand and the Philippines, in a security grouping dominated by Western nations. Two purely regional attempts have been made, ASA, the Association of Southeast Asia, which for a time brought together Thailand, Malaysia, and the Philippines, and the so-called "Maphilindo" (Malaysia-Philippines-Indonesia). Both were born, and have so far foundered, on the rocks of intraregional politics. A new Association of Southeast Asian Nations (ASEAN)— Malaysia, Singapore, Thailand, Indonesia, and the Philippines—was formed in the fall of 1967. Regional economic cooperation is in any case seriously hampered by the fact that, unlike Western Europe for example, Southeast Asia consists of basically competing rather than complementary economic units. It is too early to know whether the ambitious, multi-national Mekong Valley Project, undertaken with international financial and technical support and, indeed, on outside initiative, will succeed in laying the groundwork for a pattern of lasting interstate cooperation.

Even under optimal conditions, Southeast Asia's decolonization course will, then, in all likelihood be strewn with innumerable and complex obstacles. It promises to be relatively smoother in those countries where political continuity and social stability have already facilitated the transition from colonialism to independent nationhood, but even there it may become progressively problematical. The prospects appear dimmer still wherever accelerated disintegration is precluding an early consolidation of political and social life. The building of viable nation states, however, is not a task to be accomplished overnight. If all is said and done, colonialism and decolonization together are no more than a brief interlude in the long history of the peoples of Southeast Asia. Their individual and collective genius may yet succeed in welding these most recent experiences into a brighter and fuller future, into a proper synthesis between old and new.

Annotated List
of Readings

BIBLIOGRAPHY

Hall, D. G. E., ed., *Historians of South-East Asia*. London and New York, 1962. An interesting series of essays on the historiography of Southeast Asia.

Hay, Stephen N., and Margaret H. Chase, *Southeast Asian History: A Bibliographic Guide*. New York, 1962. A useful guide to standard books and articles on Southeast Asian history.

Soedjatmoko *et al.*, eds., *An Introduction to Indonesian Historiography*. Ithaca, N.Y., 1965. A comprehensive survey by 22 scholars of Asian and Western primary and secondary materials relating to the history of Indonesia.

PERIODICALS

Journal of Southeast Asian History. Department of History, University of Singapore, 1960—present. Published in two parts annually, this journal gives a good coverage of recent work on the history of Southeast Asia.

GEOGRAPHY

Hall, D. G. E., intro., *Atlas of South-East Asia*. London and New York, 1964. A useful book for the student of Southeast Asian history.

Fisher, C. A., *South-East Asia: A Social, Economic, and Political Geography*. London and New York, 1964. A comprehensive study.

McGee, T. G., *The Southeast Asian City: A Social Geography of the Primate Cities of Southeast Asia*. London, 1967. A study of the major features of urbanization in Southeast Asia.

Robequain, Charles, *Malaya, Indonesia, Borneo, and the Philippines; A*

Geographical, Economic, and Political Description of Malaya, the East Indies, and the Philippines (2nd ed.). London and New York, 1958. A useful geographic and political appraisal by the Professor of Tropical Geography in the University of Paris.

GENERAL HISTORIES

Benda, Harry J., and John A. Larkin, *The World of Southeast Asia: Selected Historical Readings*. New York, 1967. A useful compilation of extracts from documentary sources, indigenous and Western.

Cady, John F., *Southeast Asia: Its Historical Development*. New York, 1964. A fluent survey of Southeast Asian history, including social and economic factors.

Hall, D. G. E., *A History of South-East Asia*. London and New York, 1964. A second and revised edition of the standard work on the subject.

Harrison, Brian, *South-East Asia: A Short History* (3rd ed.). London and New York, 1966. A most stimulating brief survey.

Tarling, Nicholas, *A Concise History of Southeast Asia*. New York, Washington, and London, 1966. An individualistic interpretation of Southeast Asian history with particular emphasis on the period from the mid-eighteenth century.

EARLY HISTORY OF SOUTHEAST ASIA

Coedès, Georges, *The Indianized States of Southeast Asia*, trans. S. B. Cowing, ed. Walter F. Vella. Honolulu, 1968. The classical study of Indianization in the Indochinese peninsula and in Indonesia.

————, *The Making of South East Asia*, trans. H. M. Wright. Berkeley and Los Angeles, 1966. An excellent survey for the general reader of the early history of the Indochinese peninsula.

LeMay, Reginald Stuart, *The Culture of South-East Asia: The Heritage of India*. London, 1954. A well-illustrated study emphasizing Indian cultural influences in Southeast Asia.

Wheatley, Paul, *The Golden Khersonese; Studies in the Historical Geography of the Malay Peninsula Before A.D. 1500*. Kuala Lumpur, 1966. An absorbing account of the Malay peninsula before A.D. 1500, based on Arab, Chinese, and other sources.

Wolters, O. W., *Early Indonesian Commerce: A Study of the Origins of Srivijaya*. Ithaca, N.Y., 1967. An impressively documented study of the rise of the powerful maritime empire of Srivijaya in southeast Sumatra at the end of the seventh century A.D.

EARLY WESTERN COLONIAL EXPANSION
AND WESTERN INFLUENCE IN SOUTHEAST ASIA

Boxer, C. R., *Four Centuries of Portuguese Expansion, 1415–1825: A Succinct Survey*. Johannesburg, 1963. An authoritative survey of the subject by an outstanding scholar.

————, *Portuguese Society in the Tropics: The Municipal Councils of Goa, Macao, Bahia, and Luanda, 1510–1800.* Madison and Milwaukee, 1965. An informative study of a key institution in the Portuguese colonial empire.

————, *Race Relations in the Portuguese Colonial Empire, 1415–1825.* Oxford, 1963. Exposes the myth that the Portuguese never tolerated a color-bar in their overseas possessions.

————, *The Dutch Seaborne Empire 1600–1800.* New York, 1965. A masterful study of Dutch activities overseas, including Southeast Asia.

Chaudhuri, K. N., *The English East India Company: The Study of an Early Joint-Stock Company, 1600–1640.* New York, 1965. A detailed analysis of the first 40 years of the Company's existence.

Glamann, Kristof, *Dutch-Asiatic Trade 1620–1740.* Copenhagen and The Hague, 1958. A pioneering and provocative study of the Dutch East India Company's trade with Asia, including a detailed analysis of trade in particular Asian products.

MacGregor, Ian A., "Notes on the Portuguese in Malaya," *Journal of the Malayan Branch, Royal Asiatic Society,* XXVIII, Part 2 (1955), 4–47. One of the few informed discussions of the subject.

Meilink-Roelofsz, M. A. P., *Asian Trade and European Influence in the Indonesian Archipelago between 1500 and about 1630.* The Hague, 1962. A comprehensive study of Asian trade in the Indonesian archipelago immediately before and after the arrival of the Portuguese, Dutch, and English on the Southeast Asian scene. Useful as a corrective to the book by Van Leur.

Panikkar, K. M., *Asia and Western Dominance: A Survey of the Vasco da Gama Epoch of Asian History, 1498–1945* (2nd ed.). London, 1959. "Europocentric" assessment of the Western impact on Asia as viewed by an Indian historian.

Phelan, John Leddy, *The Hispanization of the Philippines: Spanish Aims and Filipino Responses, 1565–1700.* Madison, 1959. A classical study of culture contact.

Philips, C. H., *The East India Company: 1784–1834.* Manchester, 1940. The standard work on the English East India Company.

Quiason, Serafin D., *English "Country Trade" with the Philippines, 1644–1765.* Quezon City, 1966. An exceedingly useful account of various aspects of the trade of Manila during the seventeenth and eighteenth centuries.

Schurz, William Lytle, *The Manila Galleon* (paperback edition). New York, 1959. An admirable study of the galleon trade and the rise of Manila.

Sen, S. P., *The French in India, 1763–1816.* Calcutta, 1958. A useful survey of French colonial activities in Asia.

Van Leur, Jacob Cornelis, *Indonesian Trade and Society: Essays in Asian Social and Economic History.* The Hague and Bandung, 1955. The first major challenge to the traditionally "Europocentric" treatment of Indonesian history.

MODERN HISTORY OF SOUTHEAST ASIA

Burma

Ba Maw, *Breakthrough in Burma: Memoirs of a Revolution, 1939–1946*. New Haven, Conn., and London, 1968. Autobiography of one of Burma's outstanding nationalist leaders.

Cady, John F., *A History of Modern Burma*. Ithaca, N.Y., 1958. A comprehensive account.

Hall, D. G. E., *Burma*. London, 1960. A good short analysis of Burma's history.

Maung Htin Aung, *A History of Burma*. New York, 1968. A stimulating "Burmancentric" interpretation by the former Burmese Ambassador to Ceylon.

Maung Maung, *Burma in the Family of Nations*. Amsterdam and New York, 1957. An informative study by the present Chief Justice of the Union of Burma.

Sarkisyanz, Emanuel, *Buddhist Backgrounds of the Burmese Revolution*. The Hague, 1965. A very thoughtful study by a scholar at the University of Heidelberg.

Tinker, Hugh, *The Union of Burma: A Study of the First Years of Independence* (4th ed.). London and New York, 1967. The standard work on the subject, written by a British scholar.

Trager, Frank N., *Burma from Kingdom to Republic: A Historical and Political Analysis*. New York, Washington, and London, 1966. A penetrating, detailed study by a senior American specialist.

Indochina (Vietnam, Laos, Cambodia)

Buttinger, Joseph, *The Smaller Dragon: A Political History of Vietnam*. New York, 1962. Particularly informed on the premodern period.

————, *Vietnam: A Dragon Embattled*. New York, 1967. A comprehensive two-volume account of the history of Vietnam in the twentieth century.

Duncanson, Dennis J., *Government and Revolution in Vietnam*. New York and London, 1968. An examination of the interacting Vietnamese traditions of government and revolution.

Fall, Bernard B., *The Two Viet-Nams: A Political and Military Analysis* (2nd rev. ed.). New York and London, 1967. A careful study by a leading scholar killed in the Vietnam war.

Halpern, Joel M., *Government, Politics and Social Structure in Laos: A Study of Tradition and Innovation*. New Haven, Conn., 1964. Valuable study by an American anthropologist.

Isoart, Paul, *Le phénomène national vietnamien, de l'indépendance unitaire à l'indépendance fractionnée*. Paris, 1961. Well-documented synthesis, carefully executed.

Lam, Truong Buu, *Patterns of Vietnamese Response to Foreign Intervention: 1858–1900*. New Haven, Conn., 1967. A documentary collection preceded by a thoughtful introduction. The first such study in English.

Le Thanh Khoi, *Le Viet-Nam: Histoire et Civilisation*. Paris, 1955. A massive scholarly study by a Vietnamese resident in France, especially useful for the pre-modern period.

LeBar, Frank M., and Adrienne Suddard, eds., *Laos: Its People, Its Society, Its Culture*. New Haven, Conn., 1960. A useful compilation.

Roberts, Stephen Henry, *French Colonial Policy 1870–1925* (reprinted ed.). London, 1966. General survey of French colonial policy with material on Indochina.

Steinberg, David J., et. al., *Cambodia: Its People, Its Society, Its Culture* (rev. ed.). New Haven, Conn. 1959. A useful compilation.

Indonesia

Day, Clive, *The Policy and Administration of the Dutch in Java* (reprinted ed.). Kuala Lumpur, 1966. One of the most stimulating accounts ever written in English on the Dutch colonial system in Java up to about 1900.

Furnivall, J. S., *Netherlands India: A Study of Plural Economy* (reprinted ed.). Cambridge, 1967. The standard work on the Dutch colonial system in Indonesia.

——, *Colonial Policy and Practice: A Comparative Study of Burma and Netherlands India* (reprinted ed.). New York, 1965. A brilliant study based on first hand observation of Indonesia and direct administrative experience in Burma under British rule.

Geertz, Clifford, *The Social History of an Indonesian Town*. Cambridge, Mass., 1965. Brilliant sociological-historical work.

Kahin, George McTurnan, *Nationalism and Revolution in Indonesia*. Ithaca, N.Y., 1966. A pioneering work, much of it based on local research.

Legge, John D., *Indonesia*. Englewood Cliffs, N.J., 1964. An excellent general discussion of Indonesian history and historiography.

Vlekke, Bernard H. M., *Nusantara: A History of Indonesia* (rev. ed.). Chicago, 1960. A standard work by a Dutch scholar.

Wertheim, W. F., *Indonesian Society in Transition: A Study of Social Change* (2nd rev. ed.). The Hague and Bandung, 1959. A stimulating analysis of social evolution in Indonesia by the Professor of Modern History and Sociology of Southeast Asia at the University of Amsterdam.

Malaysia

Cowan, C. D., *Nineteenth-Century Malaya: The Origins of British Political Control*. London, 1961. A brilliant analysis of the reasons for British political intervention in Malaya during the 1870's and 1880's by the Professor of South-East Asian History at the University of London.

Emerson, Rupert, *Malaysia: A Study in Direct and Indirect Rule* (reprinted ed.). Kuala Lumpur, 1964. A classic comparative study of British and Dutch colonial rule in Malaya and Indonesia published before the Second World War.

Gullick, J. M., *Indigenous Political Systems of Western Malaya*. London and New York, 1965. A brilliant account of the way in which traditional Malay government operated before the introduction of British rule in the 1870's.

Lim Chong Yah, *The Economic Development of Malaya*. New York and London, 1968. A comprehensive study covering the period from 1874 to 1963 by a scholar attached to the University of Malaya.

Mills, Lennox A., *British Malaya 1824–67* (rev. ed.). Kuala Lumpur, 1966. An excellent survey of mid-nineteenth century Malayan history.

Ratnam, K. J., *Communalism and the Political Process in Malaya*. Kuala Lumpur, 1965. An excellent analysis of the political consequences of communal divisions in Malaya since the Second World War.

Roff, William R., *The Origins of Malay Nationalism*. New Haven, Conn., and London, 1967. A unique study of the growth of communal and nationalist feeling among the Malays of West Malaysia during the present century.

Winstedt, R. O., *A History of Malaya* (rev. ed.). Singapore, 1962. The best account by one of the great British administrator-scholars of Malaya.

Philippines

Agoncillo, Teodoro A., *The Fateful Years: Japan's Adventure in the Philippines, 1941–1945*. Quezon City, 1965. A thorough piece of scholarship, combined with personal observations.

Benitez, Conrado, *History of the Philippines: Economic, Social, Cultural, Political* (rev. ed.). Boston, 1954. An original study of economic and social change from pre-Spanish times on.

Corpuz, Onofre D., *The Philippines*. Englewood Cliffs, N.J., 1965. A thoughtful interpretation of the historical and political development of the Philippines by a Filipino political scientist.

Friend, Theodore, *Between Two Empires: The Ordeal of the Philippines, 1929–1946*. New Haven, Conn., and London, 1965. A skillful analysis of the Philippines under American and Japanese rule.

Hayden, Joseph Ralston, *The Philippines: A Study in National Development*. New York, 1942. A thorough study of the American era, including the Philippine Commonwealth, by a former Vice-Governor of the islands.

Landé, Carl H., *Leaders, Factions, and Parties: The Structure of Philippine Politics*. New Haven, Conn., 1965. An important interpretation by an American political scientist.

Wickberg, Edgar, *The Chinese in Philippine Life, 1850–1898*. New Haven, Conn., and London, 1965. A pioneering work not only with regard to the Chinese and Chinese *mestizos*, but also to general social and economic history.

Zaide, Gregorio F., *Philippine Political and Cultural History* (rev. ed., 2 vols.). Manila, 1957. A detailed and well-documented account by a Filipino history professor.

Thailand

Chakrabongse, Prince Chula, *Lords of Life, the Paternal Monarchy of Bangkok, 1782–1932, with the Earlier and More Recent History of Thailand* (2nd ed.). London, 1967. Detailed treatment of Thai history in the nineteenth and twentieth centuries.

Ingram, James C., *Economic Change in Thailand since 1850*. Stanford, Calif., 1955. An authoritative work.

Landon, Kenneth P., *Siam in Transition: A Brief Survey of Cultural Trends in the Five Years Since the Revolution of 1932* (reprinted ed.). Ann Arbor, Mich., 1966. An American scholar's first-hand assessment.

Riggs, Fred W., *Thailand: The Modernization of a Bureaucratic Polity*. Honolulu, 1966. A careful analysis.

Skinner, George William, *Chinese Society in Thailand: An Analytical History*. Ithaca, N.Y., 1957. An important study.

Vella, Walter F., *The Impact of the West on Government in Thailand*. Berkeley, Calif., 1955. An excellent appraisal.

——, *Siam under Rama III, 1824–1851*. Locust Valley, N.Y., 1957. A useful work covering many aspects of Thai history during the first half of the nineteenth century.

Wood, W. A. R., *A History of Siam, from the Earliest Times to the year A.D. 1781* (reprinted ed.). Bangkok, 1959. A short history of Thailand, based on Thai chronicles, by a former British Consul-General to Chiengmai.

Index

ʿAbduh, Muhammad, 106
Abdul Rahman, Tungku, 175
Achin, Achinese, 13, 19, 49, 95, 144
Alliance Party (Malaysia), 175, 176, 177
Angkor, 5, 8, 11
Anglo-Thai Treaty (1909), 53
Annam, 8, 10, 31, 43, 57, 84, 89, 189
Anti-Fascist People's Freedom League (AFPFL; Burma), 143, 181, 182
Arakan, 39, 40, 41
Association of Southeast Asian Nations (ASEAN), 201
Aung San, 119, 142–44, 181
Ayuthia, 8, 31
Azad Hind (Free India, Provisional Government of), 129, 142

Bali, 7, 49
Ba Maw, 118–19, 142–43, 181
Banda Island, 17, 34
Bangka Island, 48, 71
Bangkok, 31, 73
Bantam, 13, 22, 25
Bao Dai (Emperor of Vietnam), 117, 148, 149, 188, 189, 193

Batavia (Jakarta), 22, 58, 73, 74
Borneo, Indonesian, 48, 49, 125
Borneo, Malaysian, 1, 39, 48, 157, 176
Bose, Subhas Chandra, 129, 143, 165
Brahmanism, 7, 9, 10
British North Borneo Company, 39–40, 53
Brooke, James, 39, 48, 53
Brunei, 1, 39, 64, 157, 176
Buddhism:
  in Burma, 94, 107, 119, 183
  in Cambodia, 7, 107
  in Indonesia, 7
  in Laos, 107
  in Malaya, 7
  in Thailand, 11, 96, 107
  in Vietnam, 9, 10, 97, 107, 108
  Mahayana, 7, 9, 10, 11, 12, 97, 107
  Sangha, see Sangha
  Tantric, 10
  Theravada, 11–12, 96, 97, 107, 200
Burma, Burmese, 1, 39, 40–42, 49, 53–55, 61, 62, 77, 86, 87, 94, 104, 120, 141–44, 150, 159, 180–83, 198, 199
  Lower, 39, 41, 77, 96, 199
  Upper, 39, 41, 42, 54